The Problem of Political Marketing

The Problem of Political Marketing

Heather Savigny

continuum

NEW YORK • LONDON

2008

The Continuum International Publishing Group Inc
80 Maiden Lane, New York, NY 10038

The Continuum International Publishing Group Ltd
The Tower Building, 11 York Road, London SE1 7NX

www.continuumbooks.com

Printed in the United Kingdom by Biddles Ltd, King's Lynn, Norfolk

Library of Congress Cataloging-in-Publication Data

Savigny, Heather.
    The problem of political marketing / Heather Savigny.
        p. cm.
    Includes bibliographical references and index.
    ISBN-13: 978-0-8264-2856-1 (hardcover : alk. paper)
    ISBN-10: 0-8264-2856-8 (hardcover : alk. paper) 1. Campaign
    management. 2. Marketing—Political aspects. I. Title.

JF2112.C3S29 2008
324.7'3—dc22

                                    2007042587

ERRATA

The editor and publisher regret the following error, to be corrected on second printing:

Contents

Conclusion: Political marketing—a challenge to democracy

In memory of my dad, Nigel Savigny

Contents

Acknowledgments

This has not been an easy book to write. There are many people to whom I am indebted, both friends and colleagues who, throughout, have encouraged and supported me, kept me sane, made me laugh, and provided inspiration. These people include: Catherine Ball, Stephen Bates, Andy Bugg, Denise and Michael Carter, Will Duff, Paul Fisher, Luke Garrod, Peter Handley, Jane and Mark Hewitt, Michael Higgins, David Hudson, Gina Irving, Mikko Kuisma, Tim and Dot Lenton, Michael Lister, Simon and Rachel Lunness, Lee Marsden, Gina Neff, Sol Nte, Lucy O'Driscoll, Chris Pike, Becky Salmon, Simon Taylor, and Chris Wilson. And those who have gone above and beyond by providing comments and critical feedback (often in a very short space of time!) on earlier versions of this work including: Tim Dant, Steve Davies, Colin Hay, Thea Hinde, Steve Kettell, Darren Lilleker, Dave Marsh, Matt Olczack, Nicola Pratt, Jean Savigny, Richard Scullion, John Street, Mick Temple, and Dominic Wring. Also, remembered here, and sadly missed, are Jane Ardley and Heather Coles.

I'd like to thank David Barker, Max Novick, and all at Continuum who have been brilliant.

However, none of this would have been possible without the very much appreciated support of my family, my late dad, my mum, and my sister, Hazel. But most of all, thank you to Sam, for being the best son a parent could wish for.

Introduction

There is a problem, a perception of crisis in politics. As Western electorates display increasing cynicism towards, their political elites and are less inclined to vote, there has been widespread concern about the character of contemporary democracy and suggestions of its decline. Discerning these tendencies, some scholars have focused attention upon the role of formal politics in the 'hollowing out of citizenship'[1], and social and economic forces (such as globalisation[2]) in accounting for a current 'democratic malaise'. Others attribute a decline in civic engagement to the impact of the media. Lewis et al[3] highlight the role of the news media in this process, whereas Putnam[4] argues that television more broadly has, and is, contributing to a more cynical, detached outlook on public life; the phrase 'video malaise'[5] has captured this trend. Some have attributed this to, among other things, changes in the demographic makeup of the citizenry[6]; the dumbing down of the media[7]; the decline of social capital as the public engage increasingly with the media rather than with politics[8]; the increase in spin and media management techniques used by politicians[9]; and the existence of a postdemocracy.[10] This phenomenon has led to academic investigation into 'why we hate politics?'[11] and has witnessed a restatement of 'why politics matters'.[12] In the practical world of politics, in a bid to reinvigorate the public, politicians are using all manner of available technologies and methods, from text messaging to blogging; also under consideration are electronic townhalls, citizen juries, Sunday voting and ballot boxes in supermarkets. Underlying all this, however, has been a profound shift in the way politics is both conceived of and practised. Politics, as both elite-level activity and the dissemination of this to the public, has predominantly become a process of marketing. The central argument of this book is that this use of marketing has played a key role in contributing to the existence of a political 'malaise' as marketing both subverts the democratic process and disconnects the public from politics.

Background

Political marketing in itself is not particularly new. As a practice and set of strategies originating in America,[13] its historical antecedents can also be seen in Britain,[14] where the techniques of marketing have been used throughout the last century.[15] However, it is within the last two decades that its usage has noticeably spread, and what is qualitatively different and is profoundly reshaping politics is the extent to which it has moved beyond a set of practices and techniques and become an overriding philosophy. The prevalence of marketing as a guiding principle of the activity of politics has become so entrenched that, as Newman observes, the question now becomes whether it is conceivable for a candidate *not* to adopt a marketing perspective in contemporary politics.[16]

In part, the use of marketing in politics has been explained, indeed 'made inevitable'[17], by the existence of a mass electorate; by changes in electoral and political circumstances; and by the growth in media and communications technologies.[18] Given this contemporary climate, the observational literature claims that the political campaign manager is assumed to face similar issues as a marketing manager.[19] These empirical reflections are entirely consistent with the view promoted within the political marketing literature that 'the problem of getting elected is essentially a marketing one'.[20]

Permanent political marketing?

There is also a sense that political marketing is not just confined to election campaigns, rather it has become a means of governance. Marketing methods have shaped the formulation and implementation of policy in office, leaving many commentators to link the use of marketing with the notion of a 'permanent' campaign.[21] This idea of a 'permanent campaign' means that electioneering is now regarded as a continual process, which occurs throughout office, not just in formally designated campaign periods. In the US, Reagan, Clinton and Bush all extensively engaged in marketing throughout their administrations.[22] On the 2nd May 1997, following a landslide electoral victory the previous day, Blair announced to the Labour party: now starts the campaign for the next election. Labour has been seen to embody the political marketing approach, both in terms of its electioneering and its 'permanent campaign' approach to government.[23]

In response to this, within the political marketing literature, advocates argue that marketing strategies should be part of not only the formal electioneering period but also should become embedded as part of the governing process. Newman described and positively advocated these techniques during the Clinton era, stating that 'the same marketing tools that were used to get Clinton into the White House could also be used to govern'.[24] As Butler and Collins argue '[p]olitical marketing is a continuous process which cannot be divorced from all the other public aspects of politics . . . [T]he electorate is the constant focus of marketers' attention. Election campaigns are continuous . . . '.[25] To this end, political marketing has been prescribed at all times, not just during election campaigns but to all areas of political communication and organisation.[26] It has been advocated that the influence of marketing 'cannot be confined to the limits of formal election periods'.[27] Not only does the political marketing literature describe campaign practice, but it is now also regarded as means of governance. It is viewed as necessary so that the candidate/party can remain responsive to the voters, while governing—enabling them to achieve the longer term goal of reelection.

This responsiveness to the public is also used as the basis for the normative defence of marketing in politics: that marketing is a 'good thing' for politics. Scholars within political science and management marketing literature claim both its benefits and advantages.[28] These normative claims centre around the notion that marketing renders politicians more responsive and accountable to the public, who at the same time are provided with a greater opportunity to participate.[29] In this way, political marketing has been presented as a panacea to cure the ills of democracy.

State of the debate

While it has become broadly accepted that the activity of politics is increasingly informed by insights from marketing, the academic literature in political marketing is not homogenous. Contributions to the literature have been made from scholars in management, communications and political science.[30] Some draw attention to extensive media and communications strategies as the driver of change and the increase of marketing in politics.[31] However, it is the theories and models from managerialist marketing which inform the dominant literature in this field. These are used to coherently describe the practice of political elites in contemporary electioneering. At the same time, these models are also used to make a series of predictive, prescriptive and normative claims, and it is these claims which form the basis of the critique presented here.

The more critical literature[32] offers a range of descriptive accounts suggesting the negative effects of increased campaign expenditure[33]; the 'packaging of politics'[34]; and the use of 'spin' in political practice.[35] There are also detailed theoretically informed critical analyses of the historical development of the phenomenon of marketing and those which highlight the need for greater theoretical and conceptual development.[36] Building on these accounts, the contention here is that marketing has become more than a set of descriptive models or a set of electioneering strategies. In transposing these managerial models into the political arena, marketing has, problematically, become the *content* of politics. At the core of this book lies the question, does political marketing subvert democracy and the political process? The answer, in its present form, is yes. Marketing has subsumed politics. While marketing may be an inevitable feature of the contemporary electioneering environment, this is not without its problems.

Aim of book

The purpose of this book is critique, but the intent is not nihilism. It is acknowledged that in the contemporary environment, political marketing forms a central part of political parties' or candidates' strategy. The main critique presented here is not in the use of marketing per se, but that marketing strategies have become dominant above all else. This is problematic, as will be shown, since many of the normative ideas within managerial marketing are essentially antidemocratic. It is contended here that what should be driving political marketing is a commitment to politics: a marketing that includes politics. It is also suggested that marketers through advocating the marketing process, and political actors in practice, have become complicit in the process of 'malaise', as marketing leaves little room for political content. That is, marketing reshapes the processes of politics, but in so doing downplays, indeed removes, the need for political content.

At the foundation of politics are distinctive sets of values and a vision of how society should be run, which are embodied in political ideology. In turn, these are articulated differently depending upon the ideological position of the candidate or party. For the party/candidate their *raision d'etre* is the achievement of office to implement politics which reflect this societal vision. For the public, political parties/candidates function to represent and protect their interests. The primary motivation of a business organisation is to make a profit. This tension between the principal objectives of businesses, political parties and the interests of the public forms the basis of the argument here. As such, the aim is to provide a critique of both the workings of the contemporary process and the marketing literature which seeks to inform and influence politics.

Underlying argument

The basic premise of this book is that political marketing, in its current form, is informed by a set of economic assumptions that are antithetical to democracy and serve to disconnect the public from the process of politics. That is, marketing in politics represents an ideology of disconnection.[37] A While the aim is not necessarily to assert causation, it is suggested that there is an undeniably strong correlation between marketing and public disconnection from the process of politics (as distinct from the content of politics). It is argued that to transcend and reclaim politics into the political sphere, discussion and debate need to move beyond the language of the marketplace.

To refer to politics as a marketing activity invokes a set of underlying principles. These, in marketing, are underpinned by neoclassical economic assumptions. Thus within political marketing, politics is referred to in terms of production, consumption, exchange and markets. The discourse of marketing seeks to present itself as a form of value in and of itself. That is, managerially informed marketing is presented as a 'good'. This discourse in turn serves to delineate the boundaries of that which is possible. This not only includes an ideal of what politics is, and what it should be, but also serves to embed ideas in relation to the primacy of markets. But as will be shown, the economic analogy and assumptions contained within marketing logically entail a suboptimal outcome for democracy. This discourse of marketing carries with it a series of problems both internally within the theoretical models, and externally, as these have implications in the wider context.

Internally, within the political marketing models and frameworks, it is shown how the managerialist marketing which now influences politics (both in analysis and practice) is founded in neoclassical economics. More broadly, in political science this influence has taken the form of rational choice theory. This teasing out and linkage of underlying assumptions between political marketing and rational choice theory performs a series of functions. First, to demonstrate how the political marketing literature can be viewed as located within, and a contemporary variant of, orthodox rational choice theory—specifically the seminal work of Anthony Downs.[38] Second, that the theoretical concerns and suboptimal outcomes, which flow from rational choice theory are equally applicable to political marketing. This theoretical connection is important, as it is informing a set of prescribed behaviours to political parties/candidates, which imply a related set of difficulties for the conceptualisation and practise of politics. Crucially, while rational choice accounts hold over time—that is, they can account for behaviour irrespective of the temporal dimension—what is qualitatively different in the contemporary environment is the way in which these assumptions are now advocated as a belief system, given the current context.

The process of political marketing, while internally problematic is also located within a broader, external discourse. This discourse of marketing itself serves to embed further the dominance and hegemony of markets as solutions to all social, economic and political concerns. Yet, politics is not only about the regulation of markets. Politics, whether about resolution of conflict or the allocation of (scarce) resources, is underpinned by the concept of power.[39] While power is a highly contested concept in politics[40], the discourse of marketing serves to locate power structurally within the economic system. Marketing in politics, then, would seem to be a logical consequence of the social, political and economic system characterised by a commitment to markets. Markets are no longer the mechanisms that governments and politicians regulate, but are now the arena in which all political activity is undertaken. In this sense, the marketing process is profoundly tied to the system of political economy and engagement with this plays a function in both reproducing and re-constituting this system.

What this means is to refer to politics in terms of marketing serves to locate politics *within* the system of political economy rather than politics operating to regulate it. It is accepted that this book provides a critique of the content of marketing while leaving its form intact; the very nature of the system that has produced marketing remains in this text and unchallenged. That is, while marketing can be seen as a function of the capitalist system, this is a critique of marketing rather than capitalism per se. It is also acknowledged that to replicate the language and terminology of marketing reinforces the notion that marketing can be applied to politics. On an idealistic level, it is argued that marketing and politics are mutually exclusive categories and therefore both ontologically and analyt-ically distinct. However, more practically, within contemporary politics, it is recognised that this needs to be reconciled with a context and neoliberal discourse which privileges markets and, more specifically, the practicalities of election campaigning in a technologically dense, media-centred environment. To this end, the assertion here is that if marketing has to be used in politics, then politics, not marketing, should form the central element of the process.

Where the term political marketing is used, it refers to the managerialist marketing models which inform politics (and are detailed in chapter 1). The purpose of this critique is not to provide an alternative to marketing, but to highlight the difficulties contained within the idea of applying marketing to politics, and thereby suggest opening a space where alternatives can be considered. In sum, this book sets out to explore what political marketing means for the content and process of politics. It suggests that political marketing fundamentally alters the idea and nature of politics, subjugating politics to marketing. In order to understand how contemporary politics is being recast and what this means for democracy, this book goes back to the first principles of political marketing. It concludes by arguing that the process of political marketing in its present form depoliticises politics as it denies the *content* of politics in the *process* of politics, which in turn can lead to disconnection and disengagement.

Notes

1. Marquand, 2004.
2. Crouch, 2004; Hay, 2007.
3. Lewis, Wahl-Jorgensen, Inthorn 2005.
4. Putnam, 2000.
5. Robinson,1976; Bennett et al 1999.
6. Franklin, 2002, 2004.
7. Franklin, 1994.

8. Putnam, 2000.
9. For example, Franklin, 1994; Jones, 1997.
10. Crouch, 2004.
11. Hay, 2007.
12. Stoker, 2006.
13. O'Shaughnessy, 1990.
14. Wring, 1996.
15. In the UK, Scammell (1995) connects marketing to the hire of professional pollsters and publicists and argues this first occurred in 1964; Wring traces the use of marketing strategies within the British Labour back to the early twentieth century, although he notes that it was only during the leaderships of Thatcher and Kinnock that the term marketing explicitly became part of organisational thinking (1996: 102). In America, Maarek (1995) and Beresford (1998) suggest marketing originated in the 1950s/1960s while O'Shaughnessy (1990) charts its usage back to ancient Greece. Nimmo (1999) provides a comprehensive historical overview and ancestry for the development of marketing techniques in both the UK and US.
16. Newman, 1994: 21, see also Hayes and McAllister, 1996: 137.
17. Harrop, 1990: 284.
18. Scammell, 1995: 291.
19. Mauser, 1983: 6; Butler and Collins, 1994: 19.
20. Reid, 1988: 34.
21. The term was initially used by Blumenthal,1980, but is now widely accepted and used within the political marketing literature see for example: O'Shaughnessy, 1990; Newman, 1994, 2001; Nimmo, 1999; Lees-Marshment, 2001a; Butler and Collins, 1994, 2001; Sparrow and Turner, 2001; Wring, 2001: 914.
22. O'Shaughnessy, 1990: 193; Morris, 1999; Newman, 2001; O'Shaughnessy and Henneberg, 2007.
23. Gould, 1998. For a more sceptical evaluation of the notion of a permanent campaign in both the US and UK, see Needham, 2005.
24. Newman, 1994: 22, see also Nimmo, 1999.
25. Butler and Collins, 1994: 30–31.
26. Lees-Marshment, 2001b, 694; 2004.
27. Scammell, 1999: 719.
28. For example, Kotler and Levy, 1969; Harrop, 1990; Newman, 1994; Scammell, 1995, 1999; O'Cass, 1996; Lees-Marshment, 2001a and b; Egan, 1999; Baines et al, 2002; Baines et al, 2003.
29. Harrop, 1990; Scammell, 1995; O'Cass, 1996; Lees-Marshment, 2001a and b; Kotler and Kotler, 1999.
30. For detailed and comprehensive review, see Scammell, 1999.
31. For example, Scammell, 1995.
32. See for example, Wring, 1997–2005; Ormrod, 2006, O'Shaughnessy, 1999, 2001; Smith, 2006; Franklin, 1994.
33. Newman, 1994.
34. Franklin, 1994.
35. Jones, 1997.

36. E.g., O'Shaughnessy, 1990; Henneberg, 2004, Wring, 1997, 2005; see also 2007 special issue of *Journal of Political Marketing* (eds. S. C. Henneberg and N. J. O'Shaughnessy) devoted to theory and concept development.
37. cf Taylor 2006.
38. Downs, 1957.
39. For discussion of what politics is, see Leftwich, 2004.
40. The debate over this highly contested concept at the heart of political analysis centres around the seminal contribution from Lukes, 1974.

1

Political Marketing: Literature and Practice

Introduction

Political marketing is the new black, or so it may seem at first glance. Widely accredited as contributing to 'New' Labour's electoral landslide in 1997 and later victories, in 2001 and 2005 (as well as extensively employed by the Conservative Party), the activity of political marketing has already significantly reshaped the political landscape in Britain. Both of the main parties in Britain (Conservatives and Labour) have embraced political marketing. As Scammell argues it was political marketing that 'provided rational strategies which helped Thatcher to become the only leader to win three successive elections [during the last] century'.[1] A detailed, proliferating academic literature has emerged as a response to these observed empirical tendencies. Marketing in political practice has become extensive and has been described in the successive US Presidential campaigns of Reagan, Clinton and Bush[2]; in British electoral campaigning[3]; and in the broader international arena.[4]

The political process is not static; politics takes place in a densely structured social, economic, political and technological environment. Political actors respond to changes in technology, adapting their style to developments in the media; politicians operate in both a national and international context dominated (certainly in the West) by neoliberal thinking both about the utility of markets and the way in which democracy and society more broadly is organised. Given this broader environment, it would seem a fairly logical response that political actors would adopt ideas and techniques consistent with this context that they are in. This includes applying marketing to the activity of politics. At the same time, these very actions serve to reconstitute and reinforce this social, economic and political context. This state of interaction and reconstitution has a series of intended and unintended consequences. For advocates of marketing in politics these consequences are democratising and empowering. However, a critical reflection upon the use of marketing in politics reveals a series of concerns in relation to the character of contemporary democracy; not least, it is argued that marketing serves to depoliticise the process of politics and contributes to a sense of democratic 'malaise'.

Political marketing is the application of practices and principles drawn from management marketing and applied to the theory and practice of politics. This is premised upon the assumption that political activity can be regarded as analogous to that of business. That is, political actors/parties/candidates are assumed to be operating in a 'marketplace'. This analogy continues with the notion that consumers (voters) purchase (exchange their vote) for a political product (party) on the day of the election. As such, this concerns the use of business models and concepts to structure political practice. The political marketing literature to date draws upon communications and election campaign literature; however, the field of management marketing makes the most significant contribution.[5] In 1969, Kotler and Levy's seminal article advanced the view that the marketing concept should be broadened to include political candidates. Since then, this phenomenon has generated considerable research, and has emerged as a subdiscipline in its own right, crossing the boundaries of political science and management.

The concepts and models that inform the political marketing literature have been used to describe contemporary political behaviour. However, they have also been used to support a series of normative and prescriptive claims: essentially that marketing is good for the activity of politics; it facilitates participation and engagement; and it should be used, both for these reasons, but primarily so that political actors might achieve their goal of winning elections. However, it is argued that the idea of a marketised politics itself serves to generate antipathy and is functioning to disconnect the electorate. While democratic malaise has been attributed to the media and the public, it is in fact crucial to restore political actors to the process and the contention here is that use of marketing is inconsistent with an activity (politics) which is not conducive to the process of commodification. In order to support the arguments contained throughout this book, this chapter sets out the central models and assumptions which inform the political marketing literature. The models, the claims and justifications made as a consequence of their usage are detailed, which in turn provides the opportunity to reflect upon why marketing may create problems for the activity of politics.

Background

Political marketing is a term which has been used to describe what politicians do in order to get elected. The phrase was first used by Kelley[6] in 1956 to describe the practices of political persuaders. Since Kotler and Levy[7] adopted the term in their seminal article, this phrase has become a common feature of political discourse and practice.

In political marketing, political candidates and parties are now assumed to be operating in an electoral marketplace where they are seeking to 'sell' their 'product' to the electorate. Marketing for some, then, focuses attention upon political parties and their attempts to influence the behaviour of the electorate.[8] It has become synonymous with spin[9], the packaging of politics[10] and broader media management strategies. This in turn has meant marketing has been characterised as the 'modern publicity process'[11] which reflects a 'crisis in public communication'.[12] This activity has been described as the behaviour of a 'public relations state'[13] or the workings of a 'public relations democracy'[14] where politics is 'packaged' for consumption.[15] Political marketing has been used as a 'catch all' term to describe the professionalisation of political communications which have included the increased use of political consultants, negative campaigning, advertising (in both paid and free media[16]) and public relations techniques. Assuming that the ultimate aim of political actors is to win elections, attention is drawn to the techniques, strategies and practices informed by marketing thinking that are used in campaigns.

But marketing politics is about more than this. It not only relates to presentational or stylistic concerns in electoral campaigning but to the methods and ways of thinking about what politics is, how it is, and how it should be conducted. Within marketing, media and communications are important, but the driver of political change is viewed as the 'campaigners' strategic understanding of the political market'.[17] This overt emphasis upon markets as shaping the activity of politics reflects a fundamental change in the conceptualisation of politics, what the form and function is, and what politics should be. This profound shift is reflected both in the academic literature and in political practice. In order to fully explore and understand how marketing is reconstituting politics, it is instructive to return to the basic principles which inform political marketing.

How politics and marketing have been linked

The central ideas and definitions of political marketing are imported from management marketing. Marketing is the application of techniques and strategies in order that organisations are able to make a profit. At first, this was connected with businesses whose primary objective was to secure commercial profit. Initially concerned to represent itself as a 'science' (consistent with the dominance of rationality and Enlightenment thinking), the management marketing literature suggested tried and tested rigorous techniques, which if applied as described, would, it was argued, lead to organisational success. Marketing scholars also proposed that the use of marketing need not be confined solely to the commercial arena and could (and should) be applied to many areas of public life, including services, people and ideas.[18] The application of marketing for nonprofit organisations has been expanded upon significantly within the management literature.[19] In their seminal article, Kotler and Levy advocated broadening the concept of marketing to extend beyond the product/profit-making arena, to include the marketing of services, persons and ideas.[20] Kotler and Levy argued that 'marketing is a pervasive societal activity that goes considerably beyond the selling of toothpaste, soap and steel.' Moreover, marketing, they argued, is not solely confined to the business arena: 'Political contests remind us that candidates are marketed as well as soap'.[21] In order to 'broaden the concept of marketing', they advocated the widening of the definition of a product, to move beyond a physical product, to also include: services (intangible goods); people (such as movie stars and political candidates); organisations (such as charities); and ideas (their example is the promotion of the idea of birth control).[22] While widening the term marketing to include both for profit and nonprofit organisations, the fundamental principles remain the same.

This approach to marketing, explicitly located within managerial thought in respect of marketing, is underpinned by neoclassical economic assumptions.[23] As such, if this approach is applied to nonprofit organisations, this suggests that the term profit be replaced by 'utility maximisation'. In this sense then, once the aim of the organisation is defined (in contrast to commercial organisations whose primary aim is to make a financial profit), it would appear that marketing scholars implicitly endorse this logic in their application of marketing to 'nonprofit' organisations. Not only has this occurred within academic literature, but marketing and managerial thinking have been employed in many areas of public life, from education[24] to health and broadcasting[25], from religion[26] to election campaigning. Marketing has been presented not only as the panacea to perceived organisational difficulties, but as a necessary condition of organisational thinking and behaviour. It has become conventional wisdom that campaign managers and political actors employ marketing strategies; these are regarded as a necessity in the contemporary environment.[27] The question that characterises much of the existing political marketing literature is not whether or not marketing should be used, but how it should be put into practice.

What is marketing?

A simplistic definition is provided by Kotler et al, who argue that '[m]arketing is the delivery of customer satisfaction at a profit'.[28] This draws attention to two key features: the organisational profit (or utility maximisation) and the consumer. The American Marketing Association concurs, stating that '[m]arketing is an organizational function and a set of processes for creating, communicating, and delivering value to customers and for managing customer relationships in ways that benefit the organization and its stakeholders'.[29] While highlighting that a set of strategies and techniques need to be employed by the organisation, the ontological assumption is that there are two actors in this process: the organisation seeking to make a profit (or in nonprofit organisations, maximise their utility); and the consumer. Marketing is conceived of as a process implying continuance over time, rather than a static, one-off phenomenon. It is a process of exchange premised upon the existence of a market comprising consumers with identifiable and expressed needs and wants. Subsequently, marketing is about the management of demand. This demand may be stimulated and increased or, conversely, may need to be reduced (through the process of demarketing—reducing services or increasing prices[30]). As Lury argues, 'Marketing is about trying to incorporate the customer into the production process in order to better satisfy them (sic) and thereby increase your chances of making a profit'.[31] This is done through the provision of a product, shaped by the consumer, in a competitive market environment, in order to satisfy the organisational goal of making a profit. This implies feedback and a dynamic, interactive, relatively equal relationship between the consumer and the organisation. Context is minimally implied as the existence of a marketplace.

While there is fragmentation within the discipline of marketing as to what constitutes the remit of theory and practice, the dominant paradigm of the managerial school of thinking uses simplistic models and focuses heavily upon marketing practice.[32] This is mirrored within the political marketing literature.

What is political marketing?

Although it is agreed that there is no one definition of the term 'political marketing'[33], the political marketing literature accepts and begins with the analogy of parties as businesses engaged in a competitive relationship seeking to secure an 'exchange' with consumers (voters). This is underpinned by the axiomatic assumption that political actors can be marketed in the same manner as any other commercial good.[34] Alongside this ontological supposition that parties can be conceived of as businesses and voters as consumers, advocates also suggest there is a similarity in the political and commercial contexts, and as such assume that business managers and political campaigners face similar challenges, and therefore similar responses/methods are appropriate.[35] Henneburg argues that a formal analytical definition is that 'political marketing seeks to establish, maintain and enhance long-term voter relationships at a profit for society and political parties. So that the objectives of the organisation are met'.[36] The key point here is that relationships with voters are instrumental and necessary only insofar as they enable organisations to achieve their goal.[37]

In this sense, political marketing is positively presented as a method which provides political actors with the 'ability to address diverse voter concerns and needs through marketing analyses, planning, implementation and control of political and electoral campaigns'.[38] Consistent with the positivist thinking which underpins the management marketing approaches, political marketing has been defined as the 'science of influencing mass behaviour in competitive situations'.[39] Again, drawing from the management marketing definition, it highlights a focus upon the strategies and techniques employed by political actors in a competitive (and minimally specified) context to achieve their goal. This goal is simply to win elections.[40] This definition and underlying analogy locates political marketing clearly within managerial marketing thinking. This is then further refined as the political marketing literature draws upon models and strategies derived from management marketing to inform its description of and prescription for practice.

Marketing: models, concepts and theoretical frameworks

There are two key aspects to the marketing process: marketing is a way of thinking and a series of techniques to implement that thinking. In order to achieve this, the management marketing literature contains a series of theories, models and frameworks. Starkly stated and consistent with the definitions of marketing, these models prescribe that placing the customer at the centre of the production process enables a firm to achieve its goal(s). To put the customer at the centre entails adherence to the marketing concept. Theoretically, this marketing concept enables models to be 'operationalised' and so doing will enable an organisation to be 'market oriented', which will in turn enable the organisation to achieve its goal. In order to be successful, actors must also believe in marketing; it must become a way of organisational thinking. Marketing is then put into practice through a series of techniques used to identify potentially profitable markets and 'target' them (known as the 'marketing mix').

Marketing as a discipline (and practice) is characterised by its recognition of the customer. Extensive research within management marketing is built upon the proposition that adopting a market orientation will improve an organisation's performance to the extent that it increases its chances of achieving its goal. In short, scholars suggest both a conceptual and empirical link between adopting a market orientation and success.[41] As other axiomatic principles are accepted from management marketing, so, within political marketing, this claim is accepted and, by some, used as a normative justification for the advocacy of the use of marketing in politics. Given this centrality of a market orientation to both management marketing and the political marketing literature[42], it is worth providing an overview of this framework.

Market orientation

A market orientation entails the identification of consumer demands, successfully incorporated into an organisation's product offering, in order for that organisation to achieve its goal. As such, it contains a number of key features: an understanding of customer demands; this then involves extensive information gathering/market research; it also provides a practical set of guidelines.[43] A market orientation reflects the successful adaptation of the marketing concept and is the means of implementing this concept.[44] Drawn from Keith's three-stage evolutionary model[45], organisations are assumed to 'evolve' through product, sales and market-oriented eras. While Keith's model was based on a single firm, this has come to be accepted as the generalised history of the evolution of marketing.[46] Organisational learning enables companies to 'evolve' to the next stage. Each stage is not discrete: companies begin with a product, pursue selling strategies, but having reached the final marketing stage, also combine this with responsiveness to the consumer. Keith's model stated that while businesses sought to retain a high standard of product, effectively promoted, the emphasis should be placed upon the needs and desires of both actual and potential consumers, and the product would then be modified to satisfy those desires. The key point was that the consumer should be placed at the centre of the production process. The shift was one from a focus upon supply side behaviour to an integration of supply-and demand-side behaviour. If demand-side wants were satisfied, the argument went, so the organisation should be successful. That is establishing consumer wants, incorporating them into the product, and communicating this back to the consumer so that in turn, s/he will buy the product, and the organisation can make a profit. To achieve a market orientation within management marketing is the optimal means to enhance business performance and profit.[47] At the basis of this three-stage model is the 'marketing concept'.

The marketing concept

Since its expression by Drucker in 1954, and despite debate as to its strengths and weaknesses[48], the marketing concept represents the philosophical and conceptual foundations to a market orientation, and provides the foundation of marketing thinking. It is the basic axiom of management marketing philosophy, forms the core of the discipline, and is central to both theory and practice.[49] Simply stated, the marketing concept holds that the needs of the customer are the primary concern of an organisation. This attention to the consumer differentiates marketing from earlier forms of organisational behaviour (such as a focus on products and sales). While the product itself and the selling are still significant aspects, these are done in conjunction with a product refined in accordance with consumer desires. This concept emphasises the centrality of the consumer to the process of exchange.[50] Businesses should, this literature prescribes, concentrate not on the product that they could make, but on the product the customer wants.

Focusing upon the customer entails the identification of expressed customer demand/preferences. It follows that the organisation will refine the product in accordance with these preferences/demands and as a consequence the customer should be well positioned to make a purchase. Management guru Drucker argued that 'the aim of marketing is to make selling superfluous. The aim of marketing is to know and understand the customer so well that the product fits him and sells itself. Ideally, marketing should result in a customer who is ready to buy. All that should be needed then is to make the product or service available'.[51] This emphasis upon the consumer contains two central suppositions: it assumes the consumer plays an active role in the production process; and that preferences are expressed, identifiable and available to be accommodated (and these two assumptions form the basis of critique in chapters 2, 3 and 5).

These conceptual tools and frameworks have been transposed into political science, and this three-stage evolutionary model, complete with the marketing concept, has provided an ordering mechanism through which changes in the nature of political campaigning and electioneering have been described and analysed. While there is disagreement within the political marketing literature as to when each of the three stages occur, there is consensus that contemporary electoral campaigning for at least the last twenty years has been characterised by a 'market orientation'. A series of scholars have used this framework to describe the developmental trajectory of electoral campaigning in both Britain and America, as candidates and parties become more sophisticated in their communications strategies, and their employment of marketing strategies and techniques.[52]

Within political marketing, the 'marketing concept' is claimed as the way in which to understand political marketing.[53] Where the marketing concept has been applied to the political process, this has been taken to mean that the activity of politics begins with the consumer (voter), not the product (party/candidate). This 'marketing concept' is used within the political marketing literature to suggest that the consumer [voter] is at the centre of the process, as such parties/candidates listen to [select] public opinion, provide the electorate with a 'product' that they want, in order to achieve electoral victory. To be successful, political candidates/parties must employ this concept—to respond to and adapt to voter demands.[54] This objective in politics is to enable the candidate or party to attract votes, and therefore win elections and gain power. As Newman observes, 'As in the business world, the marketing concept dictates what candidates do, and, as with businesses, candidates want to create and retain their customers'.[55]

In this sense, the marketing concept provides both a guiding template for action and a philosophical defence for this action. The axiomatic marketing concept then means for many marketers that 'the essence of marketing is reciprocity: "consumers" themselves bring something to bear on the selling; they are not passive objects and the process is an interactive one'.[56] This process of listening and responding is used to support the normative claim that the application of this concept enhances the political process. In this way democracy is assumed because accountability is claimed to occur as a consequence of responsiveness to public opinion.[57]

Implementing marketing

In order to implement the marketing concept, and thereby achieve a market orientation, a series of strategies and techniques are required. The principal conceptual tools are the marketing mix and market segmentation.

Market segmentation plays a crucial role in modern management marketing. As Dowling notes, 'Market segmentation is a primary way to search for and exploit market opportunities'.[58] First introduced by Smith[59], market segmentation draws attention to the heterogeneity of the marketplace; it highlights the differences between one consumer and another. This is based on three features: consumers are different; this difference influences demand; and segments of consumers can be identified within the market. Reflecting this in marketing strategy entails refining the product accordingly and communicating this to consumers. In order to establish this, data is required about both the size and structure of the market and trends that may influence demand. As such, this is a process that entails identifying differing 'segments' within a market; developing profiles to fit consumers within each segment; and evaluating the 'attractiveness' [to the organisation] of each segment. Markets are divided into smaller groups of consumers with similar demands. Traditionally markets were segmented into demographic, geographic, and socioeconomic variables. More recently, advances in both technology and practice have meant segmentation by a variety of variables, including consumption patterns and lifestyle choices. Once this is done, target markets are identified, a positioning strategy is adopted focusing on the target market and a 'marketing mix' selected.[60]

This notion of market segmentation again is one that plays a significant role in the political marketing literature. The tools and techniques of marketing are part of the political marketing process, generating three aspects to the political campaign: market segmentation; candidate positioning; and strategy formulation and implementation.[61] Acknowledging that political 'markets' are not homogenous[62], and consistent with management marketing, voters are 'segmented' into target groups (such as 'Mondeo Man' or 'Worcester Woman'). Once differing groups have been identified, then parties/candidates position (or reposition) themselves; (re)defining their product offering to target selected consumers (for example in key constituencies).

Once the consumer has been identified, the next stage is to employ the marketing mix ('controllable factors'[63]). One of the most widely used and enduring frameworks in marketing is that of the 4Ps[64] (price, place, promotion and product). For marketing scholars, effective marketing relies upon the successful mix of these four factors. This 'marketing mix' means that an organisation blends these four elements in different ways to suit the different markets at which they are aimed. This is then managed by an organisation to influence demand for a particular product or service. This 4P framework is widely used within the political marketing literature, again, to demonstrate how contemporary political actors have planned and executed campaigns. The 'product' is promoted in both paid media (for example, advertising) and 'free media' (for example, news coverage). Placement is used to refer to distribution, which includes regional networks and local campaigning activists. The price aspect is used to reflect the assumption that a vote is a 'psychological purchase'.[65] As such, once markets have been segmented, consumers are targeted through emphasis upon whichever aspect or combination of the 4Ps framework which has been identified as necessary to attract them. So for example, in the run up to 1997, Labour sought to present itself as 'New' (this perception being the 'product'); having identified key voters (segmenting the market), it focused attention upon Tory switchers (targeting). Promoting this product meant the use of professional publicists in both paid and free media, and the mobilisation of local-level activists. This was done in order to attract voters to exchange their vote (purchase) so that Labour could win the election (the ultimate aim of political marketing).

Notably, however, this strategy means that companies (political actors) do not have to compete in all markets. The notion of segmentation means that businesses/political actors only compete in segments of the total market which they consider likely to enable them to achieve their goal. In electoral competition terms this means that parties need only compete in identified key seats, rather than at the level of the electorate as a whole. This then presents a challenge to the implied pluralism of market competition. If political actors refine their 'product offering' only in accordance with voters who are likely to impact upon the electoral outcome, this is significantly different from all votes carrying equal weight in influencing the political process. The way in which marketing is implemented and these attendant concerns are explored in more detail in chapter 3.

Marketing as a philosophy

Marketing is a way of thinking and a set of tools to implement that thinking. Its proponents advocate that it forms a guiding philosophy for organisational behaviour. This means that the marketing concept detailed above is not only a means to operationalise models, but also functions as a philosophy: a template for thinking and guiding organisational behaviour.[66] Marketing itself is regarded not only as a set of guiding practices/frameworks and tactics, but normatively, scholars suggest, should form the core of organisational thinking; organisational success is only possible once a 'marketing mindset' has been achieved: marketing should be the guiding philosophy for the organisation as a whole, not only confined to the 'marketing department'.[67] Marketing should be infused as organisational culture; the ultimate philosophy for organisational success is marketing.[68]

The role of ideas and marketing as a guiding philosophy are significant here. In this sense, ideas about the activity of marketing become routinised and subsequently institutionalised within organisations. Through this process, these ideas are internalised and accepted as common sense. For marketing scholars this internalisation of ideas lends itself to organisational success. Clearly ideas do not occur in a vacuum but again are shaped both by their context and actors who hold these ideas. Further, marketing as a guiding philosophy does not remain internal to a particular organisation. An organisation operates within a set of political and economic institutional structures. These structures (in the West) are informed by ideas in relation to the primacy of the market as a mechanism for ordering transactions. As such, ideas are also externalised as competitors respond. The philosophy of, or ideas in relation to, marketing are adopted by other organisations and in turn become social 'norms'. Indeed, this would seem logical for businesses in an economic environment.

The philosophical roots of marketing are consistent with this context. Market thought and its development as a philosophy is clearly located within economic schools of thought. The genealogy of marketing provided by Jones and Monieson shows two significant schools of thinking: neoclassical economics (derived from English classical economics) and institutionalism (traced back to the German historical school of economics).[69] These twin aspects are interwoven to form the intellectual basis for the philosophical foundations of marketing. It is now accepted wisdom that the roots of management marketing can be located in neoclassical economics.

Importing models into politics in relation to marketing also entails importing their ideas and assumptions. In this sense then, ideas about the utility of marketing, if political actors want to achieve their goal, become the driving force in the political process. Therein lies the difficulty. Politics is about argument, persuasion and debate. It is normative and value laden, concerned also with the distribution and exercise of power. While politics also involves the regulation of markets, these markets are exogenous to political actors and the political process. In contrast, neoclassical economics is premised upon the rationality assumption and claims objectivity in its acceptance of the market as the mechanism to resolve all problems (which despite claims to neutrality can also be regarded as a value-laden claim).[70] Adopting neoclassical economic perspectives within politics means that the market *itself* becomes endogenous to the political process. Once conflated in this way, this fundamentally changes the nature of politics. While markets and politics may not be mutually exclusive, at the same time, to accept uncritically this fundamental shift in thinking about the primacy of the market as an organising mechanism for politics (and by extension society) arguably serves to depoliticise the political process.

There is nothing novel in the application of economics to political analysis. Indeed, rational choice accounts of political behaviour form a dominant approach within the discipline of politics. Given the underlying economic assumptions of the management marketing models, it would seem logical to explore the connection between political marketing and orthodox rational choice accounts and models of political behaviour (this is drawn out in chapter 2). What marketing represents, however, is a qualitative shift in the way in which modelling is used, given the conflation of theory with practice. This diverges from the manner in which models are employed in political science (and the rational choice subfield).

The use of models

Within the mainstream political marketing literature, there is a clear belief in the utility of marketing models being practically applied to the activity of politics.[71] Crucially, the distinction between management and political science is in the application of concepts and models. For the management marketing literature these are practical guides, while in political science they function to generate predictions or as heuristic devices. However, it is argued in this book that an uncritical adoption of these models has meant an uncritical adoption of the underlying assumptions. In this sense, marketing models for political marketing have also been accepted as templates for behaviour.

Within managerial marketing, concepts, frameworks and models are a set of directive behavioural tools, not just a means of modelling. Marketing is regarded as a practical discipline; 'mainstream managerial marketing discourse is replete with normative models of strategic managerial marketing practice'.[72] Managerialist literature argues that these models are a template for behaviour, which organisations 'must' adopt to be effective and successful.[73] Epistemological concerns in management marketing centre upon whether frameworks 'function successfully in guiding actions to fulfil intended purposes and results'.[74] As such, these models function instrumentally and prescriptively to structure and direct the activity of marketing.

Within the political marketing literature there is also an acceptance of this prescriptive basis. O'Cass notes that the marketing concept 'appears to be both a philosophical and practical guide for the management of marketing'.[75] These frameworks are regarded as both 'pragmatic and realistic'[76], with practical utility.[77] Indeed, the importance of applying these models in practice is a view that is widely held within the political marketing literature. Lock and Harris argue that political marketing 'has to develop its own prescriptive and predictive models if it is to inform and influence political action'[78], and as Lees-Marshment notes, '[P]olitical marketing can enable us to observe how organisations may lose touch with their market; maybe even to advise them how not to do so'.[79] Political marketing claims to be able to show a political party what they 'ought' to be doing[80], offering actors ways to improve their performance and manage their campaigns more effectively.[81] Butler and Collins note that 'research into the field of campaign/marketing management *must* be dominated by questions of practicality'[82] (emphasis added). Indeed this is nowhere more clearly evident than in Egan's view that politicians need marketing, lamenting the difficulties in getting politicians to accept the utility of such models in practice:

> Political marketers do not, however, always have it their own way. Politicians have a habit of taking back the reigns of electoral management particularly when things do not seem to be going to plan. This is largely political arrogance. Politicians, almost by definition, believe theirs is the right way. This confidence in their own ability leads them to believe that the solution to the problem is simply a case of explaining (usually in some detail) their position to the public at large.[83]

This quote highlights both the desire for marketers to influence that which they describe and the thought that marketing is the best way for actors to achieve their goals. Further, as Scammell notes, '[A]s the techniques of market research and market prediction become more "scientific" and precise, the more influential marketing and marketing experts are likely to become in politics'.[84] Given both the actual, and potential for, influence in political practice, it is then important to clarify and reflect upon what this may mean, entail, or subsequently imply. If models have practical utility, this raises issues, first in terms of renegotiating the function of modelling within political analysis, and second, more broadly, this suggests an internalisation and adherence to the assumptions of the models.

Simultaneously, and consistent with rational choice theorising and positivist political science, the political marketing models are also used to provide a scientific, predictive function. Lees-Marshment argues that the usage of political marketing [in the academic literature] 'offers the potential not simply to capture political behaviour but predict the consequences of certain types of behaviour—or lack of'.[85] The generation of predictions is also an explicitly stated aim; indeed, Lock and Harris note the 'dearth of published work measuring and *predicting* the effect of political advertising and other communication tools'[86] (emphasis added). However, in its use of models, this is where the political marketing literature parts company with rational choice theory. For orthodox rational choice theory, it is not the accuracy of the assumptions which is important, but the predictions which flow from this model. As Downs argues, '[T]heoretical models should be tested primarily by the accuracy of their predictions rather than their reality of their assumptions'.[87] As Hinich and Munger expand, '[F]ormal theories help scientists explore "what if" questions'[88], and this is the function of modelling, rather than to explore questions of what should be. Theory is used to describe what will happen under certain conditions, rather than what *should* happen.

The claims to science (implicit in the provision of 'generic models'[89]) are also difficult to substantiate if theories and models are 'adapt[ed] to suit different specific situations'[90] or if 'stages that are not relevant can be discarded'.[91] This highlights two critical points. First, as already noted, it is difficult to substantiate claims to predictions and generic modelling (and the implicit commitment to 'science') if the fundamental scientific rules of modelling are violated; if the models are altered to 'fit' the evidence. Second, this draws attention to the significance attached to the function of models and theory. Theoretical concepts are not, in scientific approaches, assumed to be things that exist[92] or are real. They are used to generate predictions. Whereas models in managerial marketing are used to advise upon behaviour, positivists in political science adopt theoretical frameworks in order to achieve the larger goal of prediction and generalisations.

Models perform a specific function in political science. They operate as means of organising and understanding phenomena and function as Weberian 'ideal types' to abstract from and simplify reality. They enable phenomena under investigation to be broken down into manageable components of analysis. Models are used within positivistic schools of thought for generating predictions, providing facts. Hypotheses are generated, empirical evidence collected and tested, and conclusions are drawn. In management they perform a different function, as they also operate as a prescriptive template for behaviour. It is this point which underpins part of the normative critique of much of the mainstream political marketing literature. Unreflectively importing these models from management has meant unreflectively importing their assumptions. If management are providing prescriptions and templates for behaviour, this is fundamentally opposed to using models to generate predictions. Clearly, predictions made using models prescribed to actors have the potential to lose their utility as predictions become nothing more than self-fulfilling prophecies. Moreover, to advocate these models to organisations whose primary aim is to generate commercial profit is fundamentally different from prescribing these models, complete with their underlying assumptions, as templates of behaviour to actors in politics.

It is therefore argued that not only are there normative issues (discussed below) associated with advocating marketing models and values to be incorporated into the activity of politics, but this prescription violates the fundamental function of 'scientific' modelling. Theory is used to describe what will happen under certain conditions, rather than what *should* happen. Scientific approaches also deny the possibility of influencing that which is observed. The neutrality of the observer is crucial for positivist accounts. Positivism suggests a belief in the separation of normative and empirical questions, in order that objective, value-free analysis can be undertaken.[93] If behaviour is prescribed to political actors then, as Hay notes, predictions become difficult to sustain as the reason they 'conform to political and economic practice [. . .] may well be precisely because political and economic actors have internalised such theories, incorporating them within their modes of calculation and practice'.[94] Political marketing cannot claim scientific status if it also seeks to prescribe that behaviour. As Green and Shapiro note, data that inspires theory cannot be used to test it.[95] Indeed, if academics seek to influence political practice by advocating these models, then the predictions generated once these models are put into practice become self-fulfilling prophecies.

Further, to advocate the usage of these models also entails adherence to the underlying parsimonious assumptions which inform them. As marketing is prescribed as a philosophy, in turn this means that the axiomatic simplification of reality becomes a standard by which reality should function. That is, political actors should behave in accordance with the simplifying assumptions of the models, and more significantly, if marketing is a philosophy, a set of beliefs, this in turn means internalising these simplifying assumptions. As the following chapter shows, this in turn can result in the internalisation of orthodox rational choice.

Normative concerns

Critical accounts of marketing caution against the direct importation and application of business models into political science given the implicit values contained, the limited discussion of democracy and the significant difference in context and product between commercial marketing organisations and political parties.[96] However, within much of the mainstream literature, alongside the prescription of models for political practice there are a series of normative claims, both explicitly and implicitly stated, in terms of the beneficial aspect of marketing for political actors, voters and the democratic process. Many of these have been justified through reference to the marketing concept.

The positive success of adopting a market orientation charted within the management marketing literature, combined with the utility of the political marketing literature to usefully describe contemporary political behaviour, has led some within the political marketing field to use this as a basis for normatively advocating the use of political marketing; the political marketing literature claims that it shows political actors what they *ought* to be doing to achieve their goal.[97] Marketing, it would seem, provides a template for electoral success. Levitt argues that marketing is essential for an organisation to survive.[98] This seminal article promoted one of the key themes of the political marketing literature, which states that, in order for an organisation to be successful, consumer demands must be at the centre of the production process. In turn, the success claimed by the management marketing literature provides the political marketing literature with a basis from which to prescribe its usage. The adoption of the marketing concept is highly significant for the political marketing literature in supporting its normative and prescriptive claims. Indeed, it is this notion that the consumer is at the centre of the process (the marketing concept) that the political marketing literature adopts as one of its central normative claims: first, because this is regarded as the best means to achieve the given ends for political actors; second, in order to support its pluralist democratic position; third, as noted above, as justification for prescribing the use of marketing to practitioners of politics.[99]

Advocates of marketing in politics highlight the way in which the use of marketing is an interactive process between political actors and voters. They highlight the existence of a twofold relationship between political actors and voters, in that these methods are undertaken, so that the ends of parties/candidates may be advanced 'in response to the needs and wants of selected people and groups in society'.[100] These needs and wants are identified via market research. It is claimed this provides citizens with greater opportunity to participate in the political process[101] in that they are assumed to contribute to and affect the product. Those advocating the use of marketing point to the definitions which highlight the role of the consumer. This, it is suggested, entails a positive benefit in that 'consumers' are not passive recipients in the political process; rather they are actively engaged in the shaping and production of the political product.

One of the dilemmas raised within the application of marketing is whether political actors become followers, rather than leaders of public opinion.[102] Presented as a dichotomy, many commentators regard this 'following' as evidence of responsiveness to the public, proof of marketing's democratising potential. This flows from the supposition of both the implicit and explicit acceptance of the marketing concept by political actors. This suggests that market research is undertaken to establish what the voter wants, then political product offering is refined accordingly to consumer demand. However, as will be argued in chapter 3, this strategic concern is used to imply, indeed state explicitly, that political actors are directly responsive to voters; political actors alter their product offering according to market demand. Significantly, though, what the market wants (which is accepted as a given once identified and negates the significance of actors shaping those wants) may well be very different from what the market will bear. The market may well bear marketing strategies, but this is very different from those comprising the market wanting those strategies. The opportunities to engage, flowing from the use of marketing, are unequal and uneven as the identification of preferences to be accommodated comes from focus groups selected by the party/organisation. At the same time, this redefines the activities that occur within a democracy, altering the nature of party competition, moving participation away from the electoral arena. Interactivity and participation are only occurring within a section of the electorate as strategic 'consumers' are identified, selected and targeted; their wants and needs are identified and incorporated into the political product. But these are those selected by the organisation to further their own ends, rather than to serve democracy or the citizenry. This is also reliant on a conception of democracy which is not clearly articulated but conforms to Schumpeterian notions of elite leaders competing and that democracy is best served by leaders responding to public opinion. It also relies on a participatory form of democracy: participation is assumed to represent and to be equated with democracy. If people do not participate, then does this suggest a lack of democracy? This concern is overlooked within the existing literature but is a theme throughout this book, as the idea of marketing negates broader democratic ideals which encompass informed citizenry, the realisation of ideals, ethics and values. In the managerially informed conceptualisation, all votes are assumed to be equal[103]; however, the implementation of marketing has meant that in practice, some votes are more equal than others (see chapter 3).

Proponents argue that not only are voters playing a more active role in the production of politics, but also assert that there have been improvements in the manner in which the electorate is informed about politics. It has been argued that the quality of information in election campaigns has been improved[104], as Scammell contends, '[M]arketing may bring real democratic benefits by improving two-way communications between voters and politicians and theoretically, at least, allowing both parties and voters to be better informed and make more rational choices'.[105] This raises two immediate concerns: first in terms of the essence of political communication and second in terms of the rationality of political parties and voters. Rather than expanding the opportunities for dialogue and debate and persuasion, information from political elites, Franklin argues, has been reduced and simplified into 'soundbites'.[106] This serves to diminish not only the quality of the debate, but the idea that debate itself is a necessary component of the political process as democracy requires citizens to be informed in order to make decisions about by whom they are governed.

Democracy

The normative claims within the political marketing literature suggest that '[p]olitical marketing makes parties more democratic by rendering them more responsive to voters' demands', hence enhancing democracy.[107] Parties are able to achieve their goals, whilst voters benefit from a greater opportunity to participate in the process[108], thereby impacting upon the nature of the political product. In so doing, there is assumed to be increased political responsiveness and, by implication, an increase in accountability.[109] Scholars within the political marketing field claim that political marketing has a direct benefit for democracy, as it assumes that parties accommodate voter preferences and demands. As Lees-Marshment asserts, 'The idea that political parties should design their product to suit voters, rather than argue their case, works against traditional views of politics. Alternatively it could be argued that it shows that parties are becoming more responsive to people, which is good for democracy'.[110] This suggests a move towards populist, not popular, government/party behaviour, rather than providing a vision for society, underpinned by a set of ideological beliefs and values; this suggests government by public opinion.

Scammell argues that political marketing can be located within a populist view of democracy, or 'plebiscitary democracy'.[111] Within this view, the aim of democracy is the satisfaction of citizens' individual interests; the public interest is assumed to be the sum of these. This suggests that, if all individual preferences are satisfied, this will serve the public interest. While political marketing advocates response to public opinion, this, arguably, has led to an increase in ideological populism rather than popular government/electoral competition. For O'Shaughnessy, marketing methods lead to a lack of political leadership 'since they take as their reference point a servile rather than a directorial attitude to public opinion'.[112] Populism claims to bring 'power to the people'[113] as does political marketing. While populism is traditionally considered to be 'of the people, but not of the system'[114], arguably this neatly summarises the marketing of politics. Given the underlying assumptions of marketing, while it is presented as responsive to and therefore of, or for, the people, ultimately, it is argued here, it serves to separate them from the system.

Underlying pluralism

Consistent with orthodox rational choice accounts, the political marketing literature has an underlying adherence and commitment to pluralism. Pluralism derives from Dahl's seminal work in the 1960s.[115] Dahl described the decision-making process in New Haven, as open, fluid, carried out by political elites, with a role for interest groups to influence the process and act as a countervailing balance to prevent the dominance of a single set of interests. Interest groups play a crucial role in this process, mobilising and emerging to represent a set of interests. They also function to act as a check and balance on state power. This resulted in a diversity of interests being represented and power was similarly dispersed. The state was regarded a neutral; interest groups were potentially equal in influence; no one group dominates as governments relied on a successful economy.[116] This pluralist description was also normative and prescriptive: not only was this how democracy worked in practice, but this was how democracy should work.

For pluralists the main areas of interest are elections, party competition and interest groups.[117] Elections are the mechanisms through which voters are able to participate and hold their leaders to account.[118] Interest groups are able to articulate voter demands through interelectoral periods. Interest groups are regarded as important indicators of strength of feeling in respect of a particular issue (assuming away any problems of collective action). In this way, power is dispersed and held in check, which suggests a degree of systemic fairness, as all mobilised interests are represented. Electoral accountability is important for pluralists, and representative institutions are a necessary condition for democracy.[119] Voters are assumed to exercise control through competitive elections, party competition and interest group activity. In emphasising this increased responsiveness and accountability to voters, the existing political marketing literature operates with an implicit conception of pluralism.

Politics in pluralism is seen as the resolution of conflicting interests, and groups are crucial to this process[120], reflecting the diversity of society. Pluralists argue that fluid and open structures mean that voices are heard and represented in the political system. Conflict is peacefully resolved, or demands are, in political marketing terms, incorporated into the political product, and therefore contained within parameters that do not provide a threat to political stability.

One of the significant aspects of pluralist thinking was the assertion that their description of democracy provided an ideal standard through which the achievement of democracy was assessed.[121] As noted above, the managerial models associated with marketing have also been prescribed as methods of political behaviour. In this sense, consistent with the development of pluralism, political marketing, while providing a comprehensive description of empirical reality, has also become a normative theory. Methodologically, political marketing proceeds in the same manner as pluralism. The focus is upon observable behaviour, which leads to a focus upon observable outcomes. Within political marketing, there is the assumption that the party that can be best seen to accommodate voter preferences is the party that will be electorally successful.[122] Assuming the voter is at the centre of the exchange process, with fixed, identifiable preferences, available to be accommodated into the political product, endorses the notion of observable outcomes, which are empirically testable. The focus is upon government as the site of power; the significance of electoral competition; the assumption that groups provide the site whereby competing interests are identified and incorporated into the political product. For pluralists, this means attention is focused upon 'the reality and importance of multiple channels through which citizens can control their political leaders and shape the development of public policies'.[123] For pluralists these interests are represented at the site of interest groups. For political marketers these interests are identified at the site of focus groups. Focus groups are the site where interests are assumed to be expressed and, in turn, aggregated and incorporated into the political product. This responsiveness to the electorate through the use of focus groups is regarded as something which only occurs on the day of the election, but something which informs the period of governance. This expression of voter preferences negates the need (and associated costs) for interest groups to emerge, as demands are directly expressed to elites in this forum.

Pluralist thinking conceives of democracy in the same terms that the pluralists observed democracy happening. In this sense, they negated questions as to the proper extent of participation, the proper scope of political rule and the suitable forms of democratic regulation (that have consistently underpinned democratic theory). These questions were ignored, or addressed by referring to current practice.[124] In this sense, as Held argues, '[T]he ideals and methods of democracy become, by default, the ideals and methods of the existing democratic systems'.[125] Much of the political marketing literature shares this assumption. In providing ample description of contemporary electoral practice, it fails to address these normative problems associated with pluralism. Clearly, the political marketing literature can substantiate its claim to improve the democratic process if its own standard is that which it prescribes democracy should be. It is the realism of its description of political practice that enables political marketers, as with pluralists, to argue that their models are democratic. Alternative approaches are subsequently regarded as unreal and, therefore, by implication given this starting point, undemocratic.

Conclusion

Marketing is a ubiquitous feature of contemporary politics. For some its use is regarded as inevitable, empowering and positive. This book challenges these claims. While some element of marketing may be necessary given the social economic and political environment political parties and candidates are in, it is worth considering the broader issues at stake aside from winning elections. In order to think through some of the implications of applying marketing to politics, this chapter has set out what marketing is; the simplistic models used to simplify and prescribe practice; and how these, and their underlying assumptions, have been transposed into politics. Marketers argue that politics is as amenable to marketing as any other commodity. This assumption forms the basic premise of a burgeoning academic literature. Simplistic and simplifying models are used to describe practice, but also contain a series of prescriptive aspects. In marketing management, these are templates and guidelines for organisational behaviour, advocated for success. Models are prescribed and assumed to lead to success, measured as achievement of goals. In the business world these are profits, in politics this is assumed to be success at an elite level: the winning of an election. This focus upon elite level activity, however, has meant that the implications of the use of marketing both for citizens and the democratic process has been widely neglected.

There is prolific literature detailing the use of marketing in political practice, and the aim here is not rehearse this comprehensive and detailed description. The purpose, rather, is to reflect upon a series of normative, analytical and theoretical concerns about the processes and thinking that underlie and inform contemporary elite political activity. The broad argument presented is that using marketing contributes to the depoliticisation of the political process and that this effects a series of concerns relating to the character of contemporary democracy. To make this argument, the underlying ideas, theories and frameworks that inform 'political marketing' are discussed. In order to provide the context, this chapter has detailed out the basic premises of political marketing, and the claims which are made as to its utility. It began by defining what is meant by marketing and showing how this definition and related theoretical tools have informed the development of the field of political marketing. The political marketing literature has applied models from management marketing and used them to generate a series of often-conflated claims, which are descriptive, prescriptive and normative. In disentangling and revealing these underlying assumptions, it is possible then to reflect upon the broader implications of applying marketing to politics. Each theme will be discussed in subsequent chapters, which explore the significance of underlying neoclassical economic assumptions (chapter 2); the way in which marketing is implemented in politics (chapter 3); the role of ideology in marketing and what this means for politics (chapter 4); the significance of the definitional and ontological assumptions which characterises politics as a process of production and consumption (chapter 5); and to suggest a link between the malaise characterising the contemporary political environment and the application of marketing to politics (chapter 6).

Notes

1. Scammell, 1996: 132–33.
2. Shama, 1976; Newman, 1994, 1999; O'Shaughnessy, 1990; O'Shaughnessy and Henneberg, 2007.
3. Scammell, 1995; Lees-Marshment, 2001a, 2001b; Butler and Collins, 1994; Wring, 1996, 2001; Smith and Saunders, 1990.
4. Farrell and Wortman, 1987; Bowler and Farrell, 1992; Butler and Ranney, 1992; O'Cass, 1996, 2001; Lilleker and Lees-Marshment, 2005; Strömbäck, 2007.
5. For a review of this, see Scammell, 1999.
6. Kelley, 1956.
7. Kotler and Levy, 1969.
8. Mauser, 1983: 5; Newman, 1999: xiii.
9. Jones, 1997.
10. Franklin, 2004.
11. Blumler, 1990.
12. Blumler and Gurevitch, 1995.
13. Deacon and Golding, 1994.
14. Davis, 2002.
15. Franklin, 1994.
16. Paid media being billboard posters and TV adverts, and free media being, for example, the news (electronic and print) and, increasingly, forms of popular culture, such as Blair's appearance on *Richard and Judy* and *The Simpsons,* etc.
17. Scammell, 1999: 723.
18. Kotler and Levy, 1969; Kotler and Zaltman, 1971; Shapiro, 1973.
19. Rothschild, 1979; Shapiro, 1973; Scrivens and Witzel, 1990; Gwin, 1990; Von der Hart, 1990; Lancaster and Massingham, 1993; Evans and Berman, 1994: 398; Walsh, 1994.
20. Kotler and Levy, 1969: 10; see also, Fox and Kotler, 1980; Kotler, 1979; Kotler and Zaltman, 1971.
21. Kotler and Levy 1969: 10.
22. Kotler and Levy 1969: 12.
23. Sheth et al, 1988.
24. Olssen and Peters, 2005.
25. Leys, 2001.
26. Most recently two churches in Chicago have employed marketing in a bid to improve recruitment (Marketing News, 15/5/06).
27. Kotler, 1975; Niffenegger, 1989; Shama, 1976; Lees-Marshment, 2001a, 2001b; Reid, 1988.
28. Kotler et al, 2005: 5.
29. *www.ama.org.*
30. Lawther et al, 1997.
31. Lury, 1994: 94.
32. This is widely accepted within the marketing literature. See for example Kitchen, 2003: 6; for comprehensive review of differing schools and emphases, see Sheth et al, 1988.
33. Scammell, 1999; O'Cass, 2001.

34. With the widely used example of soap powder, Kotler and Levy, 1969; O'Shaughnessy, 1990: 1.
35. Butler and Collins, 1996; Newman, 1994: 34; Reid, 1988.
36. Henneberg, 2002: 102–3.
37. See Wring, 1997: 652 and Sackman, 1992.
38. O'Cass, 1996: 48.
39. Mauser, 1983: 5.
40. Lock and Harris, 1996: 18.
41. This link was initially made by Narver and Slater, 1990; Kohli and Jaworski, 1990 forming the basis for empirical and theoretical research by Jaworski and Kohli, 1993; Greenley, 1995a; Pelham and Wilson, 1996; Baker and Sinula, 1999; Moorman and Rust, 1999; Farrell, 2000; Harris and Ogbonna, 2001; Hooley et al, 2000; Ellis, 2006; Berry, 1997; Day, 1999; Deshpande et al, 1993; Slater and Narver, 1994 and 2000.
42. Shama, 1976; Smith and Saunders, 1990; Wring, 1996, 2005; Newman, 1999; O'Cass, 1996, 2001; Lees-Marshment, 2001a and b; O'Shaughnessy, 1990; Butler and Collins, 1996.
43. Uncles, 2000.
44. O'Cass, 2001: 1006.
45. Keith, 1960.
46. Keith, 1960; Quester et al, 2004; Stanton et al, 1991; Zikmund and D'Amico, 1989.
47. Levitt, 1960; Kotler, 1984; Kotler and Andreasen, 1996; Webster, 1988.
48. See for example, Houston, 1986.
49. Houston, 1986; Keith, 1960; Levitt, 1960; McKitterick, 1957; Webster, 1988; Borch, 1957; Kotler and Levy, 1969; Ellis, 2006; Greenley, 1995a and b; Wensley, 1995; Jaworski and Kohli, 1993.
50. Keith, 1960; Levitt, 1960.
51. Drucker, 1974: 64–65.
52. Wring, 1996, 2005; O'Shaughnessy, 1990; Smith and Saunders, 1990; Lees-Marshment, 2001a and b; Newman, 1994; Shama, 1976; Dickinson et al, 1986 For theoretical discussion, see also Wring, 1996; Butler and Collins, 1994; O'Cass, 1996, 2001.
53. Scammell, 1999: 726.
54. Mauser, 1983; Reid, 1988; Shama, 1976; O'Cass, 1996; Lees-Marshment, 2001 a and b Egan, 1999.
55. Newman, 1994: 34.
56. O'Shaughnessy, 1990: 2.
57. Kotler and Levy, 1969; O'Cass, 1996; Lees-Marshment, 2001a and b.
58. Dowling, 2004: 169.
59. Smith, 1956.
60. Kotler and Andreasen, 1987: 117–55.
61. Butler and Collins, 1996; Newman, 1994: 11; see also Smith and Saunders, 1990; Smith and Hirst, 2001; Baines et al, 2002; Baines et al, 2003.
62. Butler and Collins, 1996: 35.
63. Uncontrollable factors being environmental factors, such as the political, legal, cultural, and social environment and resources available to the organisation. Hunt, 1976: 20.

64. Hunt, 1976; Dowling, 2004: 47; O'Cass, 2001.
65. Reid, 1988. For comprehensive description of the use of this framework in both Britain and America, see for example Wring, 1997; Newman, 1994 respectively.
66. Brownlie and Saren, 1997; Kotler and Zaltman, 1971; O'Leary and Iredale, 1976.
67. Kotler and Andreasen, 1996: 37; Moynihan and Titley, 1995: 193; Lancaster and Massingham, 1993: 7–18; Hooley et al, 1990: 22.
68. Webster, 1992; McKenna, 1991.
69. Jones and Monieson, 1990.
70. Within political studies there is a widespread dispute as to what constitutes the discipline. For an excellent summary and overview of this, see Leftwich, 2004, seminally brought to the fore by Lasswell, 1936.
71. E.g., Kotler and Levy, 1969; O'Cass, 1996; Butler and Collins, 1996; Egan, 1999; Lees-Marshment, 2001a and b.
72. Hackley, 1999: 722.
73. Kotler and Levy, 1969: 15; Kotler and Kotler, 1999: 6.
74. Marsden and Littler, 1996: 647.
75. O'Cass, 1996: 48.
76. Mauser, 1983: 1.
77. See also Reid, 1988; Smith and Saunders, 1990: 304; Butler and Collins, 1996: 42.
78. Lock and Harris, 1996: 23.
79. Lees-Marshment, 2001b: 706–7.
80. O'Cass, 1996: 56.
81. Maarek, 1995; O'Cass, 1996: 59; Smith, 2001.
82. Butler and Collins, 1994: 32.
83. Egan, 1999: 496.
84. Scammell, 1995: 19.
85. Lees-Marshment, 2001b: 705.
86. Lock and Harris, 1996: 21 and 23.
87. Downs, 1957: 21.
88. Hinich and Munger, 1997: 1.
89. E.g., Butler and Collins, 1994: 21.
90. Butler and Collins, 1994: 20.
91. Lees-Marshment, 2001b: 695.
92. McDonald, 1993: 553.
93. Marsh and Furlong, 2002: 22–23.
94. Hay, 2004b: 28.
95. Green and Shapiro, 1994: 35.
96. Smith and Saunders, 1990; O'Shaughnessy, 2001; Wring, 2005; Smith, 2006.
97. O'Cass, 1996: 56; Lees-Marshment, 2001a and b: Egan, 1999; Kotler and Levy, 1969; Shama, 1976.
98. Levitt, 1960.
99. An explicitly stated aim within the literature, see Lock and Harris, 1996; Lees-Marshment, 2006.
100. Newman, 1999: xiii.
101. Scammell, 1995: 298.
102. Henneberg, 2006.

103. Butler and Collins, 1996: 42.
104. Harrop, 1990: 297.
105. Scammell, 1995: xv.
106. Franklin, 2004.
107. Lees-Marshment, 2001a: 225, 228.
108. Kotler and Kotler, 1999: 3; Lees-Marshment, 2001a and b; O'Cass, 1996; Harrop, 1990; Scammell, 1995: 298.
109. Kotler and Kotler, 1999: 3.
110. Lees-Marshment, 2001b: 699.
111. Abramson et al, 1988, cited in Scammell, 1995.
112. O'Shaughnessy, 1990: 247.
113. Canovan, 1999: 2.
114. Taggart, 1996: 32.
115. Dahl, 1961.
116. Later neopluralists revised this to acknowledge the influence of business which is assumed to have a 'privileged position in government'. See Lindblom, 1977: 172. Dahl, 1982, also later revised his understanding of pluralism to acknowledge that counterveiling power does not always act as a check against the interests of business.
117. Dunleavy and O'Leary, 1987: 23.
118. Dunleavy and O'Leary, 1987: 25.
119. Dunleavy and O'Leary, 1987: 24–25.
120. Smith, 1995: 211.
121. Smith, 2006.
122. Cf. Lees-Marshment, 2001a and b.
123. Dunleavy and O'Leary, 1987: 23.
124. Held, 1997: 209.
125. Held, 1997: 209.

2

... And Rational Choice Theory

That political parties/candidates behave in a similar manner to businesses and compete around the average voter is neither an original nor startling insight in political science. This simple premise is one of the key starting points within rational choice theory, which in itself has come to play a dominant role in the analysis of politics.[1] As such, this chapter will show how the increasingly influential field of political marketing can be identified as a contemporary variant of this theoretical approach. By rendering this link explicit, it is then possible to demonstrate how political marketing in its current form has inherent, and as yet unexposed, weaknesses.

As demonstrated in chapter 1, essentially the political marketing perspective is premised upon an analogy: political marketing comprises a series of tools and techniques that are used to promote a political 'product' in a political 'marketplace'. Consistent with economic analyses of politics, the focus is upon the production and consumption of politics. Underlying this is the unquestioned notion that competition is occurring in a marketplace. Attention is drawn to the existence of a political market, with actors/parties competing for votes. Underpinned by neoclassical economic assumptions of rationality, political actors adopt rational means-end behaviour in order to achieve their goal: to win elections. Political marketing is clearly underpinned by assumptions drawn from neoclassical economics. First, this is evidenced implicitly by the use of frameworks drawn from management marketing, which are derived from economic philosophy and business practice. These accounts begin from the central assumption of analytic rationality on the part of the consumer and the business.[2] Second, these neoclassical economic roots are explicitly accepted within some of the political marketing literature and the link to earlier economic models of political behaviour has also been acknowledged.[3] These analytical claims, and underlying economic assumptions, can be considered to be analogous, and have been linked to, those of rational choice theory, in particular the seminal work of Anthony Downs' (1957) *An Economic Theory of Democracy*. Rendering this explicit facilitates the identification of, and the opportunity to reflect upon, a series of difficulties highlighted by rational choice accounts and implicit within the political marketing literature. This link means that the use of marketing can be seen to institutionalise the process by which party platforms come to resemble one another, thereby reducing the choices available to the voter. The adoption of marketing as a philosophy can by extension be viewed as the internalisation of rational choice theorising. In short, the more parties conform to the prescriptions of marketing models, the more their behaviour becomes consistent with the theorising of Downs. Not only can this lead to partisan convergence in terms of electoral competition, but it is argued that if voters perceive political actors to behave in a manner that is consistent with rational choice theorising, then it becomes rational for voters to behave in this way too. Rational choice theorising also draws attention to the paradox of voting, that the cost of voting exceeds the benefits; therefore, a rational voter will not vote.

Given the emphasis upon the 'consumer' influencing the nature of the product, this chapter also reflects upon how economic accounts deal with the issue of preferences. The following chapter addresses how preferences are identified and fed into the political 'product', but this chapter provides the theoretical background and as such draws attention for the potential for manipulation of preferences by the organisation.

As such, this chapter sets out the way in which neoclassical economics have been used to inform political science and draws out two of the key concerns this raises: in respect of the nature of party competition and the paradox of voter turnout. It then explores the inherent structuralism within rational choice which suggests that actors have little 'choice' available to them, and that they are operating within a climate that privileges ideas in relation to markets. This would suggest that the adoption of marketing and by extension the internalisation of rational choice assumptions becomes less of a choice but the optimal route available to political voters and actors alike. This has an impact not only in terms of the potential effects upon electoral turnout, but also raises broader concerns in the manner in which democracy is characterised, conceived of and practised.

Economic models in political analysis

The use of economic behavioural assumptions to inform political analysis is nothing new. Most prominently these accounts in political science are located within rational choice theory. Rational choice adopts the methodology of neoclassical economics and seeks to model the behaviour of individuals. This begins with the assumption that individuals are rational actors, seeking to maximise their utility, who have expressed identifiable and transitive preferences. They use means-ends strategies in order to achieve their goals. As such, rational choice provides a model, or series of models, through which the use of parsimonious assumptions facilitates the simplification of reality. This is done in order to explore the way in which actors optimally adapt to their circumstances and pursue the rational course of action available to them. This enables analysts to account for (and explain) political behaviour and generate predictions. As with marketing, this approach has a normative aspect in that it suggests how actors should behave in order to achieve their goals; prescribing a focus on the means of achieving goals, rather than what those goals should be. These approaches are also positive in that 'what is' and/or 'what if' questions are addressed; implications are deduced from a set of premises.[4] Rational choice is both a theory and a method. It is a method of studying politics using a particular set of assumptions. These assumptions are used to construct models from which deductive explanations of individual behaviour are produced. It is also a theory because the use of these models has generated a set of coherent arguments about the nature of political competition.

Methodologically both approaches proceed in the same manner. Political marketing models begin with a series of simplifying assumptions used to produce generic models from which propositions are deduced, and are then tested against the empirical evidence to produce retrospective predictions.[5] Despite the parsimony of these assumptions, it is their applicability and testability that are assumed to establish the validity of the theory (consistent with the Downsian view).[6] However, it is the contention of this book that the use of this modelling also raises a series of implications for the democratic process. The basis of the argument presented here is to extend analysis to that of the model itself. Rather than using the model to generate post hoc predictions and descriptions of political behaviour, and given the prescriptive character of these models, it is argued here that this modelling also contains a series of implications for the way in which the activity of politics is perceived by analysts, practitioners and the public.

The following sections will highlight the convergence between the political marketing literature and orthodox rational choice accounts (summarised in table 2.1). This will be done with particular reference to the seminal rational choice account of electoral competition. As such, it will proceed initially by identifying the underlying assumptions within the political marketing literature. Subsequently, it will outline Downs' model of electoral competition and party behaviour, before finally discussing the assumptions made about voters. Consistent with orthodox rational choice, this agency-centred approach is reflected within much of the political marketing literature, which assumes that actors are relatively unconstrained by their environment.[7] However, as has also been noted, there is an inherent structuralism in rational choice theory[8], and this point will inform the critique offered of the political marketing literature.

Table 2.1. Convergence between orthodox rational choice theory and political marketing modelling

Key Aspects of Orthodox Rational Choice Theory[9]	Political Marketing
Assumption of rationality	Evidenced through acceptance of underlying neoclassical economic assumptions
Individuals are units of analysis	Attention is drawn to political actors (parties and candidates) and voters
Models use simplifying assumptions to produce deduction	Marketing models imported, simplifying assumptions accepted, with the explicitly stated aim of generating predictions (see chapter 1)
Predictions are post hoc	Description of campaigns using models is used to justify the utility of marketing as an explanatory tool with predictive capacity
Individuals are seeking to maximise their utility	Political actors employ marketing for the purpose of winning elections
There is a clear hierarchy of transitive and expressed preferences that are identifiable	Voter preferences are identifiable through market research and available to be accommodated
Normative in prescribing means to achieve goals (without specifying what goal should be)	Accepts this normative aspect; prescribes marketing to win elections

Key Aspects of Orthodox Rational Choice Theory[9]	Political Marketing
The behaviour of political parties in electoral competition can be predicted given the distribution of voter preferences	Given this identification, the adherence of political actors to the marketing framework can mean electoral victory (see chapter 1)
Draws attention to problems of collective action	Attention to the underlying assumptions of political marketing can draw attention to the collective action problem of voter turnout (see chapter 6)
Limited awareness of discussion of broader contextual factors	Assumes political actors and voters in a market. Minimal specification of context.
Implausible theoretical assumptions	Simplistic and simplifying models adopted from management, premised upon rationality assumption

Table 2.2. Specific theoretical assumptions

Rational Choice	Political Marketing
Parties behave as if businesses	Parties behave as businesses
Voters behave as if consumers	Voters are consumers
Political actors pursue policies to win office	Political marketing is necessary to achieve office
Preferences fixed, expressed, identifiable and transitive, and available to be accommodated	Focus groups, opinion polls and market research identify expressed preferences. These preferences are then incorporated into the political 'product'
Unimodal distribution of preferences	Unimodal distribution of preferences
Unidimensional space (characterised by political ideology)	Unidimensional space assumed (characterised by marketing ideology)
Voter choice based on ideology (not policy)	Voter choice based upon brand (not policy)
Policies 'bundled' into ideological package	Policies 'bundled' into a brand image

The nature of party competition

In economic accounts of two-party competition, parties are assumed to converge and compete around the median voter. Preference accommodating strategies are pursued in order for parties to seek to maximise votes. These frameworks are described in order to (a) demonstrate how the political marketing literature and this economic modelling are analogous, as summarised in tables 2.1 and 2.2 and (b) to argue that the use of marketing institutionalises the process of partisan convergence. This in turn reduces the 'choice' available to voters.

Existing political marketing research overtly identifies its foundations in neoclassical economic thinking.[10] Congruent with rational choice theorising, the principal assumption that informs the political marketing literature is: parties behave like businesses competing for votes in an arena which is analogous to that of a commercial marketplace. One area of analysis within rational choice theory is a focus upon spatial models of competition. While initially derived from economics, these have been extensively applied to the activity of politics. Spatial models of electoral competition assume that parties compete in a 'space'. The primary assumption here is that political space can be mapped as a linear, one-dimensional spectrum. This is conceived of as an ideological continuum. In orthodox economic accounts of politics, this is from extreme left to extreme right with positions in between. Candidates/ parties thus position themselves within this space in order to define their competitive stance. There are three main components to this model: (1) that voters will choose the candidate or party most able to maximise their own utility; (2) that parties will maximise their utility by seeking to attract the greatest number of voters; (3) that assuming a unimodal distribution of expressed voter preferences, parties will converge and compete around the centre ground. This was first articulated by Downs, who provided the seminal and enduring work on electoral competition and provides the starting point for theories, methods and assumptions from economics to be explicitly applied in attempts to account for political behaviour.[11] This modelling of party competition begins with the analogy of parties as if businesses and voters as if consumers operating within a marketplace.

Downs and party competition

Downs drew from Hotelling's[12] work to offer the insight that electoral competition can be modelled and described in a manner analogous to that which occurs within an economic market, with political parties behaving as if they were businesses, and voters assumed to behave as if they were consumers. In this sense then, the political market is assumed to comprise buyers and sellers actively engaging in a process of exchange. This is governed by a set of rules, and the process of exchange is influenced by supply and demand.[13] Parties were assumed to be unitary rational actors, motivated by the desire to maximise their utility (votes) in order to achieve their goal (office). Politicians would identify voter preferences in order to seek to incorporate them into party programmes. This would be done so that popularity, and hence votes, would have the potential to be maximised, in order for political actors to achieve their goal. In a two-party system, both parties would seek to accommodate the preferences of as many voters as possible. Voter preferences were assumed to be (a) identifiable and (b) distributed unimodally in a 'bell curve' distribution in a one-dimensional space. This then would logically suggest the convergence of electoral programmes as parties competed around the median voter.

Political marketing accepts the underlying conception of rationality, and marketing is used to provide 'rational'[14] strategies for behaviour. Political marketing assumes in its prescription of these models (indeed this is also explicitly stated) that the party best at marketing will win the election—voter preferences are assumed to be susceptible to comprehensive marketing strategies. Voter preferences are also assumed to be fixed and identifiable through the choices they make. Parties are office seeking, and, therefore, need to accommodate voter preferences in order to maximise the number of votes they receive in order to achieve office. To attract voters, in rational choice accounts, policies are part of loose ideological bundles. This is regarded as a cost-saving device for voters. In political marketing terms, the brand replaces ideology as the cost-saving device for voters.

Context and conception of democracy

Consistent with the minimal specification of context, the key components of the political market are 'the existence of a mass electorate; competition between two or more parties for the votes of this electorate; and a set of rules governing this competition'.[15] Following Downs, and Schumpeterian conceptions of democracy, the political process is regarded as a 'democratic method [which] is that institutional arrangement for arriving at political decisions in which individuals acquire the power to govern by means of a competitive struggle for the people's vote'.[16] This instrumentalist conception of democracy is implicitly accepted within the political marketing literature. Democracy is not imbued with an intrinsic value; rather, it is a mechanism through which competition is structured and facilitates the means through which actors can achieve their goal. That goal is assumed to be electoral victory.

The Downsian account assumes a single dimension within which competition occurs. This is a consequence of assuming a unimodal distribution of voter preferences. This would suggest that parties are responsive to voters, positioning themselves around the centre ground, and that political conflict can therefore be mapped in a single-issue space. This leads to parties locating themselves around the centre ground, in order to compete for votes that are thought to exist in a single peak. The political marketing literature also assumes a single peak, as parties compete around the median voter. The unidimensional space in political marketing is a marketing, not a 'political', ideological one, though. Political marketing alters this Downsian assumption of 'space', as the site where competition occurs is assumed to be characterised by marketing, this renegotiation is discussed later (see chapter 4).

Emergent issues

Policy substance, within the political marketing perspective, is only regarded as important in terms of its effect upon party image. This would suggest that political marketing again fits with the Downsian assumption that 'parties formulate policies in order to win elections, rather than win elections in order to formulate policies'.[17] In two-party systems, political actors are not directly motivated to give voters the policies or product that they want, rather they offer the 'product' as a means to achieve their primary goal—to maximise votes and win elections. As has been noted, substantive policy debates are less likely to be the focus of marketing.[18] Scammell argues that 'policy discussion is related not to intrinsic merits or national interest, but to potential effects on party images'.[19] In emphasising the importance of image, political marketing implicitly accepts the orthodox rational choice assumptions about voter 'rationality'. Downs argues that the costs of acquiring information are greater than the benefits derived from voting. Therefore, voters make their choices based upon ideologies, or in political marketing terms, brand images, saving themselves the costs of gathering detailed information about policy stances.[20] This is done in order to appeal to voters who are assumed to cast their vote affectively. In this sense, this might suggest that competition becomes peripheral, that rather than seeking to differentiate their 'products', leaders become content to offer stylistic changes.[21]

If, as rational choice implies, competition between parties is perfect, this indicates that, ultimately, parties will offer identical solutions to political problems. Logically developed, this implies that, whichever party wins the electoral competition, policy outcomes and subsequent individual utility will be the same, regardless of the party in office. Thus, the costs of mobilisation considerably exceed the benefits, and it becomes rational for the individual not to vote. The paradox, that it is rational not to vote, goes to the core of rational choice critique and is something which many attempts have been made to overcome.[22]

Spatial models of electoral competition are operationalised, premised upon the assumption of a median voter.[23] That is, voter preferences are represented on a unidimensional ideological spectrum and are assumed to exist as a single peak. So, there is the assumption of a unidimensional ideological spectrum; a single dimension of political conflict. For spatial models of electoral competition to be applied, parties and voters must fit along a single ideological dimension. As the parties converge ideologically (assuming a unimodal distribution of voters), their relative position provides less opportunity to make a distinctive choice and, thus, the act of voting becomes less than rational.

The act of voting

Rational choice predates political marketing in its assumption of the voter as consumer. Tullock notes, 'Voters and customers are essentially the same people. Mr. Smith buys and votes; he is the same man in the supermarket and the voting booth'.[24] Downs (and much of the political marketing literature also shares this assumption) assumes voters behave in a rational manner. Voters will vote for the party which provides them with the most benefits.[25] Voters are also assumed to vote either in favour of, or against, the incumbent administration. To vote in favour, signals the desire for a continuation of existing policies, to vote against means that the opposition will be required to make changes once in office.[26] This also means that, despite the convergence around the median voter, there is a difference between the two parties. For Downs, it does matter, and does make a difference, which party is elected.[27] Voters, however, are regarded as 'not interested in policies *per se*, but in their own utility incomes'.[28] Assuming costless and complete information, voters then assess the present utility under the incumbent administration and the potential utility from the competing party. Voters then establish a preference between the two, consequently voting for the party that s/he prefers.[29] This assumes that choices are equal to, and reflect, expressed preferences. The assumption of costless information, for Downs, makes voting a rational act.[30]

Voters, for Downs, are assumed to vote affectively; that is, they are assumed to identify with a 'brand' image. They are not assumed to assess rationally the costs and benefits of each policy (this is consistent with Downs' explanation for the adoption of ideology). Spatial models of electoral competition suggest that voters choose parties based upon ideology. They do not assess each policy in terms of its distance from themselves. To make a choice based upon policy requires too many costs. Therefore, the space in which political competition occurs is an ideological space rather than a policy space. Within political marketing competition is assumed to occur between brands, not policies. As with Downs' model, voting within much of the political marketing literature is assumed to have an expressive function. Political marketing assumes the existence of a political market; this is the electorate.[31] However, despite being regarded as consumers, within political marketing the vote is regarded as 'a forceful social and ideological affirmation'[32] and a 'psychological purchase'.[33] Major social cleavages are thought to be expressed in elections, with votes reflecting identity before issues.[34] Party image is considered a more significant factor for voters than policies.[35]

Retrospective voting is accounted for within the political marketing literature (not unlike Fiorina's retrospective model of voting behaviour). While voting is a one-off activity every four or five years, the decision for whom to vote, within the political marketing literature, may depend upon the service received over the previous electoral period.[36] Consistent with rational choice revisions, political marketing focuses upon the benefits and costs to democracy and the role of civic duty. Yet, this is problematic in itself. To assume that the voter is a consumer and that voting is an act of consumption, denies the civic responsibility attached to the notion of citizenship (see chapter 5).

The utility of Downs' model stems from the fact that it provides a formal and deductive explanation of voters and parties in an analogous marketplace. Rational choice modelling allows for a less static and deterministic interpretation of electoral activity. In highlighting the importance of party competition and its potential impact upon voting behaviour, this model goes beyond the traditional party identification perspective which argues that voting behaviour is sociologically structurally determined as a result of historical conflict resolution.[37] However, while rational choice accounts seek to explain voting behaviour as a rational act, given that the costs of the act of voting invariably outweigh the individual benefits, paradoxically it becomes rational not to vote, but to 'free ride'.[38] Downs acknowledged this and reverted to sociological explanations of time- and cost-saving mechanisms (as indicated above), although to some extent, this undermines his original premise that all action is based upon the individual as a rational actor.

Voting also has a broader systemic function, and for Downs this activity makes democracy possible; without it, the system collapses. He assumes that 'citizens of a democracy subscribe to its principles and therefore derive benefits from its continuance'.[39] He argues that despite the costs of obtaining information, and the assumption of voter rationality, this would rationally lead to voter abstention, given that the costs outweigh the benefits. Given the limited likelihood of a single vote making any difference to the electoral outcome, it is rational for individual voters to abstain, letting others bear the costs of voting, while benefiting from the continuance of the democratic system. Downs argues that voters do, however, vote. Voters are assumed to be motivated by a sense of 'social responsibility' leading them to behave in a manner that contradicts the assumptions of rationality. They vote for affective/emotional reasons, rather than 'rational' ones. Further, Downs seeks to overcome the problem in respect to voting by giving participation a structural property. 'Participation in elections is one of the rules of the game in a democracy, because without it democracy cannot work'.[40]

The motivation for voter behaviour has been an issue which has plagued rational choice theorising. In an inductive attempt to overcome 'the paradox that ate rational choice', Fiorina sought to provide a more realistic explanation of voting.[41] He argued the voter acted instrumentally, rather than rationally, and voted retrospectively. Voters considered the past performance of the party, not just the present. Voting was not a new decision at each election but resulted from the development of party identification and retrospective evaluation. Voters were directly influenced by retrospective judgements and, subsequently, were assumed to reward governments for good times and punish them for bad times. This implied that citizens/consumers made an informed decision. Building on this, Himmelweit et al developed the consumer model of voting, as a systems account, from a social psychological approach. This allowed for the interdependence of the individual and society by examining social reality and individual experience of that reality.[42] This model was predicated upon the axiom of the voter as an informed consumer. In accepting a changing environment and an individual's perception of that environment, they argued that their framework provided an essentially cognitive model.[43] Voting was assumed to be an individual and active, rather than a passive, activity, with emphasis placed upon policy preferences. From this perspective, individuals were assumed to assess the ability of parties to implement their proposals before casting their vote. Voters consciously and instrumentally decided for whom to cast their vote. While accepting that voters may have developed 'brand loyalties', Himmelweit et al argued that 'each election is like a new shopping expedition in a situation where new as well as familiar goods are on offer'.[44] They dismissed the notion of partisan identification, arguing it was not central to explanations of voting behaviour. Further, they argued that their findings suggested that '*in the future the influence of the individual's past habit of voting on his or her subsequent vote will, if anything, decrease further*'.[45] These assumptions of issue-based voting have been adopted within the marketing literature, although the 'issue' is not one of policies or politics, but primarily focused around a brand or an image, emphasising style over substance, image over policy content.[46] This is done to connect with the 'consumer' who 'purchases' ahistorically, without sense of political loyalty, in a manner akin to any other consumer purchase, such as soap powder. Given the fluidity of cognitive and affective components which motivate this choice, the preferences of voters need to be expressly incorporated into the political product, the assumption being that if voters perceive a political actor/party has accommodated their preferences, this will motivate the voter to vote for that particular party/actor.

Voters within political marketing are assumed to have identifiable and expressed preferences or wants. Therefore, extensive research, through focus groups, opinion polls and market research, is used to identify these voter preferences. As Shama argues, the 'marketing concept is interested in the basic political needs and wants of the voters with the intention of offering them candidates who are capable of satisfying these needs and wants'.[47] Once these needs and wants, or preferences, are identified, the political product is refined accordingly in order to accommodate them. The point is to offer a candidate/party who satisfies voter demands, or appears to accommodate voters' expressed preferences. The party that accommodates them most successfully will be the party that wins the election. Or, in political marketing terms, the party/candidate that most successfully utilises marketing will be the one which wins the election.[48]

The way in which these preferences are identified and incorporated into the political product, or the way in which marketing is implemented, is discussed in the following chapter. However, given the significance of voter preferences in shaping the political 'product' and providing a rationale for voting behaviour, it is useful to understand what is meant by voter preferences.

Assumptions about voter preferences

The political marketing literature makes a series of key implicit assumptions in respect of preferences. Consistent with orthodox rational choice assumptions, preferences are taken as a given. They are also assumed to be fixed, expressed and identifiable. In assuming that voter preferences are fixed, the options available to political actors in electoral competition are limited. This would suggest that political actors then pursue preference-accommodating strategies. The successful identification and accommodation of these preferences is assumed to enable the party or candidate to maximise their utility. Parties redesign their 'product' to fit expressed voter preferences (identified through opinion polling and focus groups); the party which offers the best 'fit' is assumed to gain the most votes and, therefore, win the election. Political actors identify what voters want, then provide a 'product' that reflects these preferences; preferences appear to be accommodated in order that organisational objectives may be achieved.

In both the rational choice model and the political marketing literature, preferences are assumed to be single peaked. In both rational choice terms and political marketing terms, it is the distribution of preferences that determine the party's positioning. The direction of causality is from voter to party. This again confirms the preference accommodation thesis. If the preferences are assumed to be distributed bimodally, parties will compete around the left and right poles. The political marketing literature notes the assumption of the bimodal distribution of preferences in the 'product' and 'sales-oriented' era of its framework. This leads the party to focus on their product, and the selling or promotion of it, assuming a market in which voters are located at either the left or the right. Parties assume they are accommodating the preferences of voters at either end of this ideological spectrum.

Preference shaping

The management marketing literature (and its political marketing derivative) claims a normative justification for the adoption of marketing strategies in the satisfaction of consumer demands. Consumers are assumed, by the management marketing literature, to impact upon the process of producing the product. However, not only must identifiable and expressed consumer wants and needs be accommodated and satisfied[49], but there is also space for an element of manipulation, as the organisation may seek to shape those wants and needs.[50] Marketers, advocating an ethnographic approach to marketing[51], note the importance of consumer involvement with the idea of the product, that they should be involved is beneficial, as this then makes them much more receptive to the promotion of that product. As Dowding notes, 'Preferences and power are intimately linked . . . for we assume that people generally act in order to promote their wants. However, individual wants are not merely givens which themselves require no explanation. Actions are explained by examining beliefs and desires'.[52] These actions and beliefs can be shaped by organisations and political parties in order to further their own interests.

Subsequently, this would suggest that voters' behaviour must also be shaped so that it is influenced favourably towards the product made available by the organisation. In political terms, this suggests that political actors also must seek to engage in preference-shaping strategies, prior to presenting a product that supposedly accommodates preferences. Consistent with revisions made by Downs[53], values and beliefs become an important part of the process. Marketing as a philosophical position then has a potential social and political impact. Indeed, Edwards goes as far as to suggest that marketing 'remains central in shaping our conceptions of ourselves, past and present'.[54]

So, this is not the equal relationship that is first implied. The ultimate goal of marketing is the influencing of behaviour and, while the primary objective is not to educate or to change values, this may be done as a means of influencing behaviour.[55] The marketing literature argues that marketing is 'concerned with the process by which people adopt, maintain, or discard patterns of behaviour—or accept ideas and beliefs that are precursors to behaviour'[56], advocating a more preference-shaping role for actors than explicitly acknowl-edged in the political marketing literature. Within this literature, preferences must be shaped by an organisation before they are accommodated. Preference-shaping *precedes* preference-accommodation. In political marketing terms, this would suggest that prior to explicitly claiming to accommodate voter preferences in terms of a political product, polit-ical actors must first shape those preferences, through proselytisation and/or persuasion. If it is not political actors who seek to shape those preferences, then consideration must also be given to the role of other actors (for example, the media and business). What this means is that the reciprocity and transparency first suggested by placing the consumer at the centre of the process becomes asymmetric.

Preferences: critique

As noted in chapter 1, there is space within the marketing literature for the organisation to manipulate the preferences of the consumer, as the organisation may seek to shape those wants and needs.[57] This is less explicitly acknowledged in the political marketing literature, which suggests that marketing is used only to identify expressed wants and needs, and sub-sequently to accommodate them, in order that the party (organisation) may achieve its objective (win an election). The political marketing literature operates upon the assumption that preferences are identifiable and available to be accommodated. It is unable to account, however, for the source of these preferences. How are preferences formed in the first in-stance? Adopting this simplified assumption of preference accommodation negates the ability of actor's with state power to pursue preference-shaping strategies.[58] Further, if voters are assumed to cast their vote affectively and rationally, the information that they receive in order to do this is provided through the mass media. It is acknowledged that the media and politicians each have their own agenda, yet the information through which the citizen makes his/her informed choice for whom to vote is mediated and represented through the mass media. This provides the media with an opportunity to play a role in preference-shaping strategies, and to define the parameters of available preferences. Political marketing deviates from orthodox economic accounts in discussing how preferences are identified and incor-porated in to the political product through the collection of public opinion using opinion polling and focus groups. This provides political marketing a means through which to claim a normative defence; that is, the claimed responsiveness to public opinion. However, if the site of preference expression occurs outside of the electoral arena, this in turn affords the possibility of greater influence to those involved in focus groups and the generation of public opinion data, undermining the ideal of equality at the ballot box.

Problems also arise in rational choice accounts in respect of assumptions made about the nature of preferences. The basic Downsian model does not account for where preferences come from, or how they are determined and identified. This perspective assumes that pref-erences are exogenously fixed and unaltered by participation. This approach further fails to allow for parties manipulating the structural bases of preferences[59]: how do parties attempt to shape voter preferences by altering the environment within which these preferences are formed? Downs later acknowledged the problems associated with assuming preferences as a given; accepting that their nature and changes may in fact impact upon economic and political behaviour.[60] He also admitted nonrational factors into analysis, arguing that 'the central institutions that constitute democracy probably cannot be sustained for long without both reinforcing its key social values in the minds and hearts of existing citizens, and inculcating those values in the minds and hearts of future citizens as they grow up'.[61] This means that while voter preferences may need to be accommodated, this is not a straightforward process. There is an acknowledgment that preferences are not preexisting but may shaped within a broader context.

Political marketing and orthodox rational choice: critique

Having shown how the political marketing literature can be considered analogous to rational choice accounts, these accounts are now developed through critique in order to highlight the importance of a given context in structuring choices available to political actors. These theoretical issues are teased out in order to provide (a) a more systematic and detailed theoretical framework for analysis and (b) a more comprehensive understanding of political action.

Structural limitations

The limitations of rational choice theory may also be levelled at political marketing. In adopting simplifying assumptions, and reducing analysis to the level of the individual actor (parties are assumed to behave as unitary actors), rational choice theory tends to neglect the specificities of the broader institutional context in which such rationality is exercised.[62] By focusing on observable behaviour, political marketing misses the role of structures and the dynamic of structures impacting upon and affecting individual behaviour. Yet, rational choice theory claims to seek to 'illuminate how choices are made within structures, the agenda sometimes stretching to the consideration of how rational choices reproduce or transform structures'.[63] Dowding acknowledges the latent structural elements of rational choice in arguing that *'it is the structure of the individual choice situation that does most of the explanatory work. It is the set of incentives facing individuals which structurally suggest behaviour to them; by studying those incentives together with assumptions about the way actors make decisions we come to understand why people act as they do'.*[64] However, he goes on to deny the significance of structures in explaining outcomes, arguing that 'the form of explanation I am associating with rational choice uses explicit assumptions about behaviour and in them it is the actions which are the causes of outcomes and not the structures'.[65] Dowding here reaffirms agency as causal for explanations of behaviour in rational choice accounts. This agency is accepted in much of the political marketing literature which emphasises the behaviour of agents as determinants of outcomes.

If rational choice theory (and by logical extension, political marketing) is broadened to acknowledge the introduction of behaviour as a dynamic process, then it becomes apparent that individuals interact with and are affected by, yet may also reproduce and transform, the structures within which they operate. However, this broadening has been rendered difficult by the existing dominant ontological and epistemological position of political marketing. If it is accepted that individuals operate within given structures, which may impact upon their behaviour, yet may not be directly observed, this has two implications. First, in order to fully explore the consequences and potential impact of political marketing, it is necessary to move beyond a focus on observable behaviour, and to analyse such behaviour with an explicit acknowledgement of the existence of unobservable structures (such as ideology) which may impact upon such behaviour. Second, it is necessary to acknowledge the impact of ideational elements in affecting behaviour and the context in which actors operate, or *perceive* that they operate. Thus, structures and institutions may shape preferences and frames of reference through which actors view the context within which they find themselves.[66] For example, it may be necessary to consider the role of other actors in constructing the preferences of the electorate, i.e., the media, and the constraints that this may impose upon political actors. Further, the language used to describe this process is part of a broader discourse which defines the parameters of choices available to all actors. Actors are clearly not autonomous individuals but are connected to their environment which in turn structures the choices available to actors. This is not to suggest a structural determinism, but that there is a dynamic at play which privileges some choices over others. In this way, actors, by making those choices interact with and reconstitute that environment, which in turn structures or inhibits subsequent choices. That is, this is a dialectical and continual process which impacts over time.

While the political marketing approach adds to orthodox rational choice models in providing rich descriptions of contemporary electoral behaviour, it may need to be broadened in order to increase its descriptive capacity. It may need to borrow from other perspectives in order to explain where preferences and interests come from and to recognise the constraints and opportunities afforded within the densely structured political environment in which actors find themselves operating. While acknowledging the existence of other actors in the political market, their role in the exchange is regarded as limited, as rational choice accounts separate action from structure. This serves to downplay the dynamism of the context in which political actors operate. To assume a direct, two-way relationship between political actors and voters is to neglect the complexity of a densely structured political environment. Surely if other actors exist in a marketplace, they too have the potential to 'consume' the product and to engage in more subtle exchange relationships with the producer of the product. This raises questions as to the nature of the exchange with these other actors. What do they bring to bear on the political product? How are their preferences accommodated? How does this conflict with accommodating voter preferences? Does this mean that the voters' preferences ultimately are shaped in order to accommodate the preferences of other actors within the market?

Political marketing, with its implicit assumption about preferences, also equates material preferences with interests. This has two significant impacts. First, it downplays the role of the ideational in the analysis. Second, it conforms to the classic pluralist assumption about power. Here, interests are identifiable, agents (negating the impact of structures and the potential latent exercise of power[67]) exercise power through observable conflict. In adopting simplifying assumptions, and reducing analysis to the individual actor, this negates the broader institutional context in which such rationality is exercised.[68] Context is crucial in understanding the actions of an individual. Rational choice suggests a certain path dependence, whereby there is a rational course of action available to an actor in a context which is taken as a given. Therefore, the political marketing derivative also implicitly accepts that the rational course of action available to political actors, in the contemporary environment, is to adopt marketing strategies in order to accommodate market preferences.

In some respects this becomes contradictory. On the one hand, there is the suggestion that structures define the rational course of action available to an actor. Therefore, if the structure (or context) is known, this negates the need for agents, as there will be only one given course of action available. This can be read from the structure/context. On the other hand, a dynamic is introduced, implying the capacity of individuals, making rational choices, to transform the structures within which available rational choices may be made. If rational choices transform structures and alter the context in which rational strategies may be selected, this highlights the significance of ideational analysis. By reducing analysis to the material, it assumes that actors have a perfect knowledge of the context in which they find themselves, paradoxically reducing the role of agency. Agents' behaviour becomes determined by the context. To introduce ideational variables into the analysis enables the recognition of differing motivations for behaviour, with the potential for a variation of outcomes. Moreover, this begins to enable an understanding of how actors are motivated, and how different motivations may produce alternate outcomes, as opposed to the path dependency assumed in rational descriptions.

The role of modelling

Downs notes that the function of economic analysis is to (a) identify the ends which an actor is pursuing and (b) to analyse the means of achieving them.[69] This is an analytical toolkit, however, rather than a template for behaviour. Downs' model is positive, in that it shows what will happen under a set of conditions. Simplifying assumptions are used to abstract from reality—they enable a focus upon the key components of phenomena. Downs' work is also explicitly presented as a model. It is a device through which reality can be simplified and used to facilitate predictions. The instrumentalist assumptions are simplified versions of reality for the purpose of modelling, not prescriptions for action.

Rational choice theory prescribes behaviour in order to achieve aims; it does not prescribe what those aims or end goals should be.[70] Political marketing prescribes behaviour in order to enable political actors to achieve their end goal (to win elections). In order to maximise their utility (vote maximise/win elections), the political marketing literature suggests that political actors need to adopt marketing strategies. Rationality is means-ends, in that certain strategies (means) are selected instrumentally in order to satisfy given ends—marketing strategies are selected to enable political actors to win elections. As rational choice theory provides a method by which an actor can adapt optimally to his/her circumstances, so political marketing provides a set of tools and techniques to enable political actors to adapt within a given environment. Rational choice models seek to identify logical possibilities rather than statistical predictions. The purpose of rational choice models, therefore, becomes not actually to measure voting behaviour empirically in order to make predictions, but to provide an analytic framework of possibility. It becomes important, therefore, not to overemphasise the empiricist application of rational choice theory; this point can also be extended to the political marketing literature.

Conclusion

Theoretically, political marketing can be demonstrated to have its roots in orthodox rational choice theory, and is able successfully to describe contemporary electoral behaviour. However, it mistakes evidence consistent with its account as a normative defence of its contribution to democratic practice. Rational choice uses reason, raising analytical onto-logical questions. Rational choice accounts claim to demonstrate how choices are made.[71] Linking these two literatures together demonstrates how political marketing, as a contemporary variant of orthodox rational choice, faces a series of challenges. The key concerns stated here then are that by locating the political marketing literature within rational choice accounts, a concomitant set of problems arise. First, rational choice theorising illustrates how party platforms and competition can converge around the median voter, limiting choice available to voters. In terms of electoral competition, the basis of marketing can be seen to be following the Downsian trajectory of competition around a single peaked distribution of voters, mapped along a unidimensional space. This means parties compete around a median voter. As parties move closer to each other, differences between them become peripheral. Competition becomes about stylistic differences rather than policy substance. In this way, it can be argued that the use of marketing, in practice, merely institutionalises the processes by which party platforms come to resemble one another. Second, this median voter is assumed to have preferences that are expressed identifiable and available for accommodation, negating the possibility that these may be shaped. Third, it can be seen that once this centripetal competition occurs, there is little or no incentive to deviate away from the centre ground. As such, fourth, there becomes an institutionalisation of the processes by which party platforms converge. To highlight the importance of structures illustrates how actors may have little 'choice' available to them. In turn, this means that an awareness of the broader material context in which politics takes place, enables an understating of the context in which it would appear to be a logical, rational response of political parties/candidates to adopt marketing.

Attention is also drawn to the problem of prescription. As these underlying assumptions become internalised (as advocated by marketing practitioners and academics alike), further difficulties arise. Orthodox rational choice modelling has developed not only to account for party competition but voting behaviour too. Here then to advocate marketing to political actors is to prescribe rational choice theorising. To internalise this and pursue this as a guiding philosophy conflates normative and positive accounts. This has further implications. The more that voters perceive political actors behaving in a manner consistent with rational choice theorising, the more likely it is that voters will behave this way too. This means that voters are likely to perceive the costs of voting as outweighing the costs of participating. Not only does this reinforce the paradox of rational choice—that it is rational not to vote—this also renders these models ontological rather than analytical, and violates their functions. Yet, for the political marketing literature to assume that voters do vote fails to address the empirical reality of declining turnout (see chapter 6). Significantly, these underlying economic assumptions in rational choice theory are divorced from their context. First, this inhibits comprehension and analysis, but second, this reinforces the methodological individualism of economic accounts. Orthodox economic accounts deny a broader context of political, social and cultural practices. In so doing, the individual is isolated and disconnected from this context. Advocated as practice then, this in turn suggests that individuals should be isolated from the wider society, concerned only with their individual self-interest, disconnected from the processes of politics and society more broadly. This practice is discussed in the following chapter.

Notes

1. It is particularly dominant in American political science, Green and Shapiro, 1994, and in Britain is one of the main areas within which contemporary research is published, see Marsh and Savigny, 2005.
2. O'Driscoll and Murray, 1998: 407.
3. Mauser, 1983; Newman, 1994; Butler and Collins, 1999: 55; Scammell, 1999: 726, 739; Lees-Marshment, 2001b: 694; Wring, 1997.
4. Hinich and Munger, 1997: 1.
5. Butler and Collins, 1994; Lees-Marshment, 2001b: 705.
6. Downs, 1957: 21.
7. For exceptions, see e.g., Wring, 1997; Butler and Collins, 1994.
8. Cf. Hay, 2004b; Tsebelis, 1990; Dowding, 1991, although while Dowding and Tsebelis acknowledge the existence of context in structuring choice, their accounts are still intentional, in contrast to Hay, 2004b.
9. Rational choice aspects adapted from Hay, 2002: 8–9.
10. Mauser, 1983; Newman, 1994; Wring, 1996; Butler and Collins, 1999: 55; Scammell, 1999: 726, 739; Lees-Marshment, 2001b: 694.
11. Downs, 1957.
12. Hotelling, 1929.
13. Downs, 1957; Scott, 1970.
14. Scammell, 1996: 132.
15. Gamble, 1974: 6.
16. Schumpeter, 1947: 269.
17. Downs, 1957: 28.
18. Butler and Collins, 1994: 27.
19. Scammell, 1995: xii.
20. Downs, 1957: 98.
21. Scott, 1970: 17–19.
22. For a summary, see Whiteley, 1995.
23. This is a convenient assumption, for the purposes of enabling mathematical modelling to be formulated.
24. Tullock, 1976: 5.
25. Downs, 1957: 36.
26. Downs, 1957: 41–42.
27. Given that 'if the opposition wins, it is sure to carry out policies different from those the incumbents would have carried out had they been re-elected'—Downs, 1957: 42.
28. Downs, 1957: 42.
29. Downs, 1957: 49.
30. Downs, 1957: 261.
31. Butler and Collins, 1999: 62.
32. Butler and Collins, 1999: 62.
33. Reid, 1988.
34. Butler and Collins, 1999: 63.
35. Egan, 1999: 496.
36. Egan, 1999: 498.
37. Cf. Lipset and Rokkan, 1966.

38. Olson, 1965, argued that it is rational for self-interested individuals to 'free-ride' rather than join organisations to pursue collective goods. Mobilisation is explained through the provision by the organisation of selective material incentives. In terms of electoral competition, free riders would let others bear the costs associated with voting, given that they would continue to receive the same benefits irrespective of their participation.
39. Downs, 1957: 261.
40. Downs, 1957: 267, 269.
41. Fiorina, 1989.
42. Himmelweit et al, 1985: vi.
43. Himmelweit et al, 1985: 2.
44. Himmelweit et al, 1985: 12.
45. Himmelweit et al, 1985: 205, original emphasis.
46. Harrop, 1990: 279.
47. Shama, 1976: 771.
48. Lees-Marshment, 2001a, 2001b.
49. Levitt, 1960.
50. Kotler and Andreasen, 1991; Lovelock and Weinberg, 1988.
51. Woolgar, 2004.
52. Dowding, 1991: 30.
53. Downs, 1991.
54. Edwards, 2000: 58.
55. Kotler and Andreasen, 1996: 38.
56. Lovelock and Weinberg, 1988: 9.
57. Kotler and Andreasen, 1991; Lovelock and Weinberg, 1988.
58. Dunleavy and Ward, 1991: 112–44.
59. Dunleavy and Ward, 1981: 351–80.
60. Downs, 1991: 145.
61. Downs, 1991: 165.
62. Hay, 2002: 9.
63. Ward, 1995: 84.
64. Dowding, 1991: 18, original italics.
65. Dowding, 1991: 24.
66. Hall and Taylor, 1996.
67. Cf. Lukes, 1974.
68. Hay, 2002: 9.
69. Downs, 1957: 4.
70. Elster, 1986: 1.
71. Parsons, 2005: 6.

3

Implementing Marketing in Politics

While the previous two chapters were concerned with providing an overview of the models and the underlying assumptions which inform political marketing, this chapter is concerned with exploring how marketing is put into practice. The political marketing literature claims that while political marketing may build on rational choice assumptions, it provides a broader picture of party behaviour; in particular, showing *how* parties identify the demands of the median voter.[1] In this sense, political marketing claims to provide both a method and a description of that method.

Within these political marketing models, politicians are assumed to identify voter preferences in order to incorporate them into party programmes. While marketing techniques are being used, and the political marketing framework provides a means of describing the extent to which parties' behaviour has been informed by marketing, it also remains connected to the rational choice literature in the assumption that voter preferences are fixed and available to be accommodated. The simplistic assumption in marketing is that once identified, these preferences are fed back into and reshape the 'product' offering. As noted in the previous chapter, however, preferences may also be shaped. The contention here is that political elites also attempt to shape voter preferences at the site of public opinion collection. Yet, if preferences are also shaped at the site of expression, the accommodation of these preferences is skewed to the interests of the political parties/candidates, suggesting a 'mobilisation of bias'[2] in the incorporation of voter preferences into the political product. This chapter explores how voter preferences are identified, and how actors use this information to inform their campaigning; in so doing, the methods of opinion data collection associated with marketing are discussed and it is argued that this process is antithetical to the ideals of democracy espoused by adherence to the marketing concept. Putting marketing into practice involves a variety of techniques and strategies, but given the emphasis upon the consumer's interactive role in the creation of the 'product', this chapter will explore (1) how public opinion is identified and fed into the 'product'; (2) how the product is then 'targeted' at key sectors of the electorate in order to mobilise electoral support; and (3) the antidemocratic consequences of this.

Background

The use of marketing techniques has enabled strategists and commentators alike to claim that contemporary campaigns are now centred on the voter in that 'the candidate must define themselves in the voters' eyes in a way that is consistent with their thinking. The challenge to the candidate becomes one of structuring an image consistent with focus group results and tracking polls'.[3] In the UK and the US, marketing has been a regular feature[4]: Reagan's period in office was heavily informed by focus group findings; Clinton's presidency relied upon extensive market research into the impact upon public opinion each policy proposal may have. Bush is also known to rely heavily on poll data, repositioning himself, for example, on environmental issues, in accordance with this. It is also widely acknowledged that in the UK, Labour's modernisation process was heavily influenced by focus group findings. The extensive findings from these focus groups influenced not only policy content but significantly, presentation and image construction, down to the minutiae of Blair's tone and language.[5]

On the surface, this behaviour is consistent with the ideals of the marketing: 'The marketing concept holds that the needs of the consumers are of primary concern and should be identified, and attempts made to satisfy the identified needs'.[6] The centrality of marketing to Labour's thinking is evidenced by Philip Gould, one of Labour's chief strategists during the modernisation process, who argued

> With the emergence of a new more responsive relationship between government and citizen, the public has a right to be consulted on issues that will directly affect them. If changes are to be made to the NHS or schools, we should first listen to the people who use those services. More and more users of public services will behave increasingly as consumers: demanding the best on their terms, instead of what others think is best for them. Market research has a crucial role to play in making this process work.[7]

This adheres to political marketing models which prescribe the centrality of public opinion for the construction of the political 'product'.

While a number of strategies are employed to collect this opinion, the marketing models assume and imply a straightforward input; that identified voter preferences directly shape and influence the political product. This is then communicated back to the consumer. However, there are tensions between the identification of public opinion and how it is collected and used to the advantage of the political party. The mainstream political marketing literature relies heavily on the notion that parties respond to public opinion, and make normative claims in respect to the benefits this provides for democracy.

Given the prominence of focus groups in marketing research, and their essential function in both the construction of the political 'product' and campaign strategy formation, this chapter will begin with an overview of the focus group method and its underlying assumptions. This is done in order to draw out, first, how the use of this influential method has been used symbolically to claim credibility (through reference to the underlying scientific principles) and second, how they are used to support the aforementioned normative claims. This discussion is illustrated with reference to Labour's modernisation process in 1997, given the extensive influence of these findings on their electoral strategies. To identify public opinion is only one part of the process, and the way in which this opinion is used by political actors is highly significant. The second part of the chapter draws out the way in which increasingly sophisticated technology has been used to support the implementation of marketing, and building on the illustration of the Labour party, reference will be made to their 2005 election campaign. Finally, this chapter will provide a critique and argue that there is a crucial significance not only in how and what data are gathered, but how both the data and the method are represented in both theory and practice, and these are antithetical to democracy.

Identifying voter preferences: focus groups

Identifying public opinion is an essential aspect in informing campaign strategy and is consistent with the principles of marketing. Surveys and databases are used to identify, collate and store public opinion data, but it is the usage of focus groups that has accelerated over the last two decades. On one level, this can be attributed to broader questions in respect of the reliability and perceived inadequacies of other methodologies in politics (for example, following 1992 when the polls famously 'got it wrong'[8]). However, this can also be seen as a logical consequence of the growth in the application of marketing in politics, which itself is heavily reliant on this methodology.[9]

While polling can still be used, it is largely triangulated with findings from qualitative research. Quantitative data is collected through a process of sampling which establishes demographics of given 'segmented' target groups. These demographic categories have become increasingly diverse as technology has advanced (as will be illustrated below), but focus groups have become an essential means through which political actors can establish their campaign strategy.[10] Marketers have emphasised the importance of ethnographic aspects of marketing; listening to the consumer, but recognising that the ideas of the consumer also play a fundamental role in the acceptance of the product.[11] Focus groups play an important role for the marketing strategist, and given the influence of marketing in politics, it is unsurprising that this methodology has also been transposed into the political arena. As noted, this gathering of public opinion is claimed as evidence of the normative utility of marketing; that is, this method is used not only functionally to generate data in a manner which is regarded as scientific and therefore credible, but also symbolically as evidence of adherence to the marketing concept. As this method is largely uncritically accepted as performing these two functions, and as this is a claim which is contested within this book, it is worth providing a brief overview of the foundations and development of focus group methodology.

Underlying metatheoretical assumptions of focus groups

Despite adopting a seemingly qualitative approach to data collection and analysis, the use of focus groups, alongside opinion polls, are regarded by many as a scientific method of generating information. Indeed, the symbolic function of being 'scientific' is as significant (albeit implicitly) as the method itself. While highlighting the strengths of qualitative methodology, and the yielding of rich data in respect of observable behaviour, there is also a desire to adhere to make qualitative research 'more scientific'.[12] This is largely in response to the positivist critique that qualitative data is 'soft' data; no more than a series of personal anecdotes, and subject to the bias of the researcher. As such, this data, for critics, is regarded as lacking reproducibility, generalisability and can be regarded as 'unscientific'. In order to address this, focus group research can be, and is presented within academic literature as 'scientific', due to the rigorous nature of the techniques and the influence of logical positivism.[13] Focus group research, from this perspective, adopts two key principles: researcher neutrality and systematic procedures. Researcher neutrality is essential (rejecting any notion of subjectivity of the researcher or moderator) in order that the findings are not influenced in any way.

While the data that is produced is qualitative rather than quantitative (traditionally, although not exclusively, associated with 'scientific' approaches), the systematic collection of the data is done in a scientific manner. Although more interpretivist approaches have been incorporated to generate data, the claims to knowledge themselves are still presented as 'scientific'. As King et al[14] suggest, qualitative research can adopt the standards of scientific research by focusing upon observable data, testing it within falsifiable theory, acknowledging the need for reproducibility, the potential for generalisations and, significantly, offering the capacity to explain phenomena (thereby implying a causal relationship). As will be demonstrated, the manner in which focus groups are perceived in the practice of politics also adheres to this positivist approach. While the aim may not necessarily be to produce generalisations, Krueger and Casey do emphasise the notion of 'transferability'.[15] They argue it is the larger theoretical points, if not the specific findings, which may be transferred into another environment or situation. There is also an emphasis upon 'truth', 'value' and the 'believability' of the findings.[16] As such, it can be argued that while these qualitative methods are traditionally associated with non-naturalist positions, practitioners and researchers in the field of focus groups do seek to align this apparently qualitative method with positivist approaches and underpin their methodology with the notion of 'scientific rigour'.

Much of the criticism levelled at focus groups within the literature tends to focus upon the lack of 'science' associated with focus group findings. Advocates of a positivist approach to the use of focus groups suggest that adherence to a rigidly structured format overcomes the critique of qualitative methodology.[17] Structured focus groups seek to establish scientific credentials, in that exact questions are repeated. With a series of listed questions, participants are encouraged to keep to areas tightly controlled by the moderator. This enables focus group method to be regarded as scientific; while the research may be qualitative, it follows the 'laws' of natural sciences, it focuses attention upon the observable, it is repeatable and generalisations can be made. It is this notion of focus groups as a scientific approach, yielding qualitative data, which underpins management marketing methodology, which in turn, informs much of the political marketing literature and has influenced the way in which the findings have been used and presented as credible, given their scientific basis.

The focus group method

The focus group method itself was developed during World War II. Some of the first studies were undertaken by Merton and Kendall[18], and many of their assumptions and techniques underpin current focus group activity. Focus groups are accepted within marketing and market research as providing believable results at a reasonable cost; they are also assumed to reflect an adherence to the scientific principles of research.[19]

Focus groups are now a significant tool for political marketers and have been widely used in political practice both in the US and in the UK. Focus groups are drawn together for a specific purpose. The aim is to provide a forum for information to be gathered and views to be aired in order to gain an insight and understanding as to people's opinions on a particular issue. They are used to 'elicit people's understandings, opinions and views, or to explore how these are advanced, elaborated and negotiated in a social context'.[20] This is facilitated through the leader of the focus group, the moderator, who creates a 'permissive' environment, whereby participants are encouraged to put forward their views and opinions. It is the interaction of the group that itself provides the key to the production of the data. The context of the group provides a site where ideas and beliefs can be explored, with active encouragement by the moderator, in a manner that is not always possible in a one-to-one interview. A focus group 'taps into human tendencies. Attitudes and perceptions relating to concepts, products, services or programs are developed in part by interaction with other people. We are the product of our environment and are influenced by people around us'.[21] A key feature of focus groups then is the active encouragement of group interaction among participants.

This group setting means that ideas and beliefs can be fully explored and justified; participants are encouraged to provide the reasoning behind their answer and reaction. In business organisations, a more interpretivist/ethnographic approach has been adopted, so that the marketing/positivist application has been downplayed (although significantly this has not been allowed to influence the claims made as a consequence of the data generated). Rather than directly enquire about, for example, an advert or a specific product, a more informal context is established. Questions used in focus groups are open-ended and one-dimensional (with no hidden meanings). They are short, clear, sound and conversational, using words that participants themselves would use. Pictures and imaginary scenarios can also be used, in order to encourage the participants to talk and develop their arguments and gain as much information from them as possible. This kind of discussion is repeated across groups, so that trends and patterns can be identified. They are generally used to generate qualitative data as a tool for exploring people's perceptions and beliefs.[22] Their use is to uncover factors that influence opinion, behaviour or motivation and as a site to test ideas. Focus groups can also uncover feelings about issues, not only in relation to the product, but also in relation to the brand.[23] Importantly, they *do not* function to educate or to produce consensus.

The moderator plays a crucial role in the conduct of focus groups. For positivists the moderator is objective and occupies a neutral role. Positivists using focus group methodology argue that in adhering to a rigidly structured format, they are able overcome the critique of qualitative methodology. Scientific approaches to focus groups are also premised upon the notion of observer neutrality. This means that the moderator asks questions only, and repeats the same questions across each focus group conducted. The moderator can be directive, exercising considerable control and using structured questions.[24] Much of the literature addressing the methods adopted to conduct focus groups advocates a structured format. These underpinnings mean that findings can be quantified, with methods repeated and treated in a value-free manner. The neutrality of the moderator is important in order to support the identification of objective and observable 'facts' about social and political behaviour.

In contrast, a nonpositivist moderator can be nondirective. This means asking few questions and probing on a limited basis. The moderator can be passive, but become active when necessary.[25] A less directive and minimal role on the part of the moderator enables the participants to take the groups in directions they regard as relevant. As Merton and Kendal argue, '[A] successful interview is not the automatic product of conforming to a fixed routine or mechanically applicable techniques'.[26] Indeed, less direction from the moderator/ researcher may well encourage respondents to develop their views in greater depth. The smaller the role played by the moderator, the less chance there is to lead participants towards a certain response. Moreover, as Hydén and Bülow suggest, individuals may act in different capacities within focus groups.[27] As such, the context of the focus group itself may generate certain outcomes. Attitude shifts and repositioning of beliefs occur as a result of the inter-action within the focus group.[28] The role of the researcher, therefore, is more complex in that s/he needs to establish not only what is being said, but to understand whether the views expressed represent the demographic group, or are as a result of the structure of the focus group itself. If the purpose of the group is to generate data based upon the interaction of those within the group, it is important to let the group discuss without too much intervention from the moderator.

As such, the moderator plays a significant role in setting the agenda for discussion and keeping the group 'focused' upon the generation of data. It is the extent to which the mod-erator intervenes, how the findings are used, or the claims to knowledge that are made from the findings, which are then significant in terms of the potential ability to make claims to 'science'.

Many marketing techniques are traditionally associated with positivism (e.g., sampling, opinion polling)[29], and the use of focus groups in marketing and political marketing can be largely located within this paradigm.[30] This is consistent with other methods that have sought to quantify public opinion. Opinion poll usage also implies the existence of, and the ability to quantify, an objective truth. Polls have been criticised as a method of providing data to be used to predict rather than describe public opinion.[31] While the adoption of focus groups has, on the one hand, been presented as a means to remedy these inadequacies, their usage and application, on the other hand, has followed a similar trajectory to that of opinion polls.

Focus groups are widely used in contemporary political practice. They are seen as es-sential in electioneering[32] and a central part of the process of governance.[33] In order to overcome the inherent problems of qualitative methodology (of unreliable 'soft' data, that are merely interpretations of interpretations), the political marketing literature accepts the dominant assumption in the focus group literature that this approach is scientific. Observers/moderators are regarded as neutral and objective, and the methodology is pur-sued in a rigorous and scientific manner. As Newman notes, there has been 'a general shift in recent years from reliance on polls to predict voters' behaviour to the use of marketing research to provide explanations behind the prediction'.[34] This explanatory and predictive role is thus regarded as an important, if not *the* function of focus groups, reinforcing the commitment to science.

Focus groups and the 'new' Labour project

Focus groups were widely used to inform Labour's transformation into 'new' Labour and became an increasingly influential source of data. Philip Gould, one of the key drivers behind this modernisation process, emphasised the significance of public opinion in shaping party image. Gould argued that if Labour had paid greater attention to qualitative research findings in the 1980s, they would have realised how unelectable they had become.[35] Focus groups became a key element in the development of 'new' Labour as a brand to be sold to voters. They were used extensively to plan electoral strategies, and to assess the impact of party leadership and to test policy proposals.[36]

As Wring notes, '[I]t has become a journalistic truism that Tony Blair and "new" Labour are obsessed or motivated by focus groups'.[37] In preparations for the 1997 election, Labour paid significant attention to focus groups comprising 1992 Conservative voters who were considering switching to Labour, particularly those in marginal seats.[38] These findings extensively influenced the repositioning of Labour and its representation as 'New' Labour. Blair used information from these groups to create an image of change and modernisation, removing symbols of the past, such as Clause IV,[39] and renaming (rebranding) the party as 'New' Labour.[40] In removing Clause IV, Blair consolidated the modernisation begun under Kinnock.[41] A priority was to remove the reasons that voters gave for not supporting the party, which included fears of union dominance and tax increases. A further element of this strategy was the use of an inclusive language; the suggestion that New Labour offered something for everyone, speaking for 'middle England', for 'one nation', using New Labour[42] wherever possible, and using 'fairness' instead of 'socialism'.[43]

In order to identify the preferences of these voters, focus groups were selected from the target 'middle England' that Labour sought to attract. Gould attached great significance to the data generated by this method, and its utility in gauging public opinion in order to inform Labour's election campaign. As such, he conducted focus groups, with carefully selected participants, once a week for three and a half years prior to the 1997 election. Then during the six and a half weeks of the election campaign, they were undertaken six nights a week. When these groups were conducted, Gould took an interventionist methodological approach. He challenged participants: 'I do not just sit there and listen. I challenge, I argue back, I force them to confront issues'.[44] Yet, this extensive intervention on the part of the moderator has a number of implications. First, it undermines the claims to science, as observers are, in scientific approaches, neutral and objective. Observers in a positivist's school of thinking cannot intervene and influence that which they observe; this would negate their claims to a scientific method. Second, this changes the purpose and function of focus groups. Rather than being a site to generate and gather data, it becomes a site through which voter preferences may be shaped. As noted earlier, focus groups do not function to educate or persuade. Clearly, the findings from focus groups also influenced the nature of Labour's image. If they were directly responding to focus group findings, and focus groups that comprised middle England, 'Tory switchers', Labour's rightward trajectory would come as no surprise. Policy was formulated and tested in these groups, however, not to establish its viability or reflection of ideological commitment, but rather to assess the impact upon the party's image (or brand) to those voters who were considered to have an impact upon the potential for Labour to achieve its goal: win the election.

The symbolism of focus groups

In order to present the perception of being in touch with the 'consumer', focus groups also perform a significant symbolic function, in theory and practice. Focus groups are used, not only to establish customer demands, to listen and to respond to these demands, but to demonstrate to customers that they are listening and making effective changes in accordance with identified customer demand.[45] They are used by organisations to show a commitment to the customer; to establish a linkage with a brand identity, and the credibility of a brand. Fairclough notes that Labour used focus groups as part of their 'experiments in democracy' in order to incorporate public opinion from the start.[46] While discussing the usage of focus group to inform campaign strategy, Gould notes the twofold function of this method. Focus groups were a site where policy could be generated, but for him 'the issue [was] not the promise, but *making the promise credible*'.[47] As Dunleavy notes, '[P]olicy making by focus group was introduced allowing the Labour leadership to fine tune their commitments so as to remove or marginalize unpopular commitments'.[48]

Critics suggest that there is a gap between focus group theory and practice. Rook argues that they have evolved into cost-saving ways of information collation rather than in-depth analyses that observe both the dialogue of the group members and the interaction between them.[49] This reinforces the notion that it is the symbolism of the use of focus groups, rather than the data generated, that is important. If used underpinned by positivism, then, they can be used not only symbolically to indicate a commitment to the consumer, but also to indicate the ability to generate truth. In marketing, this truth is adopted to inform the production process, which then enables the product to be branded in a manner that is credible to the consumer. Labour used focus groups not only to inform their campaign and party policy, but also to symbolise that they were 'listening' to the public. Using methods associated with the collation of credible data can be regarded as part of Labour's strategy to generate a perception of being a credible party of government (the latter being an explicitly stated aim). Focus groups were used by Labour as much to play a promotional role as a dialogical one. The use of focus groups theoretically implies a commitment to a 'science' of gathering and analysing public opinion, to generate a credible truth. This is also used within the political marketing literature to symbolise responsiveness to consumer demand, accountability and the placing of the consumer at the centre of the product.[50] These twin aspects, of science and a commitment to democracy, underpin the perception of credibility and legitimacy that political actors seek to promote to the broader electorate.

Moderator intervention

One of the more understated difficulties of focus groups is the 'informational' role that they implicitly contain. Question guidelines can mean too much focus upon what the researcher is interested in and not enough of what is of interest to the participants. Focus groups play a function in informing participants about a particular product. Each question tells the participant that 'this is relevant and important'.[51] In this sense the moderator sets the agenda defining the areas of significance. If the moderator does this, there is little room for preferences to be articulated outside of the agenda that has been set. For example, as noted with Labour's use of focus groups, Labour defined the issues for discussion. Gould also used focus groups as a site to test his own ideas.[52] Rather than listening and collecting the opinions of the selected public, this was significant in communicating to participants what was important. Gould's interventionist approach, to argue and challenge participants, further meant that discussion could be inhibited. Particular viewpoints could be prevented from being expressed.[53]

As is also noted above, the context of the focus group itself plays a crucial role. This would suggest that preferences and interests are not only expressed and identified, but that there is also potential for preferences to be shaped, first as a result of the context of the focus group itself, and second as a consequence of intervention by the moderator. This latter point in particular highlights the potentially subjective role of the moderator and, again, seriously undermines the 'scientific' neutrality of the moderator (particularly in respect to Gould's application of this method). As highlighted earlier, focus groups in theory should not function to educate or produce consensus. Yet, in political marketing terms, and as put into practice by Philip Gould for the Labour party, focus group usage can become a two-way process. Not only have they been used as sites to collect data about public preferences, but also as a site whereby political actors seek to shape voter preferences. The initial one-way flow of information, from 'consumer' to 'producer', is altered because the preferences and attitudes of the consumer/voter are shaped, not only within the context of the focus group, but also through intervention from the moderator.

Focus groups and democracy

Democracy relies upon active and engaged citizens. The essence of democracy is choice. Electoral competition is the site where political actors are held accountable to the electorate. Neoclassical economic accounts of electoral competition point towards the marketplace as a mechanism through which political actors respond to identified consumer preferences (in order to achieve their goals). This implies choice, opportunities for citizens' engagement and elite responsiveness. Democracy in this sense is an institutionalisation of a method: the choosing of elites and leaders, which occurs through electoral competition.[54] For economic theorists, responsiveness occurs as politicians seek to incorporate public opinion into their electoral platforms. These functions are implicitly endorsed in the usage of focus groups in practice, and the acceptance of them as a method within the political marketing literature. As noted above, focus groups play a significant symbolic function in terms of demonstrating a political actor's responsiveness (and implicit commitment to democratic ideals) to the political 'consumer'.

Theoretically, the focus group is used to establish the product that the consumer wants, which has been used to suggest that political actors are responsive to the electorate, incorporating voters' demands into the political 'product'. Whereas once electoral strategy was determined by party leaders, it is now increasingly influenced by media professionals, reliant on in-depth focus group surveys.[55] This, according to Gould, is because focus groups 'enable politicians to directly hear the voters' voices'[56], and have been used to describe 'how' parties determine consumer wants. Gould argued that focus groups were an essential part of the democratic process, part of a 'necessary dialogue between politicians and people'. [57] However, this suggests responsiveness is occurring outside of the electoral arena, comprising selected members of the electorate. Further, this selection is not in accordance with standard sampling techniques, which seek to ensure some kind of demographic equality, rather focus groups comprise tactically significant voters. For Labour in 1997, these were 'Tory switchers'. This group is not demographically representative of the population/electorate at large; rather it was a targeted group, selected not for its democratic utility, but to enable Labour to achieve their goal: win an election. Focus groups, in practice, suggest the 'mobilisation of bias'[58] with certain interests (those of the focus group organisers) 'organised in' to the conduct of groups, with the interest of the electorate at large, whose votes were less strategically important to the electoral outcome, organised out. Clearly this undermines the electoral process, with only a few selected citizens having the opportunity to engage, rendering it difficult for the use of focus groups to be a means of enhancing the democratic process.

Theory and practice: implications for science and democracy

'New' Labour's use of focus groups has a number of implications for claims to democracy and science. First, intervention by the moderator (Gould) also undermines claims to be 'scientific'; the moderator did not observe neutrally. Second, this intervention altered the nature of the focus group, not as a site to only accommodate preferences but was used as a site to shape them as well. Third, as Scammell notes, rather than providing a site for discussion of policy content—their usage is directed towards determining presentation, suggesting the 'stance or tone' of policy.[59] Focus groups then are used to determine image and presentation, rather than substantive policy content. This would suggest that focus groups are employed to assess image, rather than to engage the selected participants in active political and democratic debate. Fourth, this also raises normative questions: is it realistic to base democratic representation on the views of a statistical sample, rather than the electorate as a whole? Significantly, membership of focus groups was not based on a statistically representative sample as required by 'scientific' approaches. Rather they were based on, and representative of, potential Tory switchers. This meant a skewed sample. This is problematic both in terms of claims to be a science of public opinion and a process that enhanced democracy (as the sample was neither random nor representative).

Labour's use of focus groups can also be considered to have performed a symbolic role. They were used in order to provide an image/perception that Labour was listening to the electorate as a whole. In fact, it listened to a minority of the electorate; the floating voters in marginal seats. It is conventional wisdom that the peculiarities of the electoral system mean that it is voters in a few marginal seats that determine electoral outcomes. Thus, marketing meant encompassing the views of voter groups in key seats. The data generated by these focus groups informed the manner in which the 'new' Labour product was presented and the image that Labour sought to project to the key groups of voters who were significant in influencing the outcome of the election. This was then translated into electoral strategy. Campaigning was limited in 'safe' seats and largely ignored where Labour acknowledged it had no chance of winning'[60]—a theme continued and exacerbated in the 2005 election.

This clearly is at odds with those who advocate the marketing concept as a pluralist normative ideal. First, rather than political actors responding to the electorate, they are responding to a minority of the populace who have the ability to influence the electoral outcome by virtue of their geographical location (marginal seats). Second, if responsiveness is to a minority of the population who express their views in focus groups, this undermines the fundamental democratic principle that political actors are held accountable through the process of elections. Third, to focus on Tory switchers and floating voters would indicate that in listening to the values of these voters, and seeking to present itself as congruent with the values of the voters, Labour would, of course, have to move 'rightward', reducing the choice available to voters between the two main parties. This creates problems for democracy, given its essence is choice. Fourth, Gould's strong leadership approach to focus groups meant that he set the agenda for discussion. In this kind of environment, there is little opportunity for alternative issues to emerge and reach the agenda, undermining democratic dialogue. Labour clearly had an agenda of findings that it sought to generate. It also used focus groups as a site to try to seek to shape voter preferences, as well as a site through which to refine its product (and accommodate expressed preferences). This would suggest that political debate was stifled (a) beyond the agenda defined within the focus group and (b) for the broader electorate who did not take part in these focus groups.

Clearly focus groups are not the only method through which opinion data is gathered and used. Marketing draws attention to the notion of market segmentation and targeting which informs both the use of focus groups, above, and is supported by technological developments which will be discussed below. Again, what is at stake here is not only the method of opinion collection but how that data is used once collated.

Other methods of data collection and its use: segmentation and targeting

Collecting public opinion and feeding it into the 'product' is only one half of the implementation strategy. The other part involves communicating this 'product' to the electorate; segmentation and targeting play a salient role in this process. As discussed in chapter 1, to facilitate the collection of public opinion, data markets are 'segmented'. That is, they are divided into categories based upon demographic data; public opinion is identified and fed back into the marketing strategy. According to the marketing literature, this means that public opinion is fed back into the product, the product is reshaped and the marketing mix is employed to 'target' specific sections of the public who fit the demographic profiling and are as such likely to be amenable to the 'sale' of the 'product'. Once data in respect of voter preferences has been collected and fed into the 'product', the next stage in the electioneering process is to mobilise support. The electorate is viewed as a 'market'—this market is assumed to comprise differing groups which can be isolated and targeted. The first group which identified is that of key voters. These are those in marginal seats, or strategically necessary for an election victory. Once these voters have been identified, they are then further segmented into demographic groups, reflecting not only socioeconomic class but also detailed lifestyle preferences and consumer habits. Following this further segmentation, strategies are then employed to specifically target these differing segmented groups. To segment the market, means to identify key strategic voters and for marketing advocates, this means that limited resources may be used more effectively.[61] The message is 'tweaked' according to the segmented groups these strategically significant voters belong to, in order to attempt to secure electoral support.

Crucially, there are two key issues which emerge here. First in terms of the selection of data which is employed to inform development of the product and second, in terms of the way in which this 'product' is then targeted. The normative claims made as a consequence of the use of the marketing concept applied to politics suggest a degree, responsiveness, accountability and pluralism. However, the findings of public opinion are used selectively, and targeting happens in politics only towards selected groups, crucially, who are important in terms of electoral victory. The 'product' is only targeted towards those groups who are in marginal seats, those groups for whom it is necessary to win the election. Public opinion data, rather than suggesting a responsiveness, is used for the ends of the politician, to win over a marginal seat, in order to gain electoral victory. Notably, this is qualitatively different from the implied pluralism within the marketing concept.

The following section then shows how these strategies have been employed by the Labour party in the UK. Given the already detailed literature surrounding the use of Labour's implementation of marketing strategies in the 1997 election[62], and given the increasingly sophisticated technology that has become available to support the implementation of marketing, the following section will describe Labour's implementation strategies in the most recent, 2005 general election. Segmentation and targeting occurred on an unprecedented level at the 2005 election, as both Labour (and the Conservatives) pursued strategies reflecting the recognition that their resources could be employed far more effectively by primarily seeking to engage and mobilise floating voters in key seats. This serves to illustrate not only how marketing techniques are used, but the extent to which they have become entrenched in organisational thinking.

The political context of the 2005 campaign

It is important to note that Labour does not operate in an isolated vacuum, rather in a densely structured context. Labour learnt lessons from its own organisational history, the opposition (the Conservative Party) and was heavily influenced by American campaign strategists. Labour was also responding to a media which had historically been hostile to the possibility of a Labour victory coupled with a largely conservative British electorate. Contextually, at the social and economic level there was a stable economy, parties were appealing to a relatively prosperous middle-class electorate, and this meant that campaign resources were better focused elsewhere. In terms of party competition, there was fundamental agreement over basic issues on the agenda: the economy, health, immigration and crime (and those not on the agenda—Europe, environmental issues). This consensus on issues that both did and did not reach the campaign agenda meant that this campaign saw very little opportunity for real public political debate. As a result of this seeming convergence on policy issues, and those on which no policy was discussed, commentators and pollsters suggested the decision for voters was to decide 'which campaign team [had] implemented the best marketing strategy'.[63] The institutionalisation and almost hegemonic acceptance of marketing being used by political actors was reflected by the commentary at the time.

Segmentation and targeting in the 2005 election campaign

Research undertaken for the Labour campaign team partway through the election campaign indicated that there were not strong regional variations in voting intentions, but that 'local factors' were important. This was considered particularly significant in marginal seats.[64] Labour's lead was only a few points, and while victories 1997 and 2001 were thought to be a foregone conclusion, the Conservatives had recovered sufficiently to be taken seriously, or at least pose a threat to Labour. Labour's small lead and concerns over low voter turnout meant that both parties were aware that the election could be won or lost in around one hundred key Labour/Conservative seats[65], and more narrowly than that, it would be decided by the floating voters within those marginal constituencies.

Crucially, then, campaign resources and marketing strategies were heavily directed towards these key voters in the marginal constituencies. Campaigning also became highly personalised as a consequence of the use of the marketing techniques of segmentation and targeting. Markets were segmented, divided into common denominators of particular groups that shared common characteristics—for example, the 'Mondeo man' of previous elections. In this sense, the 'product' was refined, the image 'tweaked' and targeted according to the demand associated with that identified group. This led to something qualitatively different: highly personalised, individual campaigning. The two main parties relied heavily on sophisticated databases to produce in-depth profiles of voters, which based not only on known political/voting behaviour, but also premised upon information relating to an individual's lifestyle. It was believed that this combination of information could be used to accurately assess an individual's preferences, so that highly personalised messages could be targeted towards identified strategic voters.

In part this was a consequence of organisational and technological learning from American counterparts. In the US, technological developments were used in the 1996 Clinton campaign to move towards a focus on 'local' markets. The polling team of Mark Penn and Doug Schoen and the firm Squier, Knapp and Ochs Communications in Washington were all extensively involved in public opinion analysis based on extensive detail in relation 'lifestyle' analysis.[66] The company QRS NewMedia also worked with campaign staff, using new technology databases that were used to analyse local news broadcasts so that the campaign message could be specifically tailored to that audience. This localised targeting started to reshape the way in which US campaigning was conducted, but this change was not only in America. In 1997 the UK Labour party were advised by Penn and Schoen and other American campaign strategists and consultants, and as a result, this increasingly sophisticated technology and strategies were also employed in the UK. The Conservatives, following consultation with the (former) Republican strategist Karl Rove, used US Republican's software, 'Voter Vault'.[67]

In a similar vein, Labour had the 'labour.contact' database, although this was thought to be less advanced than that of the Conservatives. Labour's database had become widely used since 2003 to profile, then target, floating voters. In order to identify the preferences of the target floating voters, both Labour and the Conservatives had purchased a profile of every postcode in Britain from the marketing company Mosaic. This was used to classify postcodes, enabling firms to target or avoid certain types of customers. Stored on Labour's (and the Conservatives') database, this information was then checked against the party's own history of voters. In the year prior to the election, both the Conservatives and Labour made millions of canvassing calls, enabling them to build up databases of information and identifying where swing voters were located. The aim was to compile a list of target voters and contact them by phone, mailshot and on the doorstep. The use of electoral records and data from commercial suppliers enabled both parties to build up a precise picture of these groups through analysis of credit history and purchasing habits, combined with information gained from the doorstep and through telephone canvassing. This meant that target voters were no longer identified by traditional social class, but by much more distinct and discrete categories. This technology facilitated further market segmentation, with over sixty-one different groups being identified. Those targeted by Labour included, for example, 'symbols of success', 'upscaling new owners', and 'affluent blue collar'.[68] This enabled a highly personalised direct campaigning strategy which was targeted at specific voters. The cap on campaign spending equivalent to 40p per voter[69] meant resources needed to be used effectively; as such, the telephone became a significant tool in election campaigning. Issues that were significant to voters were identified through continual telephone canvassing from national telephone banks, which were in place more than six months before the date of the election. Labour's call centre in Gosforth, Tyneside, employed over one hundred staff.[70]

This technology enabled the parties to identify the key/ swing voters crucial to the outcome of the election. Marketing meant identifying these voters, their wants and preferences and then targeting them accordingly, with direct reference to the specific issues raised in the process of market research. As such, spending on direct mail increased considerably during this campaign, and during the first two months of 2005, Labour had already spent £222,000 to fund 370,000 pieces of direct mail.[71] Campaigning was highly individualised, leaflets, videos and dvds were targeted, and personalised letters (sent with handwritten addresses), on issues that these key voters had identified as important. This also meant that the campaign message could reach the voter without mediation through traditional media forms.

Despite this extensive marketing (or maybe because of), the 2005 election saw only a marginal increase to 61.3 percent voters turnout (following the previous postwar low in 2001 of 59 percent). In 2005, Labour was returned to office with a majority of sixty-six seats on a record lowest 35.2 percent of the vote. On one level, this is clearly a consequence of the peculiarities of the electoral system, with turnout averaging considerably lower in safe seats (the lowest ten safest seats averaged 51.4 percent turnout, compared with 68.8 percent average in the ten most marginal seats[72]). However, it is also argued that an analysis of marketing itself may also enhance understanding.

Segmentation and targeting in 2005: a critique

In the first instance, it is suggested that market segmentation deviates from the implied equality within the marketing concept in two ways. First, by focusing resources on and identifying preferences of only a small proportion of the electorate and second, by tailoring aspects of the image (product) to suit the preferences expressed by a few individuals, rather than the expressed preferences of the electorate as a whole. The practice of marketing in campaigning suggests that rather than the demands of the polity being at the centre of the political process, it was the voters whose votes mattered to the election outcome that were at the centre of the process, not the polity, or the interest(s) of the polity as a whole. That is, the voters whose preferences were accommodated were in key or marginal constituencies.

Campaign resources were targeted for the purpose of enabling politicians to win seats and voters. In 1997, campaign resources had focused on ninety key seats.[73] In 2001, there were 'no key seats only key voters', and the 2001 'Operation Turnout' targeted weak and wavering Labour voters.[74] This meant that rather than the political consumer (voter) being at the centre of the product, less than 2 percent of the electorate were at the centre of this process. So this direct form of marketing is far from identifying and incorporating the demands of the populace, rather about refining and presenting a message to a small minority of the population.

This localised and heavily individualised strategy, and technology, was premised upon the notion that consumer habits could be equated, or at least, seen to be indicators of, political beliefs and potential voting behaviour. This reinforces the perception of linkage and overlap between market and political thinking; indeed, this idea suggests that beliefs about markets precede and inform beliefs about politics, reinforcing the notion that both marketers and politicians perceive politics as merely another commodity to be sold for consumption.

Conclusion

The concern of this chapter has been to explore how the marketing concept is operationalised both in theory and in political practice. This process of listening and responding is widely used to support the normative claim that the application of this concept enhances democracy—parties respond to the expressed preferences of the voters. However, what has been argued here is that this represents a far more complex process, with the potential for less than democratic outcomes. First, at the site where preferences are expressed and incorporated into the political 'product' and second, when the 'product' is then targeted towards a section of the public in order to mobilise electoral support.

Focus groups are a central method used by marketers and political practitioners to gauge public preferences. However, while this usage for advocates of marketing suggests the opportunity for the public to input directly into the political process, the contention here is this is not the equal relationship first implied. Elite actors select focus group participants, not as a method of establishing the wants of the collectivity, rather as a means of establishing how political candidates/parties can improve their electoral strategy with the aim of winning elections. Focus groups are used to symbolise democratic exchange and dialogue, but this is a site where elites determine the parameters of debate, and, within those boundaries, elites also are seeking to shape and manipulate preferences (as both Gould has done for the Labour Party, and as marketing accepts as a viable part of the process). Moreover, where findings are incorporated into the political 'product', these are skewed in favour of focus group participants, so even where public preferences are incorporated, these reflect the aspirations and interests of a sample identified by elites for their own benefit.

Wring highlights the nature of this concern and observes that 'political marketing techniques are less about understanding the electorate as a whole and more about cultivating and maintaining support in key segments of the populace'[75] which encourages parties to 'concentrate their most serious efforts on winning support from the elusive, undecided or floating voter'.[76] Implementing marketing deviates from the underlying equality implied by the marketing concept, as politics becomes driven by elites, directed at a minority of the populace. In sum, this is a consequence of the twin aspects of: first, preference accommodation at site of focus groups, which means that the 'product' is skewed to those particular interests of the elite-selected participants and that there is the potential manipulation of those interests by elite actors. Second, once these interests are reflected in a 'product', this presentation of the product becomes refined to attract and mobilise support of only key segments of the population. This means that not all 'consumer' preferences are accommodated. Crucially, a select group of key voters have their views represented, yet the perception is promoted that the preferences of the entire electorate are being accommodated. Political actors construct an image centred on the views of floating and marginal voters, using focus groups and opinion polls. Where political actors are responsive, this is to a small percentage of the electorate, rather than to the entire citizenry. This individualisation of the campaign process not only conforms to the methodological individualism of neoclassical economic accounts, but also serves to reinforce the primacy of individual interests over any sense of collective good.

Notes

1. Lees-Marshment, 2001b: 694.
2. Cf. Schattschneider, 1960: 71.
3. Newman, 1994: 21.
4. In the US, see Niffeneger, 1989; Morris, 1999; Newman, 1999; for the UK, see Gould, 1998; Wring, 2003, 2005.
5. Butler and Kavanagh, 1997: 61, 65.
6. O'Cass, 1996: 46.
7. Gould, 1998: xviii.
8. Moon, 1999; Sparrow and Turner, 2001.
9. Bartos, 1986; Morgan, 1988; Morrison, 1998.
10. Scammell, 1995: 274.
11. Woolgar, 2004.
12. Goodwin and Horowitz, 2002: 36.
13. Bulmer, 1984; Krueger and Casey, 2000: 198.
14. King et al, 1994: 24–30, 100–13.
15. Krueger and Casey 2000: 203.
16. Leininger, 1994: 105.
17. Carey, 1995; Kennedy, 1994; McDonald, 1993; Smith, 1995.
18. Merton and Kendall, 1946.
19. Bulmer, 1984; Krueger and Casey, 2000: 6.
20. Wilkinson, 1998: 187.
21. Krueger, 1994 :10–11.
22. Merton, 1987; Morgan, 1988; Kitzinger and Barbour, 1999.
23. Duckler, 2003: 29.
24. Frey and Fontana, 1991.
25. Goldman and Macdonald, 1987; Stewart and Shamdasani, 1990.
26. Merton and Kendal, 1946: 544.
27. Hydén and Bülow, 2003: 306.

28. Bristol and Fern, 2003: 450.
29. Bulmer, 1984.
30. For exception, see, for example, Wring, 2003, 2005.
31. Lewis et al, 2005: 54.
32. Scammell, 1995: 274.
33. Newman, 1994.
34. Newman, 1994: 40.
35. Gould, 1998: 327.
36. Gould, 1998; Burnham et al, 2004: 106.
37. Wring, 2003: 1.
38. Gould, 1998: 204, 329, 350.
39. Labour's ideological commitment to the ownership of the means of production.
40. A central element of the process in seeking to promote the distinction between the party 'then' and 'now'.
41. Who was able to do this as a result of internal party changes that had strengthened the role of the leadership.
42. The theme of 'New Labour, New Britain' was launched at the 1994 party conference. The word 'New' was used 37 times in the conference speech and 107 times in Labour's *Road to the Manifesto*. Butler and Kavanagh, 1997: 64.
43. Bartle, 2002: 61.
44. Gould, 1998: 327–28.
45. Strother, 2003: 16.
46. Fairclough, 2000: 5.
47. Gould, 1998:2 71.
48. Dunleavy, 1997: 129.
49. Rook, 2003: 12.
50. Lees-Marshment, 2001a, 2001b; O'Cass, 1996; Scammell, 1995.
51. Walvis, 2003: 405.
52. Gould, 1998: 328.
53. Cf. Schattschnieder, 1960.
54. Cf. Schumpeter, 1947.
55. Scammell, 1995: 288.
56. Gould, 1998: 326.
57. Gould, 1998: 328.
58. Schattschnieder, 1960: 71.
59. Scammell, 1995: 10.
60. Pattie, 2001: 48, see also Seyd, 2001.
61. Yorke and Meehan, 1986: 67.
62. Smith and Hirst 2001; Butler and Kavanagh, 1997; Wring, 1996, 2005.
63. Shakespeare, 2005.
64. Wintour and White, 2005.
65. Jones, 2005.
66. Novotny, 2000: 18.
67. This technology had helped the Republicans win crucial swing seats, such as Ohio, in the 2004 presidential election.
68. Wintour, 2005.

69. *The Economist*, 7 April 2005.
70. Wintour, 2005.
71. Barnes, 2005.
72. Electoral Reform Society, 2005 http://www.electoral-reform.org.uk/article.php?id=83.
73. Seyd, 2001: 54.
74. Labour Party, cited in Seyd, 2001.
75. Wring, 2001: 925.
76. Wring, 2002: 32.

4

Ideology

The way in which marketing is implemented is not only about technology, techniques and strategies. For marketing scholars, for marketing to be successful, marketing must be adopted as a mind-set, an ideology, a guiding philosophy. This has permeated the political realm to such an extent that as Harris and Wring observe, there is now a perception that 'managerialism has to some extent replaced traditional forms of ideology as the driving force within modern politics'.[1] The techniques of marketing referred to in the previous chapter emphasise the importance political actors attach to marketing and managerialism driving the process and activity of political campaigning. These form the visible elements of deeper ideological commitments: to the primacy of the market in all aspects of public life.

But if marketing as ideology is prominent in the political realm, what does this mean for the content of politics? This chapter explores this issue first, by detailing what ideology means in marketing/political marketing accounts. It then sets this against traditional economic accounts of electoral competition, given their shared underlying assumptions and explores the similarities and contradictions between the two approaches. This usage is situated within the broader context and, building on the previous chapter, suggests that the extensive employment of marketing materials and strategies reveals an underlying ideological adherence to neoliberalism, and the primacy of the market over and above a commitment to democratic debate and party competition. Much of the political marketing literature is silent on the ideological content of politics. Where it is referred to, the suggestion is that it provides a 'package' in which politics is presented and is fluid, implying that ideology can be adapted to fit electoral strategy. Political ideology is regarded in this way as a tool within the marketing process, something that is malleable and can be altered in response to changing demands and preferences.

Marketing is assumed to provide actors with a method of achieving power, and does not provide a method for prescribing to actors how that power should be used. While political marketing prescribes the use of marketing once in office, this is only insofar as the next election impacts on strategic thinking. In this way, the ideological underpinnings of political marketing are, within much of the political marketing literature and practice, empirical questions in relation to the proper extent and usage of marketing in politics, rather than a political vision of what society should be.

While there may be some disjuncture between political marketing and economic accounts over the prominence and function of political ideology, what both share is an underlying adherence to economic principles. As this is promoted within marketing as a driving force, a guiding philosophy, this suggests in the political sphere an internalisation of orthodox rational choice, which by extension, also implies disengagement from the political process. First, it encourages political elites, and electorates, to behave in a manner consistent with Downsian thinking. This in turn encourages parties to pursue centrist strategies and fails to resolve the voter paradox. Second, because neoclassical economic ideology per se, with its focus upon the individual devoid of any context, can be regarded as an ideology of disconnection.[2]

Ideology

Although it is recognised that ideology is a highly contested concept, the term more broadly refers to systems of shared beliefs and internally consistent sets of ideas. In politics, this tends to take the form of a vision for society, about what is right and wrong/good and bad; how and why resources are distributed; and it can offer insights into the location of power (where it does and should reside). This usually takes the form of a coherent set of political belief systems, e.g., conservatism, liberalism, socialism, and embodies consciousness, ideals and values. Ideology functions to structure and constrain or facilitate thought, but at the same time it has a legitimation function. It serves to legitimate power held by a group or class or set of elites. Ideology also has a *self*-legitimating function: it serves to exclude alternate sets of ideas, to naturalise a particular belief system, to render that belief system common sense, so that alternate views may be prevented from reaching the agenda. In this sense, it can distort, obscure and shape reality in a manner conducive to its own survival.

Ideology can be conceived of as a consequence of the social system/structures within which actors exist and operate. However, as Mannheim[3] notes, in contrast to Marxist accounts, while ideas may emerge from a social system, they are not reducible to these origins. Although ideas/ideologies may originate from and be part of a society, they may also exist, survive and evolve independently of that system. While ideology cannot be seen, its effects are visible. In its most advanced form, ideology can be conceived of and experienced as 'common sense' (for example, that liberal democracy is *the* ordering mechanism for society). This 'common sense' approach is encompassed in the Gramscian notion of hegemony. Here, consensus is sustained through the presentation of the interests of a particular group as the interests of the society as a whole. That is not to say conflict is nonexistent. Conflict may take place between dominant and subordinate groups (e.g., class, gender); however, this consensus is maintained through the negotiation of this conflict, and within certain boundaries. That is, for example, the unquestioned acceptance of the existence of class and/or gender divisions. This is not necessarily imposed from above but can be a consequence of lived social practices, in this sense 'in ideology men [sic] ... express, not the relation between them and their conditions of their existence, but the way they live the relation between them and their conditions of existence'.[4] That is, ideology is operationalised through lived relationships, reinforced through daily practices and actors' perceptions of the world around them. Ideology can also function to position people within a particular system.[5] Ideology provides a coherent set of ideas which may shape social practices, be reinforced by social practices, yet at the same time, functions to position people within those social (or political) practices.

Marketing/political marketing and ideology

For marketing, these lived practices take the form of engagement with a marketplace. Leading marketing scholars claim that for marketing to succeed, it must be adopted as a 'mindset; a guiding philosophy'.[6] In this sense, marketing ideology also contains a much more prescriptive function. It is claimed by marketing scholars that in order to be effective, marketing values and ideology *must* be internalised. The marketing literature prescribes that successful marketing occurs when a 'marketing mindset' has been adopted. Marketing must be viewed as a coherent philosophy that underpins the thinking and behaviour of organisations.[7] The content of ideology in marketing is that of ideas in relation to the utility of marketing practice. As has been noted, for scholars within marketing, the set of practical guidelines also operate normatively. But this marketing 'ideology' plays a broader functional role in that it also serves to legitimate to marketers the activity of marketing.[8]

Marketing changes the emphasis of politics, both as an activity and in terms of analysis. Marketers downplay the role of ideology; regardless of a candidates'/parties' ideology, they are assumed to face similar strategic decisions, not dependent upon their ideological vision for society but based upon their respective market positions.[9] Normatively, political ideology is regarded as redundant; it has been claimed that 'if politics is to do anything for the people of this country, it must deliver what they need and want, not just discuss political ideologies remote from their everyday lives. Political marketing has the potential to do this'.[10] This suggests that 'political' content is less important for political marketing and implies a post-ideological politics, where political ideology is a (minor?) technique of marketing. Smith and Saunders acknowledge that there may be ethical concerns in adopting marketing strategies, if this is seen to influence policy, and that marketing may be a threat to ideology, in the sense that it replaces the consistency and values of a political ideology. However, they argue that, in order to build brand loyalty, 'the political party (brand) must have an enduring ideology (image); it must be consistent and have credibility'.[11] The emphasis on building and sustaining brand loyalty over time, therefore, means for them that political actors will remain image, rather than ideologically, focused. Political ideology, in this case, however, is regarded as only part of the method of building an image. The image is constructed for no other reason than to win elections. Ideology becomes another tool in the marketing process, with little recognition of it possessing any underlying normative content, rather than a set of underlying political beliefs and principles.

In marketing/political marketing and economic accounts, there is a distinction then between the way in which ideology is used. In this sense there are two differing meanings to the term ideology, although these remain largely conflated within the literature (and indeed, in practice). Ideology as used largely within economic accounts of political behaviour refers to *political ideologies* (e.g., liberalism, conservatism). In contrast, management marketing defines ideology as 'a relatively stable set of arguments accounting for the marketer's commitment to marketing (management)'.[12] Both are normative and contain a set of guiding principles. Both also perform a legitimation function, in that they legitimate actions and serve to legitimate the system itself. However, the content of ideology is qualitatively different. Management ideology contains ideals about how to effectively achieve the aims of marketing and serves to legitimate the activity of marketing per se, whereas political ideology contains ideals in respect of a vision of society and in turn functions to legitimate the political system.

Two problematic issues emerge here for political marketing. First, political ideology is simply another technique at the disposal of political actors used to mobilise support. It is connected with presentation and imagery, rather than a set of internally consistent political values and ideals. Second, that for marketers and political marketers alike, what should be driving the process of politics is a commitment to and a belief in the utility of marketing. Given the shared underlying assumptions of both schools of thought, logically developed, if the assumptions, values and beliefs, which underpin the marketing approach, must be internalised, then by extension this suggests the internalisation of orthodox rational choice theory.

Ideology in economic accounts of party competition

In formal economic analyses, ideology performs a, if not *the*, functional 'linkage' role. It links political actors with political space, and it links voters with political parties. In terms of parties, it guides and locates their position on the political spectrum, and for voters it is assumed this provides a means to connect their wants and desires with formal political activity. In this sense, ideology is a significant part of the political process, organising or guiding choice.

Downs defines ideology as 'a verbal image of the good society and the chief means of constructing such a society'.[13] This definition, then, contains both means and ends, and also implies the existence of a set of political values and beliefs. For Downs, ideology is vital given the uncertainty of the environment in which political decisions are made.[14] Ideology has significance in terms of party competition in that it guides the practice or positioning of parties in political space. Competing parties' positioning is, according to Downs (and again, in political marketing), a response to the distribution of voter preferences. The preferences of voters are assumed to be unimodally distributed along a single left-right ideological axis.[15] Conversely, a bimodal distribution of preferences would mean that parties are poles apart ideologically.[16]

Ideology serves not only to locate parties/candidates in a political 'space', but also serves to fix them within this space. This means that not all the political space along the continuum is available to them. Ideology functions to prevent parties from 'leapfrogging' each other: from moving further to the left or right of their competitor. This is a significant (a) in terms of providing system stability and (b) in order to for parties to retain some credibility with the voters from whom they need support in order to achieve their goals. Conversely, this limits the available options to parties/candidates and may constrain the amount of choices available to the political actor and in turn the voter.

Ideology plays a role in guiding future actions and facilitating and structuring thinking on future issues. It also logically implies difference and differing responses to issues by political actors. The positions adopted by parties on particular issues are dependent upon the ideology of the party. Ideology not only defines the boundaries of possible response to an issue, it also functions to identify what an issue is. For example, more ideologically right-wing parties may see immigration/race relations as an issue, whereas for left-wing groups this may not even make it onto the policy proposal agenda. Left-wing groups may see environmental concerns as an area for policy consideration, whereas right-wing parties may not consider this a political concern in any way. Ideology is used, by candidates/parties, as a measure of commitment and a guide to responses on possible issues. To this end, political actors are able to demonstrate an undertaking to particular political positions. This commitment is then in turn communicated to the voter via the existence of a particular ideological position. What this then means is that parties are able to communicate their positioning in a manner which enables to voter to behave in a cost-saving way when it comes to determining for whom to vote. Ideology then serves to reduce complex issues into a simplified 'whole'.

Although the potential for electoral destruction is assumed to prevent parties from becoming too close to each other, the problem remains that 'the closer that parties become ideologically, the more people's votes are liable to turn on something other than ideology'.[17] Whereas ideology was a device to make parties distinct from each other, increasingly centralised competition around an assumed homogenous voter can lead to an homogenisation of ideology, with little ideological differences to distinguish between the competitors. Therefore, it becomes insufficient for parties to identify and distinguish themselves from each other on an ideological basis, and so, they must find other means of distinction. For many, this reduction in ideology has meant an emphasis upon image management, leading to charges of style over substance. As demonstrated by Hay, Downs' model may well provide a surprisingly accurate description of New Labour's electoral tactics[18], reinforced by the latter's emphasis upon outputs, rather than ideology.[19] In the US, after the 1994 US midterm elections, the Democrats, following advice from strategist Dick Morris who is widely accredited with providing Clinton with the ideas and strategies behind his centrist moves, or 'triangulation'[20] (in the 1996 presidential election), can be also argued to have behaved in a Downsian manner by pursing these centrist strategies, converging around the median voter. This suggests that parties/candidates have a greater interest in their image than in ideological content to their actions. Indeed, if sharing almost indistinguishable political ideology (and if both actors are now driven by marketing) this means that parties/candidate must differentiate themselves in other ways.

Voters and ideology

Downs' model rests on the assumption that voter choice and behaviour is determined and driven by ideology; voters react to ideologies presented by parties. Parties also recognise that the voter may vote according to ideology and, therefore, according to Downs, 'fashion[s] an ideology which it believes will attract the greatest number of votes'.[21] While never internally contradictory, ideology may 'be only loosely integrated, since [it is] designed to attract many social groups'.[22] In this sense, ideology performs a functional and instrumental role.

Ideologies are used as a means of product differentiation, which can be used by the voter as a cost-saving device.[23] This saves voters the time of establishing a party/candidates position on every single issue, of collecting and evaluating policy detail and performance in government. Ideology may also provide the reason for voting, rather than a retrospective assessment of the incumbent government. Instead of comparing government behaviour and opposition proposals, the voter compares ideologies; a further cost-saving measure.[24] As Popkin observes, 'Parties use ideologies to highlight critical differences between themselves, and to remind voters of their past successes. They do this because voters do not perceive all the differences, cannot remember all the past performances, and cannot relate all future policies to their own benefits'.[25] It is assumed that voters depend on the ideological commitment of the party/candidate as a guide to what a candidate or party will do, to what they stand for, how they are likely to respond to future events.

Contrasting marketing and economic accounts

While the term 'political' is not stated in front of ideology in economic analyses of political competition, it is implied in its usage. And, despite the instrumental role of political ideology in economic accounts, its acknowledgement and presence suggests that political ideology plays a significant role in the activity of politics. In marketing analyses, however, ideology is not a political one, as discussed below, but a marketing one. Both accounts recognise the instrumental function of ideology, but its prominence varies. While there are similarities in the function ascribed to ideology, a distinction lies in terms of content and legitimation. First, for orthodox rational choice accounts, political content is important, as this provides a linkage, location and simplifying function for voters. For marketing, this is part of a broader set of techniques to attract voters; political content is less important. Ideology is part of a broader 'brand' image which attempts to achieve this linkage and simplifying function. Second, marketing ideology also functions to legitimate marketing per se; that is, it is self-reinforcing and success which flows as a consequence of using marketing becomes a virtuous circle of self-legitimation. In politics (and economic accounts), political ideology functions as a means not of self-legitimation but of political action and system legitimation. Remove this and a key mechanism of legitimating the process of politics is denied.

Prominence of ideology

Economic analyses of politics highlight the need for parties to be [politically] 'ideologically adaptable' in order to take advantage of 'strategic opportunities'.[26] This suggests that ideology is not fixed nor the driver of political behaviour, rather it is one of several means through which parties may achieve their goals. While marketing also concerns appealing to values and emotive sentiment, political ideology plays a small, ambivalent role.[27] Where it is referred to, it has a functional role as a device for 'branding' or image/presentational purposes. In political marketing terms, the role of political ideology is performed through the brand, the means to an end of obtaining votes. Ultimately, in marketing, it is material interests that dominate; ideas and ideology are reduced to playing a material, utility serving role. Policies, even if informed by political values, are a means to an end, rather an affirmation of a set of political values consistent with a coherent ideological position. The limited role for political ideology is highlighted by Lees-Marshment who argues that it is not ideology that wins parties elections, but the party that is most adept at marketing.[28] This fundamentally reshapes and redefines the activities and activity of politics.

Ideology also functions as a 'shortcut' for parties to 'bundle polices' to make them accessible to voters. This is one way in which economic accounts seek to address the paradox of voting. Ideology in both marketing and economic accounts has a functional/rational role: to facilitate the achievement of an actor's goals. These ideological distinctions are less significant in political marketing. If both main parties adopt marketing strategies, then the distinction becomes a marginal one of 'branding' and presentation. Ideology provides economic analyses with the means to overcome, or reduce the likelihood of the voting para-dox. If voters can identify with an ideological position, then this will reduce their costs and increase the likelihood that they will vote. Remove the political content of ideology, and this removes the cost-saving mechanism provided for the voters, reducing their incentive to participate.

Legitimation

In terms of the legitimation function, action is legitimated through recourse to the role of ideology. The political marketing literature accepts the Downsian assumption that feedback from the identification of consumer demands can be fed back into political party ideals behaviour, and can affect and influence the ideological presentational stance of competitor parties. This notion of consumer demands informing party behaviour is used to not only define the presentational stance of the competitor parties but serves the function of also justifying the prescription of marketing in terms of its ability to increase responsiveness and accountability. This legitimation function is an important one as it provides implicit justi-fication for action; ideology also functions to legitimate and prescribe activity and behaviour. While the content of political ideology in political marketing may be relatively unimportant and malleable for political marketing (although accepting the limitations of spatial models of competition, that in order to remain credible, parties cannot 'leapfrog' each other), the role of marketing ideology itself is much more significant. The success claimed from ad-herence to, and believing in marketing, becomes self-referential and serves to reinforce and validate the utility of marketing as an ideology.

Critique

While rational choice accounts provide a series of analytical models, the political marketing literature violates these underlying principles and goes beyond the use of such models as analytic frameworks and introduces a normative element. This thereby suggests the pre-scription of the internalisation of the above neoclassical economic assumptions. In essence, this means replacing traditional 'political' ideology with a 'marketing' ideology—that is, one which privileges the market as way of thinking about society, and the activity of politics. Again, this contains implications. To downplay 'political' ideology from party competition contributes to the further depoliticisation of politics, the emptying of political content from politics. This fundamentally redefines political activity, as political activity becomes in-formed by marketing values and ideas rather than formal political ones. Here then ideas about marketing become institutionalised, normalised and routinised. They become con-ventional norms from which there is no alternative, and become the 'common sense' way for politics to proceed. In many senses this serves to reinforce the 'end of ideology' thesis, as this suggests that since all social interests can be represented through market mechanisms, political ideology is no longer necessary to provide alternate depictions of political, social and economic order.

Yet politics is about values, as O'Shaughnessy notes. If political debate 'were simply about utilitarian appeals, most such debate would have been silenced long ago'[29], but in some senses this is one of the effects of marketing. Extensive and informed debate is being silenced, election campaigns have become contests about promotional product placement, with little ideological difference, the key aspect which differentiated political parties from all other forms of organisations. Marketing itself can also lead to unity in products if consumers are assumed to have fully expressed preferences, which are stable and hierarchical. In this sense, then, there is only so much market research can produce. It can then be limited by consumer imagination, ideas, awareness of demands and wants. If politics is driven by consumers with short-term, individual, self-interested concerns, the notion of a vision, a set of ideals for society is further undermined.

In business, ideas and values are one part of a process. In politics they are the foundation, the core of the activity. In politics, free speech is defended as the precondition for a 'marketplace' of ideas[30]—to dilute this dialogue undermines one of the very foundational principles upon which the activity of politics is premised. For some, the use of marketing can provide an alternative perception of politics, adding to the 'marketplace of ideas'.[31] The crucial point here, however, is that marketing is not providing an alternative reality; rather it is creating a single reality, where the marketplace of ideas is marketing one, containing no alternative, without political values or ideas, only marketing ideals.

As stated at the outset, ideas and ideology do not emerge from, nor exist in, a vacuum. Ideas held by actors emerge from the context and the perception they hold of the context in which they are situated. Despite these contradictions and tensions, marketing has clearly come to dominate. Ideas about the political world create a lens through which to perceive events and behaviour and inform how the world is perceived. Ideas not only about politics, what it is and what it should be, inform political behaviour, but these ideas are also shaped by a broader context. The acceptance of ideas in relation to the utility of marketing can be understood and situated in a broader context of neoliberal thinking in respect of politics, supportive of ideas about marketing. Here then is a theoretical frame which supports and privileges ideas about marketing, and reinforces the notion that marketing is not only a set of principles and practices, but a set of beliefs, a value system. This presents a 'common sense' view that marketing and its attendant principles are the way in which society should be ordered which also serves to position candidates/parties within that context.

The neoliberal context

The economic underpinnings of this managerialist marketing literature are part of a broader neoliberal discourse which has come to dominate and inform lived practises within the contemporary social and political environment. This neoliberal discourse has become institutionalised through a series of interactive processes between individuals and the context in which they operate. Through the interaction of individuals with the formal mechanisms of an institution or organisation, ideas become embedded, routinised and internalised. Yet these ideas are not static; through this interactive process, ideas and discourses evolve, responding to both endogenous and exogenous factors. The idea of marketing in politics in many ways becomes a logical response to a broader environment which is characterised by a commitment to market mechanisms as a solution to all societal problems, to privatisation of public provision of welfare, to the celebration of wealth and a focus on the individual, rather than the collective.

Wellhofer traces the existence of the market as an ordering mechanism for liberal societies back to the eighteenth century.[32] He argues that not only has the market interpretation of democracy become increasingly accepted, but it has also become increasingly appropriate in liberal capitalist democracies. This, he argues, has been 'favoured' by decline in party organization and development in techniques of mass manipulation.[33] In recent years this has become increasingly prominent, arguably, dominant. The 1980s witnessed the implementation of strategies which fundamentally reshaped the ideological terrain of politics.[34] Belief in the primacy and the utility of markets in all areas of public life came to dominate the political arena, and many areas of state engagement became subject to internal and quasi-markets from health and broadcasting to education and transport.[35] With its roots in economic and political liberalism, neoliberalism, which came to dominate political discourse during the 1980s, was underpinned by two key ideas: the limited role of the state and the promotion of individual freedom. This could be achieved through commitment to markets.

Markets were regarded as mechanism through which efficient distribution of resources could be achieved. At the same time, this was seen as a means through which the individual could be empowered and maximise their liberty. The individual would be free to enter and leave markets as they chose. Moreover, the individual would be liberated, as they were best able to identify and pursue their own interests. The idea of the individual empowerment as a result of market competition was a dominant theme and characterised much of the neoliberal/new right discourse. While in the US the main focus of this thinking was moral, in the UK, initially the primary influence of the new right was at the level of economics[36] latterly extended to the political realm.

Neoliberalism represents a linkage between classical liberalism and neoclassical economics. The underlying shared assumptions are:

- A focus on the individual who is regarded as a rational, self-interested, utility maximiser.
- Free-market economics—the market is the most efficient mechanism through which scarce resources are allocated and liberty is enhanced.
- A laissez-faire approach—markets are, and should be, the appropriate ordering mechanism. They are self-regulating, and as such, should be free from government intervention. The state should only intervene to protect the rights of individuals within that market.

Neoliberalism, however, is both an economic and political programme. At the economic level, in the UK, this was evidenced through a shift away from Keynesianism and state intervention at the economic level. In the political sphere, this was characterised by opposition to both state socialism and the idea of a Keynesian welfare state. This meant a commitment to a laissez-faire approach, the celebration of the freedom embodied by the marketplace which would be regulated by the Smithsonian 'invisible hand'.

The underlying assumptions of neoliberalism were espoused by the Thatcherite project of the 1980s. Heavily influenced by the work of Hayek, it could be argued that this became hegemonic[37] and the idea of markets as ordering mechanisms providing for individual freedom and simultaneously relinquishing state of its heavy burden became embodied in public policy. In a time when governments were facing claims of 'overload' and of 'ungovernability'[38], public choice theorising provided the means through which this issue could be addressed.

For public choice theorists, it was the absence of the market which was responsible for the growth in government. Unwieldy bureaucracies were a drain on state resources. Buchanen and Niskanen[39] were at the forefront of theorising how state inefficiency could be reduced. For them the market was the mechanism through which public life could and should be ordered. The state's role was simply to regulate these market mechanisms, and the introduction of the market mechanisms would eliminate the inefficiencies of state provision of public goods and services. Public choice theorising was the main way in which economic approaches came to be embodied and embedded in public policy. Public choice theory provided 'the new right with a particular language in which the failings of the state could be dissected and a set of policy recommendations to deal with them'.[40] The inefficient provision of public sector services were seen in large part as a consequence of the individual bureaucrats within them. The introduction of markets was seen as a means through which resources could be allocated efficiently and in turn would contribute to the empowerment of the individual. Public choice theory is highly individualistic and 'private property, the market economy and the capitalist order are acceptable if they result from the necessarily subjective choices of individuals. "Goods" and "bads" are the subjective experiences of individuals and there is no collective organic entity called society or the public'.[41] In this sense political institutions, public choice theorists argued, should be designed to maximize individual freedom. Markets were viewed as the domain of choice and freedom, the state was a site of repression from which individuals should be liberated.

While it is acknowledged that there is significant debate as to the extent that the Thatcher era marked a break with the past, and the extent to which it marks continuation of the past[42], it is undeniable that there was a significant shift towards a commitment to a neoliberal agenda. Markets as solutions to public problems became embedded, through public choice theory, in public policy. Monetarism also became the singular approach to economic policy. There was a move from a mixed economy to a capitalist one; over 50 percent of the public sector was transferred to the private sphere[43] as marketisation was introduced into many areas of public sector services. For many, this growth of neoliberalism signalled the demise of social democracy.[44] As a consequence, it has been widely suggested that a neoliberal consensus[45] has emerged and contemporary politics now takes place within this framework.

The nature of party competition

This broader acceptance of neoliberalism has clearly had an impact on the nature of party competition. The Labour party in the UK are now widely regarded as operating within and accepting this neoliberal consensus.[46] Both Labour and the Conservatives have accepted neoliberal principles: that markets should be dominant, with minimal government intervention; taxes and public spending should be kept down and trade unions should have as marginal role as possible.[47] The restructuring of Labour saw a party that would accept the market economy, have a mass membership and no trade union block vote.

Some commentators point to the structure of the market itself as the reason for partisan convergence.[48] This would suggest that policy convergence with the Tories, the use of sophisticated marketing tools and techniques, and exogenous shocks, such as repeated electoral losses, led Labour to compete around the median voter. As Butler and Kavanagh argue, '[T]he leader thought that politics at the end of the twentieth century could move beyond the battle between socialism and capitalism: Labour had to reoccupy the centre ground'.[49] Labour, it has been argued, were 'playing the politics of catch up', 'accommodating Thatcherism', and were no longer a social democratic party[50], and its policies have been identified as being around the centre of a unilinear ideological dimension.[51] However, Labour's acceptance of the neoliberal economic and political paradigm has had a broader effect and led, Hay argues, to Britain becoming a 'one-vision polity'.[52] This would suggest neoliberalism has become hegemonic; party competition is occurring within one ideological paradigm.

While these centrist tendencies conform to Downsian thinking, convergence has been not only around the median voter, but around neoliberal ideology, which narrows the ideological spectrum. The implications of this are that if Labour and the Conservatives compete around the centre ground, consensus is then reached on most areas of social and economic policy, and the key differences between them become stylistic. Elections become a competition between the most adept at the practice of marketing, rather than a competition between ideologies. As parties are seeking to differentiate themselves from each other, differences between the two become stylistic rather than ideological. For marketing, this serves to reinforce the importance of marketing as providing a means through which parties can do this.

Ideas in relation to marketing are part of a broader discourse and related set of ideas about the utility of markets and its attendant processes and underlying principles. The discourse of neoliberalism makes the ideas and language marketing acceptable, rendering them intelligible. Ideas can be both internalised by organisations and institutions, and externalised as a given set of ideas adopted by other organisations that then that become norms. The effective acceptance and embrace of marketing techniques by political actors has relied heavily upon an environment conducive to its acceptance. The lived practices of political actors within their environment draw attention to individuals interacting with a state which functions within an advanced capitalist system. This is premised upon the notions of production, distribution and consumption. It would seem a logical development within this context that ideas as to the markets, the way in which they operate and their function should also inform the political process, and that political actors themselves would embrace this market-driven approach to their own activities.

The implications of marketing as ideology

The marketisation of areas previously in the remit of government arguably marks the beginning of the wholesale adoption of marketing in other areas of political behaviour. In this way, the use of marketing itself has become an ideological act. It represents a change in the way in which the process of politics is conceived of by political actors.

Within the political marketing literature, there is a renegotiation of what 'the political' means. Politics, in liberal democracies, is arguably about reconciling competitive demands and claims for state action. Parties appeal to the electorate upon the basis of core values. Yet, according to the marketing literature, these values 'do not need to be specifically delineated. Indeed, the content of policy might appear to non-partisan observers to contradict core values . . . [T]he implication for successful management is the need to reconcile central identities with market realities'.[53] So, rather than ideological beliefs, the market dominates. Politics becomes about markets and market competition. Prescription for political action is focused on marketing values and beliefs, rather than political ones. As Finlayson notes, 'The ideological content of political marketing is not contained in the message . . . but in the very fact that politics has to go to the market in the first place, that it has to submit to that logic and cannot develop its own. Propaganda is unnecessary if the mechanisms of ideological reproduction and legitimisation can occur through the dominance of the market itself'.[54]

This use of marketing is taking place in the context of a fundamental acceptance, by the main parties, of neoliberalism, which emphasises markets as the primary ordering mechanism in society. The extent to which markets are regulated is the concern of contemporary political actors, rather than whether markets have a proper role in the activity of politics. Consequently, the focus upon the electorate as the market and the use of marketing itself becomes legitimated through discourse within a neoliberal environment. Not only does the broader neoliberal environment legitimate the actions of political actors using marketing, but this becomes dialectical. By adopting marketing as an ideology for political practice, political candidates/parties themselves legitimate and reinforce the neoliberal, market-dominated thinking about the ordering of society.

In this sense, given the clear underpinnings of rational choice accounts in political marketing, this prescription of adopting a marketing ideology and internalising marketing as a philosophy can come to constitute the internalisation of rational choice assumptions. This has a series of implications for the nature of party competition, democracy and legitimation. In this way, Downsian predictions about the nature of party competition become fulfilled. Moreover, it renders the voting paradox more plausible. The more that voters perceive political actors using marketing behaving in a Downsian manner (whether consciously or unconsciously), the more likely it is that voters themselves will respond in the manner predicted by Downs. The individualisation of the campaign strategies as detailed in the previous chapter, coupled with an ideological commitment to philosophical premises derived from the assumption of an individual as a rational self-interested actor, emphasises the primacy of the individual at expense of the collective.

In a devastating critique of rational choice theory, Taylor argues that this is an ideology[55] of disconnection because it assumes (and idealises) a world where individuals are disconnected from their own lives, from each other, and from broader social and cultural practices.[56] Marketing as an extension of this neoclassical economic ideology can also be viewed in this way. As has been noted in earlier chapters, it individualises the process of campaigning, reinforcing to the voter the importance of the individual. The voter plays an instrumental role for political parties, which disconnects the voter from both their own interests outside of those which are useful to political parties/candidates and disconnects voters and parties from any broader sense of public good (as this does not feature in marketing accounts).

Altering the form and function of ideology implies a series of consequences. First, the role of ideology, in its political form, is reduced to a tool of the marketing process. This serves to remove values and ideals from this concept, leaving little for voters to identify or connect with. Second, to replace political ideologies with an overarching marketing ideology creates problems for the legitimacy of the system. In contractual conceptions of democracy, legitimacy is conferred upon a system by citizens' participation, agreeing, giving informed consent to be governed. If there is a reduction of information, it is difficult to provide informed reflective consent. A monolithic marketing ideology in all aspects of public life provides little room for alternative perspectives, and represents, arguably, the triumph of capitalism, driving every aspect of public life, excluding alternate ideologies and providing one dominant 'market' ideology.

The redefinition of ideology can be seen as representative of the active struggle of competing sets of ideas. As currently espoused, ideas in relation to marketing and political values seem to be mutually exclusive, opposed in basic principles they cannot coexist. If ideas are reproduced and embedded through practice, then this also suggests that their lack of usage in practical terms in informing practice will lead to their disappearance. Ideas in relation to marketing are reproduced through their practice. In this way, where political space has been vacated by political ideas and ideology, this space becomes filled with images and marketing methodology. At the same time, this becomes a two-way process, reinforcing and reconstituting the use and need for marketing.

Conclusion

Marketing scholars argue that marketing, to be effective, must form a belief system of those who are employing it. In light of the changing nature of party competition as a consequence of adopting marketing techniques, and the theoretical frameworks which model and describe current behaviour, this chapter has reflected upon the role of ideology in the marketing and the political process. It is argued here that the adoption of marketing implies an internalisation of rational choice assumptions; politicians come to believe and act in accordance with the assumptions of rational choice models which in turn may serve to disconnect the public from the process of politics.

In politics, ideology is used to confer legitimacy upon a given political system. While ideology may have originated from that political system, it also evolves and is reconstituted by those who interact within that system. In this way, ideological origins may be part of a social system, but this does not mean that ideology is fixed. Importantly, however, ideology does serve to legimate and relegitimate that system. Ideology is a means of legitimating power relations. Habermas notes how 'legitimation crises' occur when 'changes in the political system ... cannot be met by the existing supply of legitimation'.[57] He suggests that advanced capitalism creates new needs that it cannot satisfy'.[58] In this sense, then, it is suggested that the advanced phases of capitalism, marked by neoliberal economic ideas in respect of the utility of the market, technological advances have combined to produce a system of thinking, namely, marketing, which while responding to perceived crises in politics (declining turnout, partisan dealignment) with marketing, is itself a product of a market-driven system. But marketing is unable to confer the legitimation function required because of a belief system profoundly different from that which it is replacing, and in this sense, marketing is unable to confer legitimacy on a system which is political. The contention here, then, is that marketing ideology undermines and delegitimates the political process and system. Its crises become manifest through increasing alienation of voters. As noted in chapter 6, while citizens may be disengaging from the formal processes of politics (again, their engagement is essential to reinforce the legitimacy of the system), this does not necessarily entail that citizens are disengaged from the *content* of politics. However, it is argued that the extensive use of marketing by political actors means that the opportunity to engage in the formal realm of politics is becoming negated by its process.

Notes

1. Harris and Wring, 2001: 909.
2. Cf. Taylor, 2006.
3. Mannheim, 1936.
4. Althusser, 1969: 233.
5. Cf. Althusser, 1971.
6. Kotler and Andreasen, 1996: 37.
7. Kotler and Andreasen, 1996: 37.
8. Marion, 2006: 245.
9. Butler and Collins, 1996: 42; Scammell, 1999: 731.
10. Lees-Marshment, 2001a: 211.
11. Smith and Saunders, 1990: 298–99.
12. Marion, 2006: 245.
13. Downs, 1957: 96.
14. Hinich and Munger, 1997: 192.
15. Downs, 1957: 115–16.
16. Downs, 1957: 118–19.
17. Barry, 1978: 105.
18. Hay, 1999.
19. Temple, 2000.
20. By this Morris meant trying to achieve key elements of Republican policy, but this would be done through Democratic means. Morris argues he saw triangulation as a way to change the Democrats; he suggested that 'a president can step ahead of his party and articulate a new position. The triangle he forms between the orthodox views of the two parties at each end of the base and his views at the apex is temporary. Either he will be repudiated by the voters and slink back into the orthodox positions or he will attract support and, eventually bring his party with him' (Morris, 1999: 80–81).
21. Downs, 1957: 100.
22. Downs, 1957: 113.
23. Downs, 1957: 98. As voters do not need to incur the costs of establishing the party position of every particular issue.
24. Downs, 1957: 99.
25. Popkin, 1994: 51.
26. Scott, 1970: 57.
27. O'Shaughnessy, 1999: 728.
28. Lees-Marshment, 2001a, 2001b.
29. O'Shaughnessy, 2001: 1048.
30. Cf. Habermas, 1989.
31. Banker, 1992.
32. Wellhofer, 1990: 9–28.
33. Wellhofer, 1990: 24.

34. Cf. Hall, 1983.
35. For empirical overview, see Leys, 2001.
36. King, 1987.
37. Cf. Hall, 1983.
38. Rose and Peters, 1977; King, 1975; Birch, 1984.
39. Buchanen, 1975; Buchanen and Tullock, 1962; Niskanen, 1971, 1973.
40. Hindmoor, 2006: 97.
41. Barry, 1978: 102.
42. Summarised in Kerr, 2001: 38–59.
43. Marsh, 1994: 1.
44. Kerr, 2001: 38–59.
45. Crouch, 1997: 352.
46. Heffernan, 2002: 743.
47. Crouch, 1997: 352. The 1997 campaign saw Labour accept much of the existing government's social and economic policy. Labour accepted grammar schools, letting parents decide their future by ballot, and agreed to accept grant-maintained schools, leaving these schools the option to convert to foundation schools. In health, while abolishing the internal market, Labour would preserve the purchaser-provider split. Existing (Conservative) legislation on industrial relations would remain largely intact. Labour (alongside the Conservatives) had a 'wait and see' approach towards the euro. The key elements of the New Labour project were the modernisation of the welfare state and the constitution; Gamble argues that New Labour is a coalition of the centre with both radical and conservative elements (1998: 27). Using focus groups comprising former Tory voters would inevitably produce outcomes that embraced 'conservatism', but requiring a strong leader. If it was Tory voters who comprised the focus groups, then it would be Tory voters who Labour were seeking to accommodate.
48. Smith, 2006: 6.
49. Butler and Kavanagh, 1997: 51.
50. Hay, 1994; Taylor, 1997. Although Wickham-Jones contests this latter point, arguing that Labour had attempted to 'recast its social democratic commitments' (1995: 701).
51. Laver, 1998, see also Hay, 1999: 108.
52. Hay, 1997: 372.
53. Butler and Collins, 1999: 65.
54. Finlayson, 2003: 48.
55. Taylor, 2006, argues that neoclassical economic theory is ideological as it influences economists' views the world and structures their behaviour.
56. Taylor, 2006: 87.
57. Habermas, 1997: 48.
58. Habermas, 1997: 49.

5

The Language of Political Marketing

The rhetoric of marketing is not simply a series of loaded metaphors; rather the terminology itself contains a series of assumptions and implications. One of the central ways in which ideas become embedded and shape social systems is through discourse, in which language plays a central role. Building on the previous chapters, this chapter looks at the way in which economic assumptions are guiding and discursively constructing contemporary politics. Clearly, language is important in politics. Labour's re-presentation, and subsequent electoral victory, as 'New' Labour bears testament to this.[1] As noted previously, marketing is regarded not only as a method, but a guiding philosophy. This is reinforced is through the use of language and terminology. Language is important for framing the context through which action takes place. Language provides the parameters for the conceivable and shapes the way through which actions and behaviours can be understood. Discourse combines both linguistic and non-linguistic aspects.[2] That is, discourse is about not only the particular word that is used, but the associated practices which give a particular word meaning.

Broadening neoclassical economic accounts, this chapter highlights the significance of the language of the marketplace in the activity and literature of politics. This chapter shows how defining politics as a process of production and consumption which occurs in a marketplace entails a series of implications. This linguistic usage has more than analytical implications, for it serves to reconstruct the nature of politics, both as an object of analysis, and as it is practised. The purpose of this chapter is to demonstrate how the language of marketing contributes to the ideological hegemony detailed in the previous chapter, and also serves to reconstitute and redefine politics ontologically. Given marketing claims the centrality of the consumer to this process, this chapter will draw out how consumers are inherently implicated and constructed by the process of production (rather than influencing the production process). This will then be contrasted with political conceptions of citizenship and suggest that to conceive of politics as a process of production and consumption serves not only to reconstruct politics as an economic activity, but serves to alienate those taking part in the process.

Rationality and discourse

The hegemony of the marketplace as an ordering mechanism has permeated both social and political spheres, and clearly this is nothing new.[3] However, it is the extent to which the market should permeate these spheres that is the concern of this book. It is accepted that the social, political and economic are not discrete categories, and their interlinkage influences and reshapes both themselves and each other. The primary starting point here is the extent to which the economic has influenced the political, and the subsequent implications of this for both the social and the political. The political marketing literature assumes the existence of a process of production and consumption is taking place within a market. This in turn has entailed the use of this terminology to describe the activities of political actors. What rationalist and economic accounts fail to incorporate is the role of discourse in constructing and creating the context within which action occurs. Rationalist accounts premised upon economic principles would at one level seem incommensurate with those which privilege discourse and the role of ideas. However, by introducing a discursive aspect, not only in terms of ideology as in the previous chapter, but also in terms of the terminology used to describe, model and analyse the practice of politics, facilitates the possibility of exploring in more detail not only what is happening to the political process but also why this might occur and with what effect.

The terminology of political marketing

Clearly, the term 'political marketing' itself creates an explicit link between politics and markets. In economic accounts, competition begins with the existence of a market. Competition occurs either in the market, or for the market. Because of the economic assumptions which drive the political marketing literature, the focus upon competition is reliant upon the existence of a market as the ordering mechanism through which politics is conducted. Politicians are regarded as actors operating in a political market, rather than an electoral arena. In political marketing not only are the models used to describe and make predictions about behaviour, but the terminology of these approaches also plays a significant function. It has the potential to shape the way in which politics itself is discussed, perceived and ultimately (given the prescriptive nature of this literature) practised.

Definitional issues

So, within political marketing, what is the political 'product' for 'sale' and who is the consumer?

The product

Within managerial marketing, organisations seek to provide a product or service to their consumers. In the political arena, the product is variously regarded as the party[4]; party behaviour at all times[5]; the candidate[6]; party membership[7]; the campaign platform[8]; person/party/ideology[9]; party image, leader image and policy commitments[10]; a service[11]; policies, communications or images[12]; or a brand.[13] Bartle argues that the 'product' comprises two elements: '1. the platform of the party which includes a) its policies on controversial issues and b) its competence in achieving consensual objectives, together with 2. the "image" of the party'.[14] Underlying this is the notion that 'marketing a party consists essentially in projecting belief in its ability to govern'.[15] While all these factors may comprise the political 'product', arguably the totality that political actors seek to 'sell' is a *perception* of a product and/or an image. Marketing is used in order to 'create an illusion that the "product" meets the desires or aspirations of the consumer'.[16] The symbolic function of the product is noted in the management marketing literature.[17] This emphasis upon image, symbolism and perception leads political marketing scholars to acknowledge that the focus of marketing is less likely to be on substantive policy debates[18] than upon the 'potential effects upon party images'.[19]

Markets and the consumer.

While the existence of five markets is acknowledged (voters; activists and interest groups; the media; the party organisation; and donors and financial contributors[20]), within the vast majority of the literature the political market essentially is assumed to comprise the electorate.[21] The consumer at the centre of the exchange process is the citizen[22] or voter.[23] The point at which the exchange central to this concept occurs, the point of consumption, is regarded as the point at which the elector exchanges their vote and purchases the political product.[24] Voting is regarded as a buying process[25], and the purchase is made on the day of the election.[26] There are a number of simplistic assumptions made in respect of the voter in the political marketplace. McGinnis argues that voters make a psychological purchase when voting: voters are uninterested in substance and subsequently candidate and/or party image is central.[27] Voters are assumed not to vote from any sense of party loyalty.[28] Further, while they are assumed to require evidence of capacity to execute policies, voters are also thought to regard policy content as secondary—for some, incidental.[29]

That politics can be conceptualised, discussed and described in the language of the markets entails an underlying acceptance that politics and electoral competition can be regarded as a process of production and consumption. While the term product is contested, what is uncritically accepted is that political behaviour at elite level is inherently tied up with the production of a product. What content the product has is less significant for the marketing literature; what is important for marketers is the production process itself. Despite the normative claims made as a consequence of the introduction of the 'consumer' into the process of production, what is uncritically accepted is that the public who take part in politics are the 'consumers' of politics. Crucially, it is this uncritical acceptance that there is a political product and, by extension, a political consumer that is significant in constructing the terrain within which politics is conducted. In order to demonstrate this, economic accounts of markets, and the process of production and consumption are set out below.

The market

The process of production precedes consumption, and this consumption is assumed to take place in a market. The market is regarded as the mechanism which keeps sellers responsive to their buyers, and producers responsive to consumers. A market is an exchange mechanism which brings together buyers and sellers. The word market means a 'meeting of people for the process of exchange'.[30] It is this exchange relationship that is at the core of the marketing approach.[31] Neoclassical economic accounts, as political marketing, begin with the existence of a market and accept this definition. In this model of the market, perfect competition is assumed; that is, it is free from constraints or intervention (usually by the state). For neoclassical economics the market precedes and facilitates competition and competition is a necessary condition of market efficiency. Markets are efficient when in equilibrium[32], but this can only occur if competition takes place. (Monopolies are an example of market inefficiency, as equilibrium is not achievable.) For this equilibrium to occur, an exchange must also take place. The allocation of scarce resources is achieved through bringing together buyers and sellers for this process of exchange, and the market functions as a coordinating mechanism. Actors in this market make strategic decisions to maximise their utility, and each decision in the market is influenced by assumptions and expectations as to how other 'players' in the market will react. Sellers set prices based on knowledge, or assumptions about the behaviour of other sellers in the market. The exchange in these economic accounts implies an equal relationship between buyers and sellers who seek to maximize their profit and buyers seek to maximize their utility (get the best possible product for the lowest possible price). That is, both the buyer and the seller are assumed to be better off as a result of engaging in an exchange within a competitive market. As such, exchange is treated as something which is mutually advantageous to all actors involved. This exchange takes place only when both parties involved agree to exchange; the buyer or seller may prevent the exchange from occurring by refusing to participate. Once costs exceed benefits for either side, the exchange may not take place. In this way, it is assumed that the existence of the market, and the competition facilitated within this market, is that which keeps firms and producers responsive to consumers. Essentially then, this simplistic model assumes perfect competition; the rationality of those involved; that the exchange is mutually beneficial; and implies an equal relationship between firm and consumer.

The ideal of the market is premised on the notion of the existence of perfect competition, which denies the possibility of exogenous influences. In neoclassical economics, and latterly, for new right theorists, in order that markets could function effectively they should be free from government intervention, as this hinders efficiency. If governments are to play a role, it is simply to ensure that markets work effectively. The pursuit of individual self-interest in early economic accounts was claimed to lead to a collective benefit to society[33], although it should be noted that collective prosperity was regarded as an unintended by-product of an unregulated market, as markets did not exist to pursue a common interest or a public good. For new right theorists, markets represented and provided for both economic prosperity and individual freedom. This was achieved through the limiting of state intervention; freedom was derived from the market, rather than state.

For Hayek[34], markets emerged spontaneously; the function of government was simply to ensure that conditions conducive to this emergence were in place. Markets were regarded as self-regulating and the laws of supply and demand would ensure quality and efficiency. In this way, markets are also assumed to be an efficient mechanism to supply information in respect of consumer demand which in turn ensured responsive producers. As Gray observes, for Hayek markets were almost Darwinian in nature, in that in a market economy the 'profit and loss system provide[d] a mechanism for the elimination of unfit systems'.[35] Unfit systems being those which were inefficient. As Weibull argues, 'Market competition is usually thought to weed out firms that are not profit maximisers and to bring about equilibrium outcomes predicted by economic theory. This is the basis for the so-called "as if" defence of economic theory, which claims that it is not important that managers think the way microeconomic theory says they do; what counts is whether they behave as if they do'.[36] This suggests producers who are unresponsive to consumers do not survive. In this sense, the operation of the market is assumed to define the parameters of that which is possible and, implicitly, desirable.

Marketing and markets

Marketing scholars continue this neoclassical economic (and, more specifically, Downsian) approach by suggesting the exchange which occurs in a political market happens on the day of the election. Economic models suggest political parties are 'an organization of men (sic) who offer a selection of products to consumers in a political market in the hope that consumption of these products, as expressed in terms of voter support, will enable the party to wield influence or assume office'.[37] This is continued in political marketing, where the assumption is that consumers (electors) 'buy' (vote for) the product (party/candidate) of their choice.[38] This exchange, for marketing scholars, is acknowledged by political actors when asking for votes[39], again, with the assumption that both sides will benefit from the exchange; otherwise it would not occur.[40]

As with neoclassical economic conceptualisations of the market, the simplistic modelling assumes the existence of perfect competition; rationality of the part of those involved; that the exchange is mutually beneficial, which in turn implies an equal relationship where rational actors benefit by pursuing their own self-interest. Consumer sovereignty is implied as voters are the ultimate purchasers of these political goods and services. If consumers do not buy a product, there is no reason for it to be present in the market, and in turn this is thought to facilitate the empowerment of the consumer. There is an emphasis upon liberty, and markets are the mechanism through which this is secured and protected. The language of empowerment via market mechanisms dominates new right thinking, and this empowerment is used to derive normative justification for marketers in politics. Through their construction as 'consumers', voters are assumed to be empowered; they are able to vocalise their interests, have them incorporated into the political product, and this mechanism (and desire for electoral victory within this) keeps politicians responsive and accountable.

The process of production and consumption

Inherently bound up in the notion of markets are the processes of production and consumption. In suggesting the politics can be described, analysed and conceptualised as an activity which occurs in a marketplace with producers and consumers, it implies/accepts the existence of the process of production and consumption. In neoclassical economic accounts, the purpose of production is to facilitate consumption.[41] In this modernist perspective, the focus is on the production of consumers. The primary function of the production process is to produce consumers for goods and products, for without these consumers there would be no profit in the process of production. Given the emphasis by the political marketing on the centrality of the consumer to the process, the following section will proceed by illustrating how the consumer is inexorably tied to the process of production, and what in turn this means for political understandings of the public as consumers, instead of citizens.

The term consumer is a generic one which, consistent with the rest of the models and concepts employed in the political marketing literature, is underpinned by neoclassical economic assumptions (as noted above). Underlying neoclassical economic accounts, and heavily influential in new right thinking, is the ideal of 'consumer sovereignty'. The focus then is upon an individual, an individual empowered through market competition. This term, however, functions symbolically, rather than having clear conceptual or theoretical basis.[42] The associated symbolism with this term implies a rational, autonomous individual able to purse and maximise his/her own self-interest, which also is used to imply empowerment.[43] In these accounts, and congruent with the assumptions made by marketing models, the cumulative decisions made by rational individuals (consumers) generate demand for a product, ensuring the success of the supply side and consequently the smooth functioning of the market. For the new right, the notion of consumer sovereignty is linked to freedom and empowerment. The individual is free to make decisions and choices in their own self-interest. The individual is autonomous, able to exercise individual will and authority.[44] This implies a degree of freedom; the individual makes autonomous decisions free from constraints. Indeed, this is implicit in the term 'free market' characteristic of new right thinking.

As such, the use of this term provides a threefold function. First, more broadly, it reinforces the new right emphasis upon markets as providing the 'solution' to societal problems. Second, it reinforces the primacy of the individual over the collective; and third, the term consumer is inherently linked to and derived from the notion of consumption. Consumption is inherently tied up with the act of production; it is the process of using and employing products. This process of consumption and production is implied and explicitly stated by both the marketing concept and scholars in the field to mean that those who consume the 'political product' are bound up with influencing its production. But consumption is the consumption of products created by another whose primary purpose is not the satisfaction of a consumer need but the securing of profit. Indeed, it is argued that this negates the notion of consumer sovereignty. Returning to the definition of marketing, the primary purpose of the marketing process is to secure a profit; the action is directed primarily at the ends of the organisation, or as the analogy has been extended into politics to the needs of the politician. The purpose of the production (and by extension, consumption) process is not to satisfy the needs of the consumer, *but of the producer*.[45] Extended to politics, this means that the raison d'etre of political marketing is to ultimately satisfy the aims of the politicians, which in turn denies the autonomy of the individual and undermines the claims that consumption is empowering.

The process of production and consumption

The economic accounts which underpin political marketing highlight this in more detail, and it is worth returning to these in order to reflect upon what is entailed in the process of production and consumption. Some economists have suggested that it is the process of production itself that generates consumer wants. Galbraith argued that 'production creates the wants it seeks to satisfy . . . Production only fills a void that it has itself created'.[46] He suggested that the process of production, promoted through advertising and salesmanship, created wants and desires. In this way, production creates not only goods, but also the wants for those goods.[47] While this suggests a largely passive consumer lacking autonomy, there is acknowledged the existence of wants outside of the production process. Galbraith suggests that 'we have wants at the margin only so far as they are synthesized. We do not manufacture wants for goods we do not produce'.[48] In this sense then, wants can only be articulated and understood through the process of production and in a manner through which producers are able to satisfy them (having generated those wants in the first instance). Wants become dependent upon production. Production functions not only to produce products, but also to produce the consumers of those products. Production does not exist to fill consumer wants and demands per se; rather it exists to fulfil demands for wants and goods that the production process itself has generated. In this sense, consumption becomes not a means of engagement, but it becomes a means through which the consumer is estranged from the production process. As will be discussed below, this inverts the marketing concept and the normative claims which flow from this.

Rather than consumer wants being at the centre of the production process and the product shaped accordingly, the above theoretical issues suggest that wants which are in existence outside of the production process can lead to an alienation of consumers and wants outside of producer interests becoming marginalized. Production generates wants to suit its own interests; the production process determines consumers' wants. Rather than emerging from autonomous consumers, this suggests that producers impose wants upon consumers. Not only are wants/preferences constructed externally, but once identified and fed back into the production process, they are moulded to suit the interest of the producer, rather than the consumer. Consumers may then become alienated from their wants and their 'true interests', as they are removed from them and their instigation. Further, preferences and wants that exist outside of this process can either be altered as they become amalgamated into the wants the process of production can incorporate, or they become marginalized. This can have a series of effects—either these wants find expression elsewhere—for example, through extremist parties or in single issue organisations/campaigns. Or they are suppressed. If political wants are not satisfied through the formal political process, then there is no reason to assume the public will take part in that process. Clearly, this does imply a lack of autonomy on the part of the consumer, and the assumption of a 'hypodermic' injection of wants and values. While the public may well not be that passive, what the discourse of production and consumption does do is to define the parameters of debate, so that the possibility of wants or preferences emerging outside of those defined by the producers are limited, and consequently have limited potential for realisation or expression within the political process.

The theoretical and discursive binding of the public into the process of production and consumption operates in contrast to conceptualisations of citizenship. In order to draw out the implications of discussing the public/citizens/voters and consumers, it is useful briefly to recap on what is entailed in conceptualising citizens and voters.

What does it mean to be a voter and a citizen?

To be a voter means to actively vote and take part in the political process. Voting is one of the expressive functions of citizenship, and as such to be a voter is inherently interlinked with understandings of what it means to be a citizen. Crucially, to be a citizen entails and suggests a political relationship with the political system and respective processes, both with obligations and duties in respect of the other. Citizenship is about membership of a community, a society, and the rights and obligations that accompany that membership. These can be defined institutionally, enshrined in law, institutions and practices that denote membership of a political community. There is also an affective aspect. Citizenship is also constituted by values, loyalties and norms.

Citizenship is predominantly linked to the notion of rights. These can be both negative and positive. Positive rights are permissive and emphasise, for example, the opportunity for citizens to vote, to hold office, to stand for election. Negative rights are protective and re-strictive, protecting the individual particularly from the state. These procedural rights were outlined in Marshall's influential conceptualisation of citizenship where three sets of rights—civic, political and social—were identified.[49] These rights were formal and enshrined by the state and bound up in the term 'citizen'.

While Marshall refers to legal, social and political rights, it is the political rights that are of interest in the first instance within this chapter. Within the political marketing literature, there is a narrow definition of the term political. Political in this sense has been used to refer to the institutions and personnel of government and the state (so a formal definition of politics). Notably, the rights of voters are not directly referred to within the political mar-keting literature. However, the use of the term 'consumer' implies consumer, rather than citizenship, rights. For Marshall, some rights arise directly from the notion of citizenship.[50] Rights can be created through being exercised, and the capacities associated with them subsequently generated through their exercise. For Isin, citizenship is the right to be politi-cal, to be an agent governing or being governed.[51] People become citizens, and part of a political community, through association and deliberation with each other. Rights are con-ferred and denied through this interaction supported through the apparatus of the state. This is a dialectical relationship which binds citizens to the state and vice versa. To refer to voters and citizens as consumers denies the both the existence of, and the opportunity to, exercise these rights. Not only can this lead to disenfranchisement, but also in liberal plu-ralism, citizens also function to keep a check and balance of power, to hold politicians accountable—again, denied in the term 'consumer'.

While Marshall's account of rights emphasises the importance of institutions, scholars evaluating the notion of cultural citizenship draw attention to the way in which society generates meaning and values, how it understands itself, and importantly draws attention to the communications channels through which 'the people' are empowered and given voice.[52] Cultural forms of citizenship incorporate an awareness of a changing environment largely driven by technological development: global media networks; instant access to in-formation at the click of a mouse; cyber communities, with national boundaries electroni-cally transcended; the relative ease of migration (compared historically).[53] This has led to some to suggest the decline in importance of the state, while others highlight the state's role as crucial. While this debate continues, what is certain is that there is a need for politicians to maintain a linkage between the state and those physically present within its borders, and that the rights of citizens are bound up in this process.

But these rights and obligations are contained in the term 'citizen'. Terminology and language form part of a broader discourse through which political realities are articulated and understood. Discourse and language are significant in that they serve to institutionalise a set of ideas and boundaries. Ideas, norms and values become routinised through everyday practice and linguistic expression. Once voters and citizens are referred to as consumers, this removes (or downplays the importance of) the links to citizenship inherent in concep-tualising the relationship between the state, political elites and the public. As has been suggested above, the term consumer is part of a broader neoliberal discourse located in new right, neoclassical economic thinking. To regard voters as consumers attributes a different set of values and ultimately serves to generate a different type of political reality. The terms citizens/voters and consumers are not 'empty signifiers, devoid of content' and as such, a series of implications follow, and by extension are also excluded (and will be teased out in the final section of this chapter).

Context and discourse

Clearly citizenship and consumption do not emerge or exist in a vacuum. Rather they are dependent upon a broader context within which they are structured. This context is complex, underpinned by discursive practices and articulated to create a particular version of political reality. As the above discussion has suggested, political actors play a role in producing citizens. In order to understand what it means to be a citizen, it is also important to have a critical understanding of the civil society in which that citizen is located. Citizenship is reliant upon an input by state actors, and civil society also structures the context in which citizenship is defined. Similarly, an understanding of consumption is premised not only on an isolated concept, but as part of a broader environment shaped, again, by political elites and a material and ideational context conducive to its development.

Contemporary material and ideational circumstances are characterised by a broader shift in the way in which politics is being practiced. The notion of the consumer is part of a broader managerialist discourse which dominates contemporary political practice. Consumption is encouraged in all aspects of life and has become almost hegemonic in its ordinariness. The market, and the idea of a market, as the solution to societal problems has also come to dominate. New public management thinking has seen market 'solutions' or (quasi) market mechanisms introduced into many areas of public life, for example: in transport; health and education; taking the form of (among others) internal markets; public private partnerships (PPPs); public finance initiatives (PFIs). Given this change in the nature of public service provision, acceptance of the dominance of markets as the means through which public goods should be organised and resources allocated has been brought about in part by a changing ideological, social, political and economic climate and by responses of political actors to that climate. It would seem somewhat logical that political actors would come to use these methods and mechanisms to inform their own electioneering behaviour. It is argued here that the language and discourse of markets and competition have been significant in creating conditions conducive to the application of marketing to formal political electioneering and more specifically in relation to this chapter, providing the conditions for the creation of consumers of politics.

What are the implications of this terminology?

The above discussion of the underlying economic process of production and consumption is useful in highlighting some of the problems associated with applying economic approaches to the activity of politics. However, these are not simply theoretical or procedural concerns. To tie the public into politics as a process of production and consumption fundamentally redefines the activity, ideologically and ontologically. Parties are constructed as businesses who are bound up in the production process. In defining voters as consumers, this links parties and voters, but the way in which they conceptually engage is within a process of production and consumption. Given the concern of this book has been the way in which politics characterised by marketing has induced malaise and disaffection with the political process, it has turned particular attention to those whom this process affects. It is argued that the political marketing literature which advocates the use of the managerialist models to practice politics, and the use of marketing by political actors, mean that these two have been complicit in the process of contributing to this malaise. The language and terminology used to characterise politics contains meaning and by extension implications.

The problem of markets

It is problematic to assume that politics can be equated with markets and market competition. The argument of this book is that politics and marketing are qualitatively different categories and as such, are mutually exclusive. While markets can facilitate competition, competition can also occur outside of a market setting, such as in an electoral arena, where a different set of motivations and issues emerge, such as the opportunity for debate, discussion and the acknowledgement of a collective good bigger than that of an individuals' own utility maximising benefit. Yet, the idea of perfect competition does not provide for either any opportunity for future investment or a common interest or public good. These may be seen as unintended by-products, but are not goals in themselves.

Markets, in perfect competition models, also fail to distinguish between large and small organisations. Large organisations clearly have greater resources at their disposal and therefore become more able to structure consumer choice favourably to their product. This can be done through advertising and persuasion of techniques, and this erodes ideals of consumer sovereignty, if preferences become shaped favourably towards an organisation by the organisation. This suggests manipulation rather than empowerment. The presumed equality of the consumer is also negated by the fact that some consumers are wealthier than others. In this sense, markets reflect the interests and wants of the rich, those who have the means to engage in the market in the first place. In political marketing terms, this can be seen in terms of the rich being similar to those targeted by political parties. The interest and wants of those in selected constituencies, key target voters, are those who are rich in an electoral market where perfect competition is assumed. If a market is assumed to function freely it will not use resources available, simply those needed by organisations to achieve their ends. In this sense, the ideas and policies that are beyond those needed to secure key voters do not reach the campaigning agenda.

Where markets as a mechanism fail, according to neoclassical economics, this is largely regarded as a consequence of lack of competition, for example, monopolies; because of the existence of exogenous factors (externalities) influencing the nature of competition; 'and when consumers have preferences for public goods the market will fail because individuals will not contribute towards the cost of goods they cannot be excluded from using'.[54] To function efficiently and effectively, the market comprises simply a buyer or seller—common interest does not exist. If a common interest does exist, this will lead to irrational action on the part of consumers and so the market will fail. This suggests for the market to work, a common interest or public good cannot exist. In order for the market to function, individuals are encouraged to pursue their individual self-interest; however, in so doing, this denies any notion of a civic society at both an ontological and an ideological level. In economic accounts, the function of government and political institutions is simply to regulate markets, not to construct and take part in a market. Arguably, rather than market failure being a problem for the activity of politics, it is the existence of the market itself which generates problems for politics, individualising interaction and negating a sense of future investment or collective benefit (such as democracy, a stable and functioning political system) and as detailed below.

The problems of production and consumption

A second set of issues arises from the idea of politics as a process of production and consumption. The above discussion demonstrates how economic accounts privilege production and that consumption is dependent upon production. It is the production process which generates consumers and consumption. This inverts the marketing concept by putting the producer at the start of the process. The producer generates consumers to enable the pursuit of the producer's interests. To tie the process of politics into the process of production and consumption raises a series of concerns in respect of the 'consumer'. Clearly, the suggestion contained within the mainstream political marketing literature is that consumption implies empowerment. A consumer has the opportunity to influence the production of a particular product, and can choose whether or not to buy. The use of the term 'consumer' serves to individualise the process of politics. To refer to politics as a process of production and consumption with attention to the demands of the consumer suggests a focus upon the individual wants and needs, rather than the wants and needs of a society. Focus is on the short-term satisfaction of interest rather than the long-term provision of a collective good.

The process of consumption is inherently bound up with dissatisfaction. For if consumers are satisfied, they will no longer consume. Therefore, the process of consumption requires a degree of dissatisfaction in order to continue. Therefore, to introduce consumption into politics means that the public can never be satisfied, as the cycle of consumption must continue. Where the marketing concept has been normatively employed, it has been suggested that the consumer is able to influence the production process, to gain the political product that they 'want'. This is consistent with neoliberal conceptions of consumer empowerment. However, if it is accepted that it is the process of production generates these wants, then the fulfilment of them by producers is a self-fulfilling prophecy. Producers cannot fail to satisfy wants that they themselves have created. This also undermines claims to enhancing accountability. If producers are creating wants, they are accountable only in the sense that they respond to wants that they have created. This is also different from citizenship conceptions of accountability which function (as above) to act as a check and balance upon governmental/elite power.

While the public may well not be that passive, what the discourse of production and consumption does do is define the parameters of debate, so that the possibility of wants or preferences emerging outside of those defined by the producers is limited, and have limited potential for realisation. What this means is that wants that exist outside of the production process are marginalized. In this way, the public can only want the politics they are given by elite actors. Rather than emerging from autonomous consumers, producers impose wants upon consumers. Consumers become alienated from their wants, as they are removed from them and their instigation. Not only are wants to constructed, but once identified and fed back into the production process, they are moulded to suit the interest of the producer, rather than the consumer. So rather than being involved, the 'consumer' is removed from the production process. What this suggests is that wants can only be determined by political actors. If wants are only assumed to be those determined by political actors, then wants which exist outside those which are defined by political actors may find expression through other mechanisms (such as extremist parties or pressure groups). At the same time, if these wants exist, but are not acknowledged in the formal process of politics, there is no reason to assume participation by those who express these wants which are effectively silenced.

To be a citizen means to take part in a formal political system and processes. If the term 'citizen' is removed, this also denies the meanings attached to it, which include both rights and obligations. To remove the obligation to take part in the formal political process generates real concerns in terms of electoral participation (see chapter 6). As such, removing the civic duty to participate formally may exacerbate this decline in the formal processes of politics.

Normative concerns: civil society

The dominant language of the market focuses on production and consumption and negates wider normative concerns. The process of production and consumption negate the notion of a public sphere or public space where political issues may be deliberated. Clearly there is a debate over the constituent aspects of politics,[55] but politics, whether about power, the distribution of resources, conflict or resolution of conflict, is inherently normative. Crucially it is underpinned by a conceptualisation of a civil society. In democratic theory the public sphere is where citizens become sufficiently informed about political elites that they may hold those elites to account.[56] It is not suggested that there was a 'golden age' of politics where this happened; however, it provides an ideal through which civil society may be conceptualised, which is lacking in the theorising of politics as a marketplace. What this does achieve is to reinforce the new right notion that 'there is no such thing as society', rather there are individuals who consume to maximise their self-interest in an open market. This market does not perform a social function nor recognise the existence of a society.

Finally, if citizenship rights are negated and consumer rights take their place, it might be worth speculating on what this may ultimately generate. Does this mean that obligations to obey laws (again enshrined in notions of citizenship) disappear? Can consumers choose not to 'buy in' to certain laws? If the public have consumer rights in respect of their political elites, does this mean it will be possible to sue/prosecute an MP? Will this marketisation mean that accountability will occur individually through the courts rather than the democratic process?

The function of discourse: ontology

In scientific accounts language functions as an instrument of communication. But language is also used to convey shared understandings and meanings.

While the objectivist approach contained within marketing management would suggest that language reflects reality, in contrast constructivists might suggest that language creates reality. The language used serves not only to describe how the political process operates but also serves to define it. Its definition in turn shapes the parameters through which compo-nent parts (i.e., voters and parties and the nature of politics) can be conceived. Language and discourse play a role in constituting what is conceivably possible and by extension, excludes certain opportunities. Discourse serves to frame and narrate norms, provide points of reference, which in turn serve to construct actors' understandings of their interests, ac-tions, and the context in which these take place. Discourse functions as a mechanism through which the world is understood by those within it. (It is also plays an epistemological function in that it is also connected with what can be known about the world.[57]) The social and political world is constructed and reconstructed according to the perceptions of those actors within it and this in turn facilitates action. Action occurs within a set of structures; these structures, for Wendt, have 'an inherently discursive dimension in the sense that they are inseparable from the reasons and self-understanding that agents bring to their actions' and while action and context/structure are 'mutually constitutive' 'each in some sense are an effect of the other'.[58]

Discourse takes place within, and serves to construct and reconstruct system(s) of meaning. All actions and structures are meaningful; they derive their meaning from their relationship to other actions and structures. Action does not exist independently of these systems of meaning; it takes place within frameworks of meaning and can only be understood in this context. That is, discourse defines systems of meaning, delineating boundaries of what is possible, what is fixed, and what is normal. In so doing, discursive structures 'exclud[e] certain options and structur[e] relations'.[59]

There is the opportunity for alternatives to emerge: '"discourses" are open ended sys-tems, always productive of new possibilities . . . There is not one discursive structure in society as a whole, or even just within the government domain, but multiple forms of "lan-guage game" and multiple rationalities that may contradict or clash'.[60] However, following Laclau and Mouffe[61] it is suggested that these alternatives are limited as the dominant dis-course functions to impose a hegemonic meaning on a set of social practices. For example, the demise of socialism, has been heralded by some as the triumph of liberal democracy[62] associated with advanced capitalism, which limits the possibility of conceiving of alternative means through which society may be organized. In this way ideas are important within political systems, as Hay notes, '[T]he development of the system depends not merely on the context, the condition of the system itself and the preferences and/or rationality of the actors within it, but on the understandings of those actors'.[63]

The terms 'consumer' or 'citizen' are part of a broader set of social relations in which its meaning is constituted and understood. So it is important to understand what the usage of the term itself implies in terms of the content of the term 'consumer' as opposed to 'voter/citizen'. This term provides a frame of reference through which understanding of the world is generated. But in turn, this also serves an ontological function in that it serves to define understanding of that which constitutes what is real. In this sense then, the usage of 'consumer', both in terms of its own meaning and related to a broader economic and polit-ical discourse, serves to construct and create the perception of the public as consumers. While an object, or indeed reality, may exist independently of its discursive articulation, it is argued here that it is the perception of that reality which serves to constitute it. As such, if voters are perceived as consumers, this in turn serves to render voters *as* consumers, thereby re-creating the meaning of the public in the public sphere and political process. In this sense, if voters are perceived and discursively constructed as consumers by political actors, this serves an ontological as well as the analytical function (at present conflated) within much of the literature.

To this end, actors adopt (and are prescribed) marketing techniques and methods to compete in this environment to achieve their goal. However, the acceptance of the existence of a market also plays a role in constructing the market. While the assumption of the existence of a market may reflect interaction of those individuals within it, this in turn means that the logic of the market also imposes itself upon the individuals within it. This means that political actors, in assuming and accepting the existence of a marketplace, in turn behave in a manner consistent with the way in which markets operate. In this sense political actors, by adopting the techniques and mindset of the marketplace, then serve to construct and reconstruct the market. If it is accepted that discourse contributes to our understanding and construction of political reality, then this represents a fundamental shift in the way in which politics is practised.

The function of discourse: ideology

Language also performs an ideological function in that it communicates a set of underlying beliefs and ideas. Language functions as part of a broader discourse, where ideals and beliefs are normalised and embodied in particular language forms, words. Following Saussarian principles, words themselves are signifiers of content. Each word has and signifies not only an object (or subject), but also contains a set of meanings. The context in which language is used facilitates understanding of that language because of a broader discourse through which social relations are constituted. That is, the term, 'political party' and 'voter' have particular meaning because of the content which is contained within the term and as part of a broader set of political practices. In this sense, words themselves are signifiers of content which contain values. However, the content of these words is not always fixed and may be dependent upon the context in which they are used. For example, a consumer in an economic marketplace may have a certain set of characteristics ascribed by rationalist foundations; however, to apply consumer to the process of politics entails the attribution of these same characteristics, yet the context of politics is fundamentally different from the context of the economic marketplace. So it is important to understand both the content of the word and the context in which it is expressed. The word serves to transmit, relay, reconstitute and reinforce the ideological assumptions and commitment which underpin it. If consumer and producer are underpinned by economic assumptions (as has been argued throughout), then the use of the term itself serves to reinforce this commitment to economic approaches to public life.

Conclusion

Democratic politics is dependent upon ideas, discussion and debate. Politics is a site where interests are represented, resources allocated, where conflict, among groups or interests and ideas, may be resolved, or at least a resolution sought. Politics is about power, its use (or not), its dispersal and the repercussions of this for those within the society which it affects. Politics is about belief systems and inherently normative; it involves an ideal about what society should be like, underpinned by contested concepts such as equality and liberty. While these concepts and ideas are contested, they do impact (even in their contested form) and shape the terrain of political debate and action. The language used to represent ideas and beliefs is significant, as use (or not) of particular terms mean certain courses of action are available, while others are excluded.

The language of the market dominates the political marketing literature. This managerialist approach to politics has largely uncritically accepted the underlying assumptions. One of the ways in which this has been done is through the acceptance of the language of marketing to describe the process of politics. First, principles accept the existence of a market (discussed in the previous chapter) and assume a process of production and consumption. This process has been rendered explicit and the implications of this drawn out. It has been suggested that production and consumption and politics are mutually exclusive, and this has been shown through a discussion of the term 'consumer'. It has been argued that to uncritically accept the term 'consumer' negates the wider issues associated with the ideals of citizenship. It also contends that to focus upon production and consumption focuses attention on the content of production, rather than the broader processes which facilitate the existence of the production process in the first place.

Within the existing literature there flows a series of definitional disputes as to what constitutes the political product, although there is greater consensus as to who the consumer is. The significance of this is in alerting attention to the role of definitions in normalising the role of marketing in politics. The political marketing literature goes beyond the analytical analogy of parties behaving as if they are businesses and voters as if they are consumers. The terms parties/candidates and businesses are conflated, as are the terms voters and consumers. This in turn serves to render these terms ontological rather than analytical. This is significant in that it can alter the way in which politics is conceived. Language and discourse play a role in legitimating, embedding and normalising ideas. Actors are positioned through this language and discourse into undertaking roles ascribed to them. In this sense, the discourse of marketing positions political parties/candidates as marketers rather than politicians. This in turn means a different set of behaviours and practices flow. It has also been argued that the terminology and language serve a broader ontological function which has contributed to redefining understandings of what politics is, which, as will be highlighted in the following chapter, provides a set of problems for contemporary politics.

Notes

1. Cf. Finlayson, 2003.
2. Cf. Laclau and Mouffe, 1987.
3. Cf. Marx, 1994.
4. Scammell, 1995.
5. Lees-Marshment, 2001b: 694.
6. Shama, 1976; Kotler, 1975; Mauser, 1983.
7. O'Leary and Iredale, 1976.
8. Newman, 1994: 10.
9. Butler and Collins, 1994.
10. Wring, 1997: 655.
11. Harrop, 1990: 278.

12. Reid, 1988.
13. Smith and Saunders, 1990; Smith, 2001.
14. Bartle, 2002: 41.
15. Harrop, 1990: 278.
16. Scammell, 1995: 20.
17. Levy, 1959; Solomon, 1983; McCracken, 1986; Belk, 1988.
18. Butler and Collins, 1994: 27.
19. Scammell, 1995: xii.
20. Kotler and Kotler 1999: 4–5.
21. Butler and Collins, 1994: 25.
22. Butler and Collins, 1994: 19.
23. Newman, 1994: 22; Lees-Marshment, 2001b: 692; Lock and Harris, 1996: 28; Smith and Saunders, 1990; Shama, 1976: 766; Butler and Collins, 1999: 55.
24. Farrell and Wortman, 1987: 297; Wring, 1997: 1133; Reid, 1988: 36.
25. Reid, 1988: 36.
26. Lees-Marshment, 2001a; Newman, 1994: 10.
27. McGinnis, 1968; see also Reid, 1988.
28. Newman, 1994: 29.
29. Harrop, 1990: 280.
30. Chapman and Cowdell, 1998: 31.
31. Frazier et al, 1991: 563.
32. Equilibrium is reached when total surplus is maximised; total surplus is the combination of the maximum benefit gained by the consumer and the maximum benefit gained by the producer taking part in this competitive market.
33. Smith, 1776, bk 4, ch 2.
34. Von Hayek, 1991.
35. Gray, 1984: 32.
36. Weibull, 1995: xiii.
37. Scott, 1970: 25.
38. Bowler and Farrell, 1992: 5; O'Cass, 1996: 46.
39. Kotler and Kotler, 1999: 3.
40. Abrams, 1980: 14.
41. Cf. Smith, 1776.
42. Keat, 1994: 27.
43. Scullion, forthcoming.
44. Fitchett, 2004: 303.
45. Cf. Sackman, 1992.
46. Galbraith, 1999: 125.
47. Galbraith, 1999: 126–28.
48. Galbraith, 1999: 113.
49. Marshall, 1950.
50. Marshall, 1950: 78, 111.
51. Isin, 2002.
52. Cf. Williams, 1989.
53. See for example, Palkulski, 1997; Stevenson, 2003.
54. Hindmoor, 2006: 84.

55. See Leftwich, 2004.
56. Cf. Habermas, 1989.
57. Cf. Dant, 1991.
58. Wendt, 1987: 359–60.
59. Howarth et al, 2000: 4.
60. Finlayson and Martin, 2006: 160.
61. Laclau and Mouffe, 1985.
62. Fukuyama, 1992.
63. Hay, 2004a: 149.

6

Marketing and Malaise

Alienation in British politics tends to be discussed in terms of declining electoral turnout, rather than as a consequence of electioneering strategies and techniques. It is has been argued throughout this book that at a conceptual level there is a demonstrable link between the two. Participation in the political marketing literature is assumed to occur in two sites: where the public influence the construction of the political product (see chapter 3) and in the act of voting. In formal political terms, this suggests a participatory rather than representative form of democracy. This participation by voters in the marketing analogy is what keeps political elites responsive and accountable. But for this analogy to work, participation by the electorate is crucial. However, the empirical reality in the UK and other Western democracies is one of declining electoral turnout and increasing disaffection and lack of trust in both politicians and the process of politics.

This chapter details these empirical observations and suggests that marketing and its use by politicians is a key aspect in the phenomenon of 'democratic malaise'. Both the malaise and the use of marketing can be seen as a consequence of material processes which are taking place in a larger political, social and technological environment. However, there are also important ideational and ideological processes at work. As has been argued, marketing as a belief system represents the internalisation of rational choice theorising. In turn, this means that the theoretical problems associated with rational choice have the potential to impact upon material reality. Within this chapter, the link between marketing and malaise is made at the ideological level. Given the interaction between the material and ideational, both conceptually and empirically, it is suggested here that a combination of material and ideational factors are discernible in the disconnection of the electorate from politics. In order to reflect this, the chapter is divided into two sections. The first addresses the material aspects of the declining participation in the political process—detailing public response to politics in the UK. It then situates this in the wider context of the 'malaise' debate and proceeds to identify the broader political, social and mediated environment within which (a) this disengagement has occurred and (b) has simultaneously provided the context conducive to political actors embracing political marketing.

The second half of the chapter draws attention to ideational aspects of malaise: specifically the beliefs in relation to marketing. The marketing literature advocates employing marketing models to construct the reality of political actors, but this is only one part of the activity of politics. Voters are also salient, and so this chapter then turns to explore the way in which voters are assumed to behave within these management marketing models and the political marketing literature. Given the underlying economic foundations of this literature, this chapter moves on to reflect upon orthodox rationalist accounts of participation. It concludes by arguing that at an ideational level, the use of marketing by political actors, rather than mobilize the public to participate, serves to reinforce the rationality of not participating in politics. While this is at a theoretical level, as earlier chapters have argued, the line between theory and practice is often conflated within the managerialist political marketing literature. In this way, highlighting the problems within orthodox economic accounts of political behaviour draws attention to the way in which marketing, as a belief system, is problematic in terms of its conceptualisation of the 'public'. Marketing as a belief system positions voters as individuals, negating their broader context, and any notion of a public good, and given the Downsian behaviour of political elites, encourages voters to behave in a manner consistent with Downsian thinking. This in turn suggests a conceptual linkage between malaise and marketing, which, given the influence of marketing ideas in practice, indicates the existence of both an ideological link and a material link between the processes of marketing and democratic malaise.

Electoral participation and disaffection

A wide academic literature has developed which discusses the public's propensity to engage in the formal processes of politics. As Parry et al argue, most studies of participation in liberal democracies assume an instrumentalist position[1]; that is, one which assumes that participation is an attempt to influence government in a way beneficial to the participant. This is consistent with rationalist, utility-maximising accounts of participation.[2] However, socio-psychological variables are also acknowledged, and the link between civic attitudes and engagement has been made by Verba and Nie.[3] They linked political knowledge and inclination to participate with socioeconomic status. While participation was thought to encompass socioeconomic variables such as race, class and gender, they also recognised the existence of affective aspects which included both personal and collective values.[4] They argued, however, that the more educated were likely to be more knowledgeable about politics and, therefore, have a greater sense of efficacy. At the same time, those with lower socio-economic status were also found to have a lesser inclination to take part.[5] In a similar vein, Lister suggests there is an inverse correlation between welfare state institutions, inequalities of social citizenship and propensity for participation.[6] In contrast, Norris highlights factors external to the formal political process and draws attention to the news media as a variable in this relationship. She argues the link between political knowledge and engagement can be made, but it is the media that are crucial in this process. As this political knowledge is largely gained via the news media, then those with a greater interest in the news media are consequently more inclined to take part in the process of politics.[7] Despite the tensions and varying points of emphasis within these accounts, what they all rely on (whether explicitly or implicitly) is that there is a perception held by the voter of the effectiveness of collective action. That is, despite the instrumentalism afforded to the act of voting, voters are still assumed to have an underlying sense of their contribution to the 'whole' democratic system—that collectively voters perceive the opportunity to produce an outcome not achievable individually.

This collective action serves the broader purpose, not only of enabling individuals to pursue their own self-interest, but it also plays a crucial role in system stabilisation. Politicians themselves recognise the importance of the public voting and the legitimation function that electoral participation confers as Harriet Harman (UK Minister for Constitutional Affairs) acknowledged, 'Our democracy lacks legitimacy if, whatever the formal rules about universal suffrage and the right to vote, people don't make it a reality by turning out to vote'.[8]

At the 2001 UK general election, turnout was 59 percent. This was the lowest of any postwar election and improved only marginally in 2005 when turnout was 61 percent. This is compared to 76 percent in 1979. This lack of turnout has been particularly problematic among younger generations[9] and Henn et al argue that 'conventional wisdom holds that young people in Britain are alienated from politics'.[10] The British Social Attitudes survey also shows that people under the age of twenty-five are becoming increasingly disinterested in politics and less likely to form attachments to political parties.[11] However, it would seem that this is part of a more general trend, as research undertaken by Ipsos-Mori, following the 2005 UK general election, suggests that large numbers of people do not see any point in voting, as they see no impact from their vote, with 14 percent of the population claiming to be 'utterly disengaged'.[12] This is supported by findings from the UK Electoral Commission which suggests only 33 percent of the public feel that getting involved in politics makes any difference.[13] The UK Electoral Commission has recently sought to measure levels of knowledge, interest and engagement with politics.[14] Their report published in 2006 sought to quantify perceptions of public knowledge and interest in politics as detailed in the following tables.

Table 6.1 Perceptions of political knowledge: 'How much do you feel you know about "politics"?'

Nothing at all	10%
Not very much	51%
A fair amount	35%
A great deal	4%

(source for tables 6.1, 6.2, and 6.3: post-election report, UK Electoral Commission 2006)

Table 6.2 Interest in politics: 'How interested would you say you are in "politics"?'

Not at all interested	14%
Not very interested	30%
Fairly interested	43%
Very interested	13%

What tables 6.1 and 6.2 suggest is that there appears to be limited knowledge of what is happening in the formal realm of politics. When asked how much they knew about politics, 51 percent of respondents replied not very much (table 6.1). At the same time, 43 percent of the population claim to be fairly interested in politics (table 6.2). This suggests, then, that around half of the population, while interested in politics, feel reasonably uninformed.

Unsurprisingly, this report also found those who were interested in politics were also those who are much more likely to vote. The report suggests a correlation between those who felt they knew about, and were interested in, politics and the propensity to vote. This is consistent with longitudinal analysis of polls, which conducted between 1973 and 2003 suggests that there has been a reasonably consistent 50:50; 60:40 split between those who say they are engaged in politics and those uninterested.[15] But when asked about the content of politics, that is, issues rather than the institutions of politics, there is a somewhat different picture. The overwhelming majority of respondents demonstrated a significant interest in local and national and international issues, as seen in table 6.3.

Table 6.3   Interest in local, national and international issues: How interested would you say you are in:

	Not very/Not at all interested	Very/fairly
Local issues	19%	81%
National issues	25%	75%
International issues	35%	65%

This interest in issues (table 6.3) suggests that the public are interested in the content of politics, but as the above tables (6.1 and 6.2) suggest, the formal mechanisms of politics are what the public are less certain of. So while the levels of interest in the process of politics appear to have remained fairly constant over the last three decades, what has changed is the proclivity for the public to act on this interest, to take part in elections. Consistent with the theme of this book, these findings suggest a distinction between the *process* of politics and the *content* of politics. The process is about the personnel and institutions of the state, while the content is about political issues, which are defined through ideological belief systems and implemented through public policy.

This lack of engagement with government, political systems and institutions is concerning not least as the legitimation of democratic systems relies, in large part, on the public endorsing a system through the mechanism of elections. However, it is erroneous to suggest that lack of participation at election time can be simply equated with political apathy. Despite the proliferation of media sources, it would seem that large sections of the public feel uninformed about politics, and politicians themselves are regarded as untrustworthy. At the same time, a high proportion of the public claim to be interested in issues which are inherently political. This would suggest that it is the process of politics, not the content of politics, which is influencing participation in elections. What this raises then is the question, if the public claim to be interested in the content of politics (political issues), why are they increasingly less inclined to take part in the formal process of politics?

Democratic malaise

At procedural level, part of the answer may lie in the electoral system itself. In part this declining participation could be a consequence of the first past the post-electoral system which favours those voting for the majority candidate; votes for other candidates may be seen as wasted votes. If the voter perceives their favoured candidate as unlikely to win an overall majority in that constituency, consistent with rational choice theorising, there is little or no incentive to vote. Electoral systems themselves are also thought to generate attitudes among the electorate: majoritarian and adversarial systems, which are thought to facilitate much less positive attitudes among the electorate than proportional and consensual systems.[16]

This systemic attribution of disengagement has also been coupled with a decline in trust in these political institutions and personnel. According to a longitudinal Mori survey, in 2003, 75 percent of the sample surveyed did not believe politicians told the truth, and this figure had been consistent since 1983. They were second only to journalists as the least trusted figures in public life.[17] This is not limited to the UK. Western democracies have witnessed a decline in trust in political leaders, institutions and political systems.[18] Newton argues that the public 'place less trust in their politicians; have less confidence in the main institutions of government; are more likely to believe that government is run for the benefit of the few big interests; and are more dissatisfied with the way democracy works in the country'.[19] The public are more likely to express satisfaction with governments they perceive to be open and fair[20], if they perceive politicians to be accountable[21], or if party systems are perceived to accommodate expressed interests.[22] And for some, it is the low levels of trust which explain declining participation in the process of politics.[23] As Dalton notes, this increasing scepticism among electorates in Western democracies has 'probably contributed to the trend towards increased issue voting and electoral volatility'.[24] Citizens have become 'distrustful of politicians, sceptical about democratic institutions, and disillusioned about how the democratic process functions'.[25]

While this disaffection has been linked with declining turnout, where this comes from is equally significant. For some, this malaise is located structurally, within the news media[26] and the broader social and economic environment.[27] For others, this is the fault of the public, too lazy to engage with politics, preferring to 'bowl alone' and watch TV.[28] Hay's insightful account of contemporary malaise notes the existence of both (in his terminology) demand and supply side interaction contributing to this process.[29] On the demand side, he draws attention to the public themselves in terms of decline in electoral participation in Western democracies, changes in linkages and allegiances to political parties and declining trust in politicians. He argues, however, that this process also needs to take account of supply side actions, that is, those of political actors. As such, he highlights the significance of marketing, policy convergence, the dominance of public choice thinking, the displacement of political responsibility to default authorities, the dominance of globalization, improper behaviour of public elites, all of which may serve to reduce public distrust. While this account comprehensively links together and conceptualises both sides of the 'coin' of influential factors, it is still couched in the language of economic accounts of politics. The rational assumptions which underpin this process, the terminology supply and demand, are inherently linked with the idea of markets. That is, more broadly, it is becoming commonplace to describe political problems in the language of the marketplace.

The material context

While the language of the marketplace has been a significant factor in creating a climate conducive to the acceptance of marketing (as noted in chapters 4 and 5), there are also material factors at stake. That is, there is a broader material context which has set the scene for marketing ideas to become embedded. This material context is one which is characterised by changes in the demographic makeup of partisan support and change within political parties as organisations. Underlying this, there has also arguably been a broader societal shift, leading some to suggest the emergence of a 'consumer society'.[30] At the same time, a proliferating media environment has meant that politicians need to harness these technologies in a bit to (re)connect with the public to encourage them to take part in the formal process of politics.

The political context

On a political level, there have been considerable changes detailed in the academic literature in relation to the way in which individuals connect, identify with or relate to, parties. Historically, it has been argued that party systems emerged to accommodate political parties.[31] These parties are elite organisations which had emerged to represent social, religious or class cleavages. There has been considerable political science literature devoted to demographic changes in patterns of voting behaviour.[32] Traditionally, voters were assumed to identify with, and therefore vote for, the party which was nearest to their social class. During the 1970s, the class/party linkage was argued to have declined. Whereas traditionally cleavage structures which were thought to structure the vote were initially thought to be frozen[33], it was suggested they had now been eroded.[34] Initially, debate centred around whether voters were 'dealigned'[35] from their traditional party identification, or whether they were merely realigning.[36] For Heath et al, one way in which this realignment can be identified is through the success of the Thatcher government in attracting the 'Essex man' vote.[37] The phrase 'Essex man' was coined by the journalist Simon Heffer to refer to voters, primarily from the upper working or lower middle classes aspiring to be 'middle class', attracted by the perception of economic opportunity (for example, the opportunity to purchase council houses and purchase shares). These voters moved towards the Conservatives (abandoning Labour) in large numbers, especially in areas such as Basildon.[38] This home-owning policy promoted by the Tories, in particular, was regarded by Dunleavy and Ward as a clear attempt to shape the electorates preferences.[39] This was a long-term electioneering strategy which essentially sought to reduce the amount of voters likely to vote Labour as a consequence of working-class identification. For it was assumed that if working-class voters perceived themselves to be middle class, then they would vote in the party who represented middle-class interests, which at the time was the Conservatives. But this social engineering had other impacts. The gradual eradication of the idea of 'class' as a societal division from public discourse led politicians to claim 'we're all middle class now'. The Labour party perceived this change in the basis of social support and now presents itself as a party located firmly within the middle classes.[40] This in turn has had a series of consequences, not least for political parties, as organisations who needed to find other methods through which to connect to and mobilize the electorate.

The demise of these party-societal links has also led to intense debate around the extent to which that the political party itself, as an organisation, is in decline.[41] This decline has been argued to be a consequence of the anti-party sentiment displayed by a disaffected public.[42] This suggests that whether a decline in partisan allegiance is equal to decline in parties as organisations per se, what is increasingly clear is that the place where identities and political allegiances were formed has now been vacated. These identities and allegiances may now come from elsewhere. In this sense, it is useful to briefly reflect on the broader societal context in which this has taken place.

The social context

At societal level there have also been broader long-term changes. The shift from Fordism to post-Fordist modes of production have been accompanied by claims that this change represents a shift from modernity to postmodernity. Modernity was characterised by focus on production; society was comprised of producers. This vision of society was driven by the desire for security.[43] Standardisation and routinisation characterised mass production, which in turn relied on the routinisation of individual behaviour, and was institutionalised through working practices. This security was linked with certainty. Certainty was associated with the long-term durability of goods and products. The focus here was on the process of production. But the production process functions to produce consumers, and in what is characterised as postmodernity, the focus is on consumption and consumerism.

While consumerism is taken to reflect a set of social processes emphasising the collectivity, consumption focuses upon the individual.[44] The notion of consumption can be viewed as a logical extension of the production process, so it serves to stabilize capitalism. For Baudrillard, needs/preferences are 'produced as elements of a system and not as a relation between an individual and an object ... [N]eeds and consumption are in fact an organized extension of productive forces'.[45] Preferences are shaped to fit the broader societal context. With an emphasis upon the role of the individual, the concern of the consumer is the satisfaction of their own individual interests, rather than a set of societal or collective needs or goods. The individualisation of this process also serves to reinforce new right principles of the primacy of the individual over any notion of a collective.

Consumption is characterised by transience, and commodities are assumed to be disposable. Simultaneously, this is thought to reflect insecurity and uncertainty (in contrast to the security and certainty associated with production). Individual identities are viewed as no longer fixed, but instead are characterised by confusion and the fragmentation of the self.[46] If this is so, the erosion of traditional forms of identity constitution leaves space for other forms of identity to emerge. Identification, then, is with products, branded goods and consumption. For some this has led to concerns of increasing space between ideals of civic commitment in the existence of consumers—suggesting a collapse of the 'social' itself.[47]

As marketisation grows and its remit extends directly into the political arena, so the notion of consumption is assumed to legitimate the system. Problems and issues are manufactured by advertising which then provides a commodified manner through which the consumer can 'solve' their problems. Commodifying social values is something not only confined to the practice of politics, but it is also a broader societal issue. What is problematic here, however, is that it is unclear that the electorate want their political experiences to be commodified. While consulting the electorate on the finer points of image, parties have negated the broader picture: that the public appear still to be interested in the political content of politics, which is informed by values and beliefs. This is noted above and evident for example in the mass demonstrations which took place against the Iraq conflict.

Yet, consumption, by its very nature, also promotes the view that 'enough' will never be attained[48], because there is a need to continue consuming rather than satisfy demand. If consumption is linked to the activity of politics, then this logically suggests disappointment and disaffection with politics.

The media context

Both by politicians and within the academic literature, the media have been largely attributed as the casual determinants of societal and political malaise.[49] While media effects remain highly contested and debated, what is significant here is that politicians clearly perceive that the media have an effect upon the public. Again, whether this is empirically provable or not, politicians behave in a manner which suggests they believe this to be true, thereby rendering it plausible. (Hence, for example, the studious courting of Murdoch by Blair in an attempt to secure the support of the *Sun*, the biggest selling national newspaper in Britain.) These issues are interlinked, as this perception of the media as responsible for 'malaise' coupled with a perception of the ability of the media to influence the public, has led politicians to engage in media management strategies which are now heavily influenced by marketing.

Curiously, however, the managerialist marketing models afford an instrumental role to the media: they are a means through which political actors 'sell' their 'product' to their target audience. Yet this fails to incorporate the motivations of the media themselves; that is, the media have their own motivations and agendas and are in a complex and dialectical relationship which serves to produce unintended outcomes. The media are not simply a tool for use by marketers and, as such, may serve to subvert the intentions of political actors engaged in marketing. The media have a differing agenda and are not always as compliant as marketing assumes. In this sense, the relationship between the media and political elites is significant in that it alters and filters the information that the public receive in respect of politics both in attempts to manage the news agenda through a process colloquially referred to as 'spin'.

Politicians and spin

Harrop claims that the use of marketing improves access to, and quality of, information.[50] Information provides the basis through which voters formulate their perceptions of the party/candidate for whom they wish to vote; it gives voters the capacity to act. However, this information and these images are mediated and represented to the public through the media. While there is debate about the effect of the media upon individuals (are the audience passive recipients or active participants?), and more broadly about the role of the media (do they impartially disseminate information or do they set the agenda?), it is, however, generally acknowledged that they are an integral part of the political process.[51]

As Kavanagh notes, for most people the election campaign is what is covered in the media.[52] With the proliferation of powerful and privately owned media with commercial interests, politicians have to respond and adapt to this environment. Elections have become regarded as increasingly stage-managed for the media.[53] The growth and expansion of access to television has led some commentators to argue there has been an Americanization of politics.[54] For some, this has meant the identification of a 'celebrity politician' keen to engage in entertainment media.[55] This has meant a focus upon media techniques and the person-alisation of politics. An emphasis on telegenic image is therefore seen as significant (and is widely accepted as one of the reasons behind Blair's ascendancy to the leadership position). While there is much debate about whether it is broadcasters who drive the politicians' agenda, or the politicians who drive the media agenda, arguably, the relationship is a di-alectical one. Consequently, the media do play a role in the political process, but this would suggest that politicians also retain some control over what is disseminated.

This focus upon the media, and particularly the attempts to use/manipulate the media, is not particularly new. What is qualitatively different now, however, is that the presentation of politicians and policy is now at least as, if not more, significant than policy content. A spin-doctor for Labour was quoted after the 1997 election as saying, '[C]ommunications is not an afterthought to our policy. It's central to the whole mission of New Labour'.[56] As Mandelson stated, 'If a government policy cannot be presented in a simple and attractive way, it is more likely than not to contain fundamental flaws and prove to be the wrong policy'.[57] Finlayson similarly notes, 'In order to get elected (to make itself electable), New Labour set a premium on appearing electable'.[58] Here consistent with marketing thinking, it is not the content of politics which is prioritised by politicians, but presentation, a per-ception of a carefully constructed image.

The media agenda

It is through the media that citizens are able to access information about their political elites. This is necessary in order that citizens are able to make informed decisions about those whom they hold to account through the electoral process. But the media are also complicit in the changing nature of communication about politics. As Simons argues, '[T]he mass media generate a pseudo-public sphere in which cultural consumption entails no discussion of what is consumed. When debate is presented through the media, the conversation itself is administered and treated as a consumer item'.[59] That is, the *content* of politics is treated by the media as superfluous to the *process* of politics.

In part, the emergence and development of the new media have been attributed as part of the reason for the dumbing down of political debate, as mass media have to appeal to the 'lowest common denominator' in a bid to attract as wide an audience as possible.[60] The structure of the market has altered also as traditional media (such as press and terrestrial television) now have to compete with 'new media', such as satellite, cable and the Internet and twenty-four hour news coverage. This has been coupled with deregulatory legislation and changes in the patterns of media ownership through mergers and acquisitions which have also increased market pressure, as news media compete for audiences in order to retain profitability. If the primary function of the media is to attract an audience (for without it, a medium does not function), then market pressures also play an important role in shaping media output. In some respects, this is impacting upon the content of political news.[61] Therefore, the demands from the market placed upon traditional media have led them to place pressure on politicians to provide items that will attract an audience (hence, for ex-ample, the rise in photo opportunities).

So, on the one hand, politicians have been pursuing the media and media-friendly images and policies to connect with the public. At the same time, it has also been argued that the media have played a significant role in contributing to the growing cynicism of the electorate.[62] Indeed, watching television has been regarded as contributing to diminishing civic engagement[63]: the more time citizens spend watching television the less time they have to consider 'civic-minded' activities.[64] Politicians themselves identify the media as contributing to a potential loss of faith in the political system. Geoff Mulgan (No. 10's director of strategy and policy) and Labour has accused the media of 'failing to tell the truth', arguing that this undermines government legitimacy.[65] Yet this suggests that the responsibility for disengagement lies either with the electorate or with the media. Blame has also been attributed to the electorate for lacking the incentive to seek out or gain information about their political elites. The electorate are assumed to prefer reality TV to serious political programming, to prefer watching television rather than engaging in community or civic activities.[66] But if this is so, it implies that the media have a significant influence over their audience.

The media and effects

There is considerable debate as to the effects of the media on the audience. The Frankfurt School argued that the media 'inject' a message into the audience. However, this was countered by the argument that the media have limited effects; the audience receive media 'selectively'.[67] They manipulate the media through their own experiences, rather than being manipulated by the media. Reinforcement theorists argue that the media reinforce existing viewpoints. In contrast, McCombs and Shaw argue that the media set the agenda: they define not only what we can think, but what we can think about.[68]

As Brookes et al note, the way in which public opinion itself (as measured by opinion polls) is represented in the media can play a significant role in constructing public opinion.[69] In terms of direct influence on voting behaviour, Harrop argues that the press do impact on voters' beliefs on issues, but only insofar as it reinforces existing intentions.[70] While Curtice and Semetko argue that the press do not directly affect voting intention, they suggest that the press do play a role in influencing voters' perceptions of political parties. However, they concur with Harrop's reinforcement argument and argue that many voters tend to 'view newspaper reports (and watch television news) through a partisan filter that enables them to ignore politically uncongenial messages'.[71] In contrast, recent research into media effects at the 1997 election suggests that newspapers have a 'limited influence on the voting behaviour of their readers'.[72] Whatever the debates over effects, politicians clearly believe the media does have an effect and exert influence over the voters[73] (or particularly floating voters). Labour openly has sought to court the press, particularly the *Daily Mail* and the *Sun*. Campbell made sure that Labour supplied these papers with information about new policy initiatives and responses to editorials or articles that were critical of Labour. He reassured editors, in conversation, that Labour could be trusted on Europe, tax and education[74], which was hoped that this would tone down the hostility of the press (widely regarded as anti-Labour especially—although not only—pre-1997).

The appeal to the mass media, in an attempt to influence voting intentions, has led many to be concerned with the emphasis placed by politicians on style over substance. Franklin argues that this focus upon presentation effectively diminishes the quality of political debate.[75] This undermines the democratic ideal of an informed citizenry making decisions about those who will govern them. In contrast, some argue this enhances the opportunity for engagement, making politics available and accessible to a wider audience.[76] Norris suggests that those who are politically interested will engage in political information anyway, and that those who are politically disengaged will not engage[77]—implying the media have little if no effect upon political behaviour or consciousness. In a similar vein, Prior argues that those who prefer to engage with entertainment, rather than serious, or 'political' media, are less likely to engage in the activity of voting.[78]

While the direction of causality (media shaping politics or politics manipulating the media) may be difficult to establish, suffice to say that both interact and influence the way in which contemporary politics is conducted and represented to the citizen. Politicians may seek to manipulate the media, but, in response to media demands, political information tends to be produced in 'soundbites'. As Street notes, 'Politics is moulded to fit the medium. But the medium is not just an instrument of the politicians' will. It creates the rules and sets the agenda for the coverage of politics'.[79] Yet, this is consistent with the rational choice view, that citizens have little time or incentive to make, dissect and study political information at length. In this view, the costs of obtaining this information far outweigh the benefits of voting, given the minimal probability of casting a decisive vote; therefore, politicians will seek to promote image, rather than detailed information.

In terms of the ability to communicate with voters, the above discussion relies upon the public engaging with the media, which promotes the message of politicians in the first instance. While some of the public may engage with the media, and so therefore there is the possibility it may have an effect (or not), what also needs to be considered is that the use of marketing per se may encourage people not to engage with the media where politicians are using these strategies. In economic accounts, the media are assumed to operate in 'two-sided' markets; that is, the need to appeal to both advertisers and attract an audience (for those advertisers).[80] Welfare for the viewer is seen in terms of cost (assuming pay-per-view) and quality of programming but a tension is introduced given the demands of the advertiser. The greater the quantity of advertising, the increase in likelihood that viewers will disengage from that programme. In economic accounts, 'disutility' is a function of too much advertising.[81] That is, there is an inverse relation between the quantity of advertising and the likelihood of effect, as the greater the amount of advertising that occurs, the less likely an audience is to engage with that medium. Where this is instructive, then, is to suggest that the activity of advertising per se serves to disengage people from watching a particular programme or channel because of the very quantity of advertising. So, applied to politics this might suggest that people are less likely to watch political programming if they are aware it is characterised by advertising, and by extension marketing. The opportunity for the media to have an effect, or to influence the public is severely curtailed if sections of the public do not engage in media in the first place.

The ideational context

This broader environment sets the scene for marketing ideas to take hold at societal level and in turn impact upon the public. As noted in chapter 4, this process is dialectical, and marketing ideas, in turn, reconstitute and redefine the material environment. The way in which social, political and technological change is perceived by political candidates/parties plays a significant role in positioning them and their response.

Where does marketing fit in this?

Given this broader material context, and the complexities political actors face in connecting with their electorates as a consequence of the above societal and technological changes, marketing is presented by marketers as one, if not *the* key method of linking publics and political elites. What is suggested here is that the ideas which underpin marketing in turn have the opportunity to effect a set of consequences where the public are engaging, or not, with politicians who are using marketing.

The marketing literature acknowledges the existence of research which highlights citizen disaffection and alienation from campaigns, elections and institutions as being at an all-time high at the end of the twentieth century, but presents marketing as a method of reconnecting with the electorate[82], rather than being a contributory factor. However, as is shown below, far from providing a means to reconnect with the public, marketing reinforces the problem of disconnection. Given the underlying economic assumptions, there are five issues at stake for political marketing: first, in assuming voters vote denies the problem of nonparticipation; second, as economic accounts highlight, the problem is actually that it is rational not to take part in politics; third, the individualisation of this process serves to negate a public good (and so reinforces point 2); fourth, that this disconnects the public from their broader context (which is largely downplayed by marketing accounts); fifth, that the prescription of these models as practice in turn serves to render the problems within economic accounts as plausible empirically.

What does marketing assume about voters?

Simply put, the marketing literature assumes that voters vote. The purpose of this vote is to enable political actors to win elections. Marketing views voting as a instrumental, as a means through which political actors can achieve their goals. From this perspective, votes are only important insofar as they enable politicians to gain electoral victory.

Henneberg claims that '[p]olitical marketing acts as a guiding theory in the development of a model [of] voting behaviour with managerial implications'[83], although this is a method of establishing voter wants and incorporating them into the political product.[84] This suggests that political marketing as a method is a means to guide and structure voting behaviour; a top-down process which can be managed. The similarity between rationalist accounts of voting behaviour and marketing consumer behaviour have been noted within the marketing literature.[85] Not only are voters equated with consumers, but they are assumed to be engaged in a buying activity on the day of the election. This endorses a position held elsewhere in political science, that '[p]arties are treated as competing products . . . Emotional ties such as party identification or class loyalty do not come into it'.[86] Assumptions of electors voting in line with class allegiance are regarded by marketers as no longer relevant; indeed, it is suggested that individuals may behave in a rational, self-interested manner when voting, but this may be affected by changes in party policy/image.[87]

As with rational choice accounts, the political marketing literature also introduces an affective aspect. Motivation for whom to vote is assumed to be 'driven primarily by the image [of a leader]'.[88] While voters are assumed to require evidence of capacity to execute policies, but are thought to regard policy content as secondary, for some, it has been claimed, this is incidental.[89] The political marketing literature assumes that 'voters are unable to unbundle the electoral product offering, the vast majority therefore choose on the basis of overall political package, concept or image'.[90] This then emphasises imagery and packaging rather than formal political content. From within the marketing perspective, this serves to validate the utility of marketing, as if voters vote as a result of imagery, then the logical marketing response is to promote imagery. However, crucially, this claim is largely guided not by empirically supported voter research but from the starting point of the tools available through the marketing process. That is, the process of marketing has led to an emphasis on imagery, and as a consequence it becomes assumed that this is what voters respond to. In this sense, it is the existence of a set of tools and techniques employed in the campaign process, which are assumed by the marketing literature to drive the rational response of voters. Interestingly, for marketers, the failure to attract votes is regarded as a failure to address the right target audience.[91]

The irrationality of voting

Far from providing powerful incentives to motivate voters, the logic within the political marketing literature merely reinforces the collective action paradox at the heart of orthodox rational choice theory: that it is rational not to vote. The two main causes of abstention in spatial models of electoral competition are (a) indifference, in that if voters perceive little difference between competitors, they are less likely to vote, and (b) alienation—if the alternatives are too far from the voter's ideal point, they are also less likely to vote.[92] The smaller the perceived difference between the competing parties, the less rational it is for voters to incur the costs of turnout.[93] If individuals are assumed to be rational, self-interested utility maximisers, then the costs of voting (e.g., collecting information and going to the polling station given the infinitesimal chance of influencing the outcome of the election) outweigh the benefits; therefore, it is rational not to vote. Therefore, the more that political parties behave in a manner that is consistent with the economic assumptions of rational choice literature (the more they adopt marketing strategies), the more likely it becomes that voters will also behave in a manner consistent with these rational assumptions and fail to participate in the electoral process.

As noted in the chapter 4, marketing ideology is advocated as a replacement for political ideology. For marketing to work it must be adopted as more than just a set of techniques and strategies but as a mindset, a belief system. Yet for economic accounts, ideology is more than just a belief system. It has a functional aspect too. For Downs' ideology functioned as a cost-saving device, a means through which voters could clearly identify policy bundles. This meant the rational voter did not have to expend vast amounts of resources in gathering information about the policy platforms of each particular party. Rather, the rational voter could look to the ideological positioning of the political party on a unilinear spectrum and make a decision for whom to cast their vote based on the party's stance on the left-right axis.

Downs relied upon the notion of civic duty and citizens' recognition of the potential for system collapse (see chapter 2) as reasons for overcoming the irrationality of voting. Other rational choice accounts have also sought to address this issue by drawing attention to bad weather[94]; time consuming or complex registration processes[95]; lack of resources.[96] Moreover, later theorists have recognised the paradox of not voting.[97] That is, if everyone behaves rationally, knowing the minimal chances of affecting the outcome, no one votes. With this knowledge, it becomes increasingly rational to vote, as the chances of affecting the outcome increase significantly, and as such, probalistic models suggest that electors may turn out.[98] Or indeed, at least, that voting is a low-cost decision.[99] While this theoretical sleight of hand attempts to address the paradox of voting, it remains the case that not all voters vote. While rational choice theorists have attempted to address this issue, political marketing has yet to develop in this area.

The adoption of marketing strategies as a means to achieve electoral victory may well produce the best outcome for each individual party. However, collectively, given the emphasis of political actors is directed towards marketing rather than political beliefs and strategies, the outcome becomes and reinforces the marketisation and depoliticisation of politics. The policies of rational choice accounts of electoral competition become brands, which voters are encouraged to identify with under the pretext of the accommodation of their preferences.

While these accounts emphasise the individual party rather than the collective system, they also individualise at societal level. That is, the act of voting is individualised. In rational choice accounts, attention is focused on the costs and benefits to the individual, rather the costs and benefits to the system or collectivity of taking part in the electoral process. While an individual may incur costs in terms of collecting information and turning out to a polling booth, the costs of that individual not participating are far greater. This theoretical individualisation is reinforced in political marketing, not only within the modelling, but in the way in which these models have been applied, as campaigns have become highly atomised and personalised (see chapter 3). While rational choice accounts acknowledge the existence of a public good, this is negated entirely within the marketing literature.

The existence of a public good

Exchange, in these rational accounts, is premised on the nation of optimisation, that leads individuals to pursue the course of action which will provide them with the best outcome for themselves. However, the difficulty lies in that the pursuit of individual optimal outcomes may lead to a suboptimal outcome for a collectivity. Crucially, markets do not recognise the existence of a common interest or a public good. In electoral competition, this public good is the stability of the democratic system.

In a competitive market, sellers have an interest in pricing goods as highly as possible. At the same time, firms also seek to sell as much as possible. These twin interests mean that the behaviour of each business or seller is opposed to that of every other seller. This means there is no common interest in the marketplace, as the behaviour of each business is opposed to that of every other competitor in the marketplace. This lack of common interest, identified in economic accounts, is highly problematic in politics. States and governments function to provide for and protect the public interest. The lack of a common interest shared by the actors in economic and marketing accounts generates a problem within the realm of formal politics. A common interest, or public good, is something which is available to all and indivisible. A public good requires the mobilisation of many individuals and represents a collective outcome that an individual alone cannot achieve. However, the nature of market competition, and the pursuit of national self-interest, means that there is a real problem both in creating and preserving the existence of the public good.

Hardin's tragedy of the commons provides an illustration of this problem.[100] Hardin argued that where a public good is available to all, ultimately, rational self-interested behaviour leads to the destruction of said public good. He illustrated this with reference to a herdsmen and the existence of a public field as pasture for grazing. He argued that the rational self-interest of herdsman would be to bring more animals to graze in this area. As more and more herdsman increase the number of animals they bring to graze in this area, ultimately the pursuit of individual self-interest leads to the degradation and destruction of the pasture. This in turn leaves all the herdsman worse off than they might have otherwise been. This parable has been extended elsewhere in relation to public goods, particularly in relation to the environment.[101] Yet, this is also able to draw attention to the damage to the public good of democracy if rational individuals choose the rational course of action (marketing) available to them. While the rationality of voting, or not voting, has been discussed, what is at stake is the extent to which the rational self-interested behaviour of individual leads to collectively suboptimal outcomes. This has become known as the problem of collective action.

The problem of collective action highlights the difficulty of mobilising groups in the interests of the public good. In his seminal account, Olson[102] argued that it would be difficult to mobilize groups, for the same reason that it will be difficult to mobilize individual voters in Downsian accounts. Individuals would recognise the negligible impact that participation would have on the ability of groups to achieve outcomes/their goals. As such, the rational response of the individual would be to 'free ride'. That is, the individual can gain the benefits of the existence of the organisation, or public good, without incurring costs. For Olson, this was illustrated through reference to trade unions. That is, a rational individual could benefit from the goals of trade unions, such as improvements to pay and conditions, without becoming a member. This was because outcomes of trade union activity would apply to all employees rather than just union members. In order to overcome this problem, selective incentives can be introduced, which benefited only, in this case, union members. These incentives encouraged others to join, and therefore overcame the problem of collective action.

In electoral competition, the decision for whom to vote can be materially incentivised. That is, parties may make promises and, such as tax breaks, to motivate an individual to select them when casting their ballots. However, to encourage participation, to encourage individuals to take part in the electoral competition itself—to actually vote, orthodox rational choice accounts revert to ideational incentives, such as civic duty. The conceptualisation of politics and electoral competition in such stark terms—parties, voters and the electoral market—neglects the existence of a public good (for example, a healthy democracy) which electoral competition stimulates and contributes to. If there is no public good, then this simply serves to reinforce the problem of collective action (alongside the voting paradox).

Critique: internalising rational choice

In an era whereby parties are unable to rely on the partisan sentiment of previous decades and a densely structured media environment, politicians and parties will seek other methods to attract voters. It can be argued this changing demographic base has contributed to the provision of a space whereby actors seek to find alternate methods to connect with voters. This implies that marketing could be viewed as a response to changing demographics. However, the demographic base does not change in isolation; rather, it too is responsive and constitutive of broader social, political and economic changes. The conventional argument is that increasing electoral volatility has led to an increase in the use of marketing techniques, a strengthened demand for advertising and a need to find some means through which the voter can become attached to the party. While perceptions of voter volatility may lead parties to alter their behaviour, conversely, this volatility may be a top-down phenomenon. Rather than parties responding to changing societal bases, parties' perceptions of changes at societal level lead them to alter their behaviour, leading voters to behave in a manner consistent with these perceptions. That is, voters behave in a volatile manner because that is how parties perceive them to be.

The inculcation of political values is a consequence of the interaction of political elites with the public. The process of communication between the two is mediated through the media. This process of action and communication is interactive and serves to construct a discourse through which politics is understood. If politics appears as a set of rational strategies pursued by political actors to achieve their goals, then it would be logical to assume that the electorate will respond in a rational manner also. As rationalist accounts suggest, it is rational for the voter not to participate given the costs exceed the benefits and the minute chance of the individual voter influencing the electoral outcome. Previous economic accounts of politics incorporated affective aspects, civic duty and ideology to overcome this difficulty. Where marketing deviates from existing economic accounts is that it removes both political ideology (as noted in chapter 4) and any sense of civic duty. The privileging of marketing and underlying economic assumptions by the marketing literature serves to reinforce that dominance of marketing and economics as a means through which politics can be conducted. In this sense, rationalist ideas become embedded, institutionalised and hegemonic.

It could be argued that if voters perceive politicians employing marketing strategies to be behaving in a manner consistent with that of orthodox rational choice theory, then so their behaviour responds accordingly. While neither voters not politicians might be explicitly aware of the claims of orthodox rational choice theory, this modelling has alerted attention to the type of behaviour which might occur given a particular set of underlying assumptions. If these assumptions are adopted as prescription for behaviour by elite actors, then it would be logical to assume that the public respond in this way. What is argued here, however, is that while the public may respond to this behaviour at election time, implying a lack of interest in politics, this is not strictly true. It is suggested that while the public may be disengaged and disillusioned with the *process* of politics, there is still considerable interest in the *content* of politics.

As has been widely noted in economic accounts, the pursuit of rational self-interest can often lead to collectively suboptimal outcomes. Hardin's parable of the 'tragedy of the commons', while debated, provides a clear account of how the pursuit of rational self-interest can lead to suboptimal outcomes for the collectivity. However, in adopting the underlying economic assumptions of marketing as templates for behaviour, political actors render these assumptions ontological. The pursuit of the rational self-interest by political actors may have led them again to electoral victory, and as such achieve their goal; however, this has also entailed a suboptimal outcome in relation to the nature of democracy. That is, if political actors behave in an ever more rational manner, so voters perceive them behaving in this way may adopt this rational behaviour themselves.

Orthodox economic accounts have provided insights as to why rational individuals may not take part in the process of politics. This does not, however, equate with apathy. Contextualising the place in which politics takes place draws attention to social and economic factors which influence the political process. Politics is not only about competition in the electoral arena between political actors and voters. The orthodox rational choice accounts problematising participation do not resolve this difficulty. Rendering explicit the underlying economic assumptions of political marketing allows attention to be drawn to the irrationality of public participation in the political process and highlights a theoretical problem for the political marketing literature. That politics takes place in a broader social, political and technological context and that the internalisation of economic assumptions serves to individualise the activity of politics to the extent that individuals are disconnected from this process.

Conclusion

Political marketing relies upon a notion of participation which assumes that voters take part in the formal mechanism of elections. This is the site where the exchange central to the process, and normative justification, of marketing occurs. Yet, turnout is regarded as important by marketers only in terms of its ability to enable a political actor to achieve his/her goal. In politics, turnout is important as it is also a means of legitimating the political system. Declining electoral participation and increasing disaffection among the public are key areas of concern for the process of politics, the legitimacy of the political system and the health of democracy. The empirical reality is that western electorates are less inclined to engage in the process of politics, and it has been argued that this in turn is linked with ideas that actors (voters and politicians) hold about their environment.

Ideas do not exist in a vacuum—they are constitutive of a material basis, but at the same time, they inform and reconstitute this material base. In this sense, these chapter has teased out the conceptual linkage between the material realm, of a changing social, political and technological environment, characterised by malaise, and the ideational context dominated by ideas in relation to the utility of marketing. These ideas in relation to marketing, as noted in previous chapters, have become embedded within this material context which again becomes reconstituted and structures the choices situation of political actors, favourably towards acceptance of ideas in relation to marketing.

At the material, political and social level, there has been a decline in partisan attachments, and a decrease in traditional class divisions, a growth of consumer society coupled with a proliferating media. The response of politicians has been to engage in marketing strategies which are underpinned by economic assumptions. This conceptual linkage of the material with the ideational has also facilitated the identification of a series of theoretical concerns which may contribute to the existence of 'malaise' which the marketing literature has failed to address. The dominant choice in the contemporary context is the use of marketing (prescribed by marketers). But this means internalising ideas associated with rational choice theory, which in turn, encourages actors to behave in a manner consistent with this theorising. Subsequently, parties can be viewed as behaving in a manner consistent with Downsian assumptions. Logically developed, then, this would suggest that voters will behave in this manner too.

Economic accounts emphasise the individual at the expense of the collective, which also undermines the potential for participation in politics to be motivated by the opportunity to achieve collective outcomes. The way which marketing adopts these assumptions negates the role of ideology and civic duty which were essential for rational choice theorising to overcome problems of collective action and voter mobilisation. Removing any 'meaning' from political electoral participation exacerbates, rather than resolves, the problem of paradox of voting. In so doing, political marketing removes incentives for individuals to take part and subsequently its use by political actors reinforces the idea of malaise.

To rationally choose not to participate does not necessarily equate with apathy. And this is not to argue for compulsory mass participation or voting (traditionally the hallmark of authoritarian democracies). Rather, it is argued that to reengage the public, attention to the political needs to be restated. While marketing may be a necessary feature of contemporary democracies, this is not all politics is about. It has been suggested that there is clearly still interest in the content of politics. Restoration of this content to the process of politics may well be what serves to reengage and reinvigorate the public.

Notes

1. Parry et al, 1992: 9.
2. See also Barnes et al, 1979.
3. Verba and Nie, 1972.
4. Parry et al, 1992: 20.
5. Goodin and Dryzek, 1980.
6. Lister, 2007.
7. Norris, 2000.
8. Harman, 2006, www.dca.gov.uk/speeches/2006/sp060116.htm.
9. Henn et al, 2002; O'Toole et al, 2003.
10. Henn et al, 2002: 167.
11. www.statistics.gov.uk.
12. http://www.ipsos-mori.com/publications/rd/new-rules-of-engagement.shtml.
13. http://www.electoralcommission.org.uk/files/dms/MORIAPEreportFinal_20376-14906__E__N__S__W__.pdf.
14. While the UK electoral commission do not provide a definition of politics, it is assumed that this represents the formal mechanisms of the state: parliaments and politicians and throughout these empirical investigations, attitudes to both the system of politics; that is, the way in which politics is practised and the content of politics are assumed to be linked.
15. Stoker, 2006: 34.
16. Lijphart, 1999.
17. www.ipsos-mori.com/publications/rmw/whomdowetrust.shtml.
18. See for example Norris, 1999.
19. Newton, 2006; see also Dalton, 2004.
20. Miller and Listhaug, 1999.
21. Weatherford, 1992.
22. King, 1997; Norris, 1999: 232.

23. Whiteley, 2003.
24. Dalton, 1996: 277–79.
25. Dalton, 2004: 1.
26. Lewis et al, 2005.
27. Crouch, 2004.
28. Putnam, 2000.
29. Hay, 2007.
30. Baudrillard, 1988.
31. Lipset and Rokkan, 1966.
32. Crewe, 1986; Heath, Jowell and Curtice, 1985; Franklin, 1992: 121, 2004; Parry et al, 1992; Dalton, 2004; Miller et al, 1990.
33. Lipset and Rokkan, 1966.
34. Mackie et al, 1992.
35. Sarlvik and Crewe, 1983.
36. Shifting support from one party to another. Heath et al, 1985.
37. Heath et al, 2001: 122.
38. Heath et al, 2001: 122.
39. Dunleavy and Ward, 1991.
40. In particular they also set out to distance themselves from their traditional basis of support that had been located in the working class, concerned with traditional class issues. Heath et al, 2001: 134.
41. Although this is not particularly new argument, it is one which continues. See, for example, Fisher, 1980; Lawson and Merkl, 1988, Webb, 1995.
42. Poguntke, 1996.
43. Bauman, 2007: 29.
44. Bauman, 2007: 28.
45. Baudrillard, 1988: 42–43.
46. Jameson, 1990; Gabriel and Lang, 1997.
47. Bauman, 1999; Touraine, 2000.
48. Corrigan, 1997: 44.
49. E.g., Putnam, 2000; Franklin, 1994; Jones, 1997; Stanyer, 2003.
50. Harrop, 1990.
51. See for example, Street, 2001; Louw, 2005 It is also worth noting that most mainstream politics textbooks also now include a chapter on the mass media.
52. Kavanagh, 1995: 177, 197.
53. Kavanagh, 1992: 84.
54. E.g., Mancini and Swanson, 1996.
55. Street, 2004; Baum, 2005; Higgins, forthcoming.
56. Cited in Gaber, 1998: 13.
57. 1997, cited in Franklin, 2001: 131.
58. Finlayson, 2003: 40.
59. Simons, 2000: 84.
60. Franklin, 1994; Barnett, 1998; Brants, 1998.
61. E.g., McManus, 1994; Rosenblum, 1993; Underwood, 2003.
62. For example, Norris, 1999; Hetherington, 1999; Kaase and Newton, 1995; Klingeman and Fuchs, 1995.

63. Putnam, 1995; Brehm and Rahn, 1998.
64. Putnam, 1995.
65. Wintour, 2004: 12.
66. Putnam, 2000.
67. Klapper, 1960.
68. McCombs and Shaw, 1972.
69. Brookes et al, 2004.
70. Harrop, 1986.
71. Curtice and Semetko, 1994: 56.
72. Norris et al, 1999: 168.
73. This is a view that can be found expressed in the press itself; for example, the *Sun's* famous 1992 headline 'It Was The Sun Wot Won It'.
74. Butler and Kavanagh, 1997: 58.
75. Franklin, 1994, although there is disagreement on this point, see for example Palmer, 2002, who argues that while there clearly has been a proliferation in the use of media technology, there is still substance behind the spin, which can be evidenced through the credibility derived through delivery of policy.
76. Temple, 2006.
77. Norris, 2001.
78. Prior, 2005.
79. Street, 2001: 2.
80. Anderson and Gabszewicz, 2005.
81. Anderson and Coates, 2001.
82. Kotler and Kotler, 1999.
83. Henneberg, 2002: 93.
84. Henneberg, 2002:104.
85. Himmelweit et al, 1985, as noted by Lock and Harris, 1996: 20; Smith and Saunders, 1990: 300.
86. Heath et al, 1985.
87. Smith and Saunders, 1990: 300.
88. Nimmo, 1970; Newman, 2001: 966; Kotler, 1982; see also Smith, 2001.
89. Harrop, 1990: 280.
90. Lock and Harris, 1996: 17.
91. Hayes and McAllister, 1996: 144.
92. Hinich and Munger 1997: 151.
93. Pattie and Johnston, 2001a, 2001b; Heath and Taylor, 1999.
94. Knack, 1992.
95. Kelley et al, 1967; Wolfinger and Rosenstone, 1980; Nagler, 1991.
96. Tollison and Willett, 1973; Wolfinger and Rosenstone, 1980.
97. Ferejohn and Fiorina, 1974.
98. Hinich et al, 1972; Ledyard 1981, 1984.
99. Aldrich, 1993.
100. Hardin, 1968.
101. See, for example, Berkes, 1985; Feeny et al, 1990.
102. Olson, 1965.

Conclusion: Political marketing—a challenge to democracy

Marketers claim that 'the main challenge facing Western democracies today is not what determines a citizen's vote but rather why so many "customers" are choosing not to "buy" anything'.[1] But maybe this is the point: to refer to voters as customers and to refer to politics as something which can be 'purchased' changes its nature. It constructs politics as something which is material, something which can be discarded when no longer of use or does not satisfy the self-interest of the individual; something which does not require loyalty, engagement or long-term commitment. However, the realm of politics contains ideas and values and a vision of what a 'good society', and this is something which is not amenable to commodification.

The contention here is that attempts to commodify and marketise the political realm are problematic because of the processes of marketisation, but more importantly, because of the incompatibility of the content of politics with the marketing process. Politics and markets are mutually exclusive, two completely different and incompatible categories. While the context is important in structuring choices available to political actors, this is not to deny their autonomy or imply a structural determinism, as there are still choices (plural) rather than a singular choice within a given context. What is argued here is that while marketing is the dominant choice, this does not deny the possibility of alternative choices being available.

It has not been the intention of this book to provide an alternative to political marketing but to draw attention to the problems that are possible once marketing encompasses the process of politics. It is also not suggested that there was once a 'golden age' of politics, where all citizens were emancipated and informed, and that democracy functioned effectively. Politics historically has been characterised by difficulties of engagement and efficacy, but as Steiner notes, '[M]arket forces tend to produce market results'.[2] What has been argued here is that the full-scale adoption of marketing strategies has indeed produced market results and exacerbated the difficulties of engagement and efficacy.

Rather than enhancing democracy, marketing politics has meant that something has been lost. The content of politics has been replaced, yet it is the content of politics which is essential for a healthy and functioning democracy. This includes a public space where the polity is informed about the decisions and actions of their elites; decisions are taken in the interests of society and a public good; and as a result, an informed collective can hold those elites to account. These ideals are missing in the process of marketing with its inherent individualisation of both the public and political actors, and emphasis upon their differing short-term goals.

To transcend marketing and reclaim politics into the political sphere, discussion and debate needs to be moved beyond the language of the marketplace. Within political marketing the discussions of politics in terms of production, consumption, exchange, markets embed ideas in relation to markets, political economy and neoliberalism. It has been argued that political actors have been complicit in this process by adopting methods, the terminology and techniques of marketing, which in turn have a detrimental impact upon the democratic process.

Summary

Underpinning this book has been a critique of the normative claims and underlying neoliberalism contained within political marketing. In order to make the above argument, it began with an overview of what is meant by political marketing. Simply put, political marketing is the application of business models and frameworks to the activity of politics. These are underpinned by economic assumptions and begin with the analogy of parties as businesses and voters as consumers in a political marketplace. Parties compete for votes to win elections. Techniques and strategies associated with marketing are then employed in order to facilitate this. The consumer is assumed to be at the centre of the production process which provides the political marketing literature with a normative defence of its contribution. That is, this literature claims the use of marketing keeps politicians accountable and responsive, and this in turn is regarded as healthy for democracy.

The purpose of the first chapter was threefold: first, to historicise and detail the models which have been used for descriptive, prescriptive and normative purposes within the academic literature. Second, to render explicit the underlying neoclassical economic and rationalist assumptions which are contained within these models. Third, to provide a critique of the way in which the managerial marketing models have been applied within political marketing. This book has argued that these models are Weberian 'ideal' types and so in this sense, abstract and simplify reality rather than reflect or create reality. While these models can be used to simplify and highlight key aspects of behaviour, they should not form the basis for templates for behaviour, as political actors do not behave in this simplified way. Political reality is more complex than this. Moreover, given the underlying rationalist assumptions of these models, this means advocating the individualist, utility maximising behaviour of rational choice theory. The latter openly acknowledges the parsimony of its assumptions; for orthodox rational choice theory it is the accuracy of the predictions of its models which is important.

Managerial marketing models have been extensively used to describe political practice, but they are increasingly advocated as prescriptions for practice. This prescriptive aspect was challenged first, as models which prescribe practice cannot be used to make predictions, since they become self-fulfilling prophecies and second, because this prescription is problematic for the process of politics, as it means prescribing economic theories to inform actual behaviour. These theoretical accounts have been shown to be both inherently antidemocratic and their application can disconnect the public from the process of politics.

As the underlying assumptions contained within these management marketing models are derived from neoclassical economic accounts, so chapter 2 showed how political marketing can be regarded as a contemporary variant of orthodox rational choice theory and that there are a series of implications which flow as a consequence of this. Explicitly demonstrating how the political marketing literature is linked to Downs' work facilitated the identification of, and the opportunity to reflect upon, a series of difficulties highlighted by rational choice accounts and implicit within the political marketing literature. As such, this chapter set out how the use of marketing implies centralising tendencies among competing political actors. While the argument that electoral competition privileges style over substance is nothing particularly new, the novelty here lay in explicitly reconciling marketing with its underlying Downsian roots and providing the theoretical context through which the implications of marketing could be thought through. It was noted that what is also significantly and qualitatively different is that marketing prescribes the use of these economic models as a set of practices and thinking.

Attention was also drawn to the way in which preferences may be accommodated and/ or shaped by actors in order to further their own interests, which are largely downplayed within the mainstream political marketing literature. Preferences are important, as one of the central tenets of marketing is the capacity of the individual to have their preferences incorporated into the political 'product'. To this end, chapter 3 explored how marketing is put into practice and the way in which individual preferences are collected and fed into the political 'product'. Preferences are expressed and collected largely through the site of focus groups and opinion poll data. This is done so that political actors may reformulate their 'product' offering more favourably, with a view to achieving electoral victory. One of the key questions to emerge is: how democratic this process is if only a select proportion of the population is having its preferences incorporated into the political product? For marketing to focus attention on small sections of the polity undermine the ideals of equality of all voters. If politicians are held accountable and responsive at the site of focus groups, this is skewed firstly to those groups, which have been selected by elites as target voters, and second, this comprises only a small section of the polity. Not only does this undermine the notion of equality of franchise, but it also distorts the electoral landscape towards the preferences of a few target voters whose preferences are shaped by elites. It was then shown that the way in which marketing is implemented, through segmentation and targeting, further serves to individualise the process of campaigning, which in turn reinforces the notion that politics can be viewed as an individual activity, negating the notion of a collective. In sum, this implementation has meant that the political terrain has been narrowly directed towards the interests of competitive political elites, rather than the polity as a whole.

In order to successfully implement marketing, marketers advocate marketing as a belief system. That is, it is once the ideas of marketing are internalised that actors are able to fully implement them. Chapter 4 explored what this meant for the role of political ideology. While rational choice accounts provide a series of analytical models, the political marketing literature violates these underlying principles, and goes beyond the use of such models as analytic frameworks and introduces a normative element. In turn, this also suggests the prescription of the internalisation of the above neoclassical economic assumptions. In essence, this means replacing traditional 'political' ideology (such as conservatism, socialism, etc.) with a 'marketing' ideology. That is one which privileges the market as way of thinking about society, and the activity of politics. Ideology provides the framework through which coherent ideals and values, the content of politics, can be articulated. Ideology also functions as a legitimating mechanism. To substitute political ideology with marketing ideology is problematic, not only for the way in which party competition is enacted and effected, but also more widely for the way in which the political system is legitimated, or delegitimated.

The rhetoric of marketing also plays a significant role in shaping conventional understandings of politics. Chapter 5 explored the language used to describe marketing in politics. The terms 'market', 'product' and 'consumers' are not empty signifiers[3] or metaphors devoid of content. Referring to politics as a process of production and consumption entails a necessarily different trajectory from that of the activity of politics. That is, by referring to parties as business and voters as consumers, marketing misses the subtleties of politics; moreover it redefines and reshapes politics as a process of commodification and consumption. Marketing accepts that production and consumption are inherently linked. The purpose of production is consumption, and consumption is necessary for producers to achieve their goals. It is argued here that this linguistic usage of parties/candidates as producers and voters as consumers redefines and commodifies the process of politics. This chapter also showed how the language of marketing has an ontological as well as analytical function, which has been conflated within the political marketing literature. Redefining voters as consumers defines away a set of rights, responsibilities and obligations tied into the political process and which flow as a consequence of a political definition of the role of the public as citizens. To treat parties *as* business, voters *as* consumers, rather than *as if* businesses or consumers, means that these simplifying assumptions are rendered ontological rather than analytical. This in turn contributes to the reshaping of the political process, creating a political reality where parties *are* business and voters *are* consumers, fundamentally redefining and reconstructing politics.

Given this ideological and linguistic recharacterisation of the political process, chapter 6 then turned attention to the phenomenon of democratic malaise. This chapter conceptually linked empirical data in respect of public participation and interest in politics to the rationalist assumptions of marketing literature. Currently, the political marketing literature assumes that voters (consumers) vote (buy). However, orthodox rational choice accounts draw attention to the 'paradox of rational choice'; that is, if voters behave rationally, then the cots of voting outweigh the individual benefits, given the likelihood of an individual's vote affecting the electoral outcome, therefore the rational voter will not vote. The contention here, then, is that if political parties/candidates behave in a manner consistent with rational choice theorising, the likelihood is that voters will too and not take part in the process of politics (in this case, elections).

It was argued that the relationship between the material and the ideational are inherently linked. That is, what can be observed is heavily influenced by beliefs and ideas not only about what is observed, but also about what that reality does and should look like. Given this conceptual linkage, the link between marketing and voter abstention and disconnection with politics was reflected upon. The argument developed through the previous chapters highlighted that the more that voters perceive actors behaving in a manner consistent with the assumptions that inform rational choice accounts, the more likely it is that voter will behave in this manner too and disengage from the political process.

The challenge to democracy

This book has argued that both the theories and methods of marketing are antithetical to democratic ideals. This has been shown by drawing attention to the way that political marketing institutionalises the process by which managerialist thinking informs political behaviour. In so doing, it has been argued that political marketing contributes to and promotes elite, rather than pluralist, behaviour, institutionalising the process whereby parties not only 'act' Downsian, but 'think' Downsian. At the same time, within politics and marketing the role of ideas and ideology are important. Increasingly as actors embrace and believe the utility of marketing, so this replaces traditional 'politics'; there is little to differentiate this type of competition from that of other actors in economic marketplaces. From the above arguments, then, a series of implications flow: parties will be rational utility maximisers, seeking to achieve their goals; they do this by employing marketing; voters perceive political actors behaving 'rationally' and do so themselves, therefore reinforcing the irrationality of voting.

In contractual conceptions of democracy, the vote provides the opportunity for individuals to express their consent to be governed. It also symbolises the desire for prevention of authoritarian regimes. Politics becomes the activity through which the opportunity to realise democracy takes place. Democracy is an ideal. It underpins a set of practices intended to materialise or realise that ideal. It involves competing visions of what society should be like. Through the formal mechanisms of elections, political parties and candidates compete for the opportunity to implement public policy in an attempt to realise their vision of society. This is aimed at improving the quality of life for those who make up that society. There are two equally important parts to this: society as a whole and the individuals who make up this society. The function of government then becomes to provide for both: to seek to provide for the best possible 'good' while at the same time recognising the importance of individual rights and freedoms which protect an individual from an overbearing, overpowerful state.

For this to work, democracy relies on an active and engaged citizenry. A dialogue is needed to engage the polity so that they can become informed and participate in the decision-making process, both by supporting elites and having the opportunity to hold them to account. This interrelationship is crucial and relies on the existence of a 'bigger picture', one which goes beyond simply assuming that the main goal of political parties/candidates is to achieve office. Ascribing these office-seeking approaches (as marketing does) negates the existence of an ideal, which is more than individuals trying to achieve power.

To refer to politics as a marketing exercise invokes a series of assumptions both about what politics is and what politics should be. By rendering these axiomatic assumptions explicit, the aim has been to highlight the difficulties, implications and consequences of the appropriation of marketing by politics. This book is not intended to provide a restatement of politics per se, but it has been argued that there does need to be political content in the political process, as to refer to politics as marketing entails a set of economic assumptions which, logically extended, functions to disconnect the public from the process of politics. As it stands, this means that marketing in politics is a problem.

Notes

1. Johansen, 2005: 102.
2. Steiner, 1952: 195.
3. Cf. Laclau and Mouffe, 1987.

Bibliography

Abrams, R. (1980) *Foundations of Political Analysis: An Introduction to the Theory of Collective Choice* (New York: Columbia University Press).

Aldrich, J. (1993) 'Rational choice and turnout' *American Journal of Political Science* 37, pp. 246–78.

Anderson, S. and Coates, S. (2001) 'Market provision of public goods: the case of broadcasting' Working paper, University of Virginia and Cornell University cited in Brown, K. and Alexander, P. (2005) 'Market structure, viewer welfare, and advertising rates in local broadcast television markets' *Economic Letters* 86 (3), pp. 331–37.

Anderson, S. and Gabszewicz, J. (2005) 'The media and advertising: a tale of two-sided markets' *CEPR Discussion paper* no. 5223.

Althusser, L. (1969) *For Marx* (London: Allen Lane).

———. (1971) 'Ideology and Ideological State Apparatuses' in *Lenin and Philosophy and Other Essays* (translated by Ben Brewster) (London: New Left Books).

Baines, P.R., Harris, P. and B.R. Lewis (2002) 'The political marketing planning process: improving image and message in strategic target areas' *Marketing Intelligence and Planning* 20 (1) pp. 6–14.

Baines, P.R., Worcester, R.M., Jarrett, D. and R. Mortimore (2003) 'Market segmentation and product differentiation in political campaigns: a technical feature perspective' *Journal of Marketing Management* 19 (1/2), pp. 225–50.

Baker, W.E., and Sinkula, J.M. (1999) 'The synergistic effect of market orientation and learning orientation on organizational performance' *Journal of the Academy of Marketing Science* 27 (4), pp. 411–27.

Banker, S. (1992) 'The ethics of political marketing practices: the rhetorical perspective' *Journal of Business Ethics* 11, pp. 843–48.

Barnes, E. (2005) 'The whispering campaign' *Scotland on Sunday* 1st May.

Barnes, S., Kaase, M. et al (1979) *Political Action: Mass Participation in Five Western Democracies* (Beverly Hills and London: Sage).

Barnett, S. (1998) 'Dumbing Down or Reaching Out: Is It Tabloidisation Wot Done It?' in J. Seaton (ed.) *Politics and the Media: Harlots and Prerogatives at the Turn of the Millennium* (Oxford: Blackwell), pp. 75–90.

Barry, B. (1978) *Sociologists, Economists and Democracy* (London: Collier-Macmillan).

Bartle, J. (2002) 'Market Analogies, the Marketing of Labour and the Origins of New Labour' in N.J. O'Shaughnessy (ed.) *The Idea of Political Marketing* (Westport: Praeger), pp. 39–66.

Bartos, R. (1986) 'Qualitative research: what is it and where it came from' *Journal of Advertising Research* 26, pp. RC3–RC6.

Barzel, Y., and Silberberg, E. (1973) 'Is the act of voting rational?' *Public Choice* 16, pp. 51–58.

Baudrillard, J. (1988) *The Consumer Society* (London: Sage).

Bauer, H.H., Huber, F., and Herrmann, A. (1996) 'Political marketing: an information-economic analysis' *European Journal of Marketing* 30, (10/11) pp. 152–65.

Baum, M.A. (2005) 'Talking the vote: why presidential candidates hit the talk show circuit' *American Journal of Political Science* 49, (2) pp. 213–34.

Bauman, Z. *In Search of Poltics* (Cambridge: Polity).

———. (2007) *Consuming Life* (Cambridge: Polity).

Belk, R.W. (1988) 'Possessions and extended self' *Journal of Consumer Research* 15, pp. 139–60.

Bennett, S.E., Rhine, S.L., Flickinger, R.S., and L.L. Bennett (1999) '"Video malaise" revisited: public trust in the media and government' *Harvard International Journal of Press/Politics* 4, pp. 8–23.

Beresford, Q. (1998) 'Selling democracy short: elections in the age of the market' *Current Affairs Bulletin* Feb–March 74 (5), pp. 24–32.

Berkes, F. (1985). 'Fishermen and the "tragedy of the commons"' *Environmental Conservation* 12, pp. 199–206.

Berry, L.L. (1997) 'The service nightmare: can we sustain success?' *Marketing Management* 6 (3), pp. 10–13.

Birch, A. (1984) 'Overload, ungovernability and delegitimation: the theories and the British case' *British Journal of Political Science* 14, pp. 125–60.

Blalock, H.M. Jr. (1984) *Basic Dilemmas in the Social Sciences* (Beverly Hills, CA: Sage).

Blois, K. (1989) 'Marketing in five simple questions' *Journal of Marketing Management* 5 (2), pp. 113–21.

Blumenthal, S. (1980) *The Permanent Campaign* (Boston, MA: Beacon).

Blumler, J. (1990) 'The Modern Publicity Process' in M. Ferguson (ed.) *Political Communication: The New Imperatives* (London: Sage), pp. 101–14.

Blumler, J.G. and Gurevtich, M. (1981) 'Politicians and the Press: An Essay on Role Relationships' in D.D Nimmo and K.R. Saunders (eds.) *Handbook of Political Communication* (Beverly Hills, CA: Sage), pp. 467–93.

———. (1995) *The Crisis in Public Communications* (London: Routledge).

Borch, F. (1957) 'The Marketing Philosophy as a Way of Business Life' in *The Marketing Concept: Its Meaning to Management* (New York: American Management Association).

Bowler, S. and Farrell, D. (1992) 'The Study of Election Campaigning' in S. Bowler and D. Farrell (eds.) *Electoral Strategies and Political Marketing* (London: Macmillan), pp. 1–23.

Brants, K. (1998) 'Who's afraid of infotainment' *European Journal of Communication* 13 (3), pp. 315–35.

Brehm, J. and Rahn, W. (1998) 'Individual-level evidence for the causes and consequences of social capital' *American Journal of Political Science* 41, pp. 999–1023.

Bristol, T. and Fern, E. (2003) 'The effects of interaction on consumers' attitudes in focus groups' *Psychology and Marketing* 20 (5), pp. 433–54.

Brittain, S. (1975) 'The economic consequences of democracy' *British Journal of Political Science* 5, pp. 129–59.

Brennan, G. and Buchanan, J.M. (1984) 'Voter choice: evaluating political alternatives' *American Behavioural Scientist* 28, pp. 185–201.

Brookes, R., Lewis., J., and K. Wahl-Jorgensen (2004) 'The media representation of public opinion: British television news coverage of the 2001 general election' *Media, Culture and Society* 26 (1), pp. 63–80.

Brownlie, D. and Saren, M. (1997) 'Beyond the one-dimensional marketing manager: the discourse of theory, practice and relevance' *International Journal of Research in Marketing* 14 (2), pp. 147–61.

Buchanen, J. (1975) *The Limits of Liberty: Between Anarchy and Leviathan* (Chicago: University of Chicago Press).

Buchanen, J. and Tullock, G. (1962) *The Calculus of Consent? Logical Foundations of Constitutional Democracy* (Ann Arbor: University of Michigan Press).

Bulmer, M. (1984) *The Chicago School of Sociology: Institutionalization, Diversity and the Rise of Sociological Research* (Chicago: University of Chicago Press).

Burnham, P., Gilland, K., Grant, W., and Z. Layton-Henry (2004) *Research Methods in Politics* (Basingstoke: Palgrave Macmillan).

Butler, P., and Collins, N. (1994) 'Political marketing: structure and process' *European Journal of Marketing* 28 (1), pp. 19–34.

Butler, P. and Collins, N. (1996) 'Strategic analysis in political markets' *European Journal of Marketing* 30, (10/11) pp. 32–44.

Butler, P., and Collins, N. (1999) 'A Conceptual Framework for Political Marketing' in B. Newman (ed.) *Handbook of Political Marketing* (London: Sage), pp. 55–72.

Butler, P., and Collins, N. (2001) 'Payment on delivery: recognising constituency service as political marketing' *European Journal of Marketing* 35, (9/10) pp. 1026–37.

Butler, D. and Kavanagh, D. (1997) *The British General Election of 1997* (London: Macmillan).

Butler, D. and Ranney, A. (eds.) (1992) *Electioneering: A Comparative Study of Continuity and Change* (Oxford: Clarendon Press).

Butler, D. and Stokes, D. (1974) *Political Change in Britain* (Basingstoke: Palgrave Macmillan).

Campbell, A., Converse, P. Miller. W., and D. Stokes (1960) *The American Voter* (New York: John Wiley).

Canovan, M. (1999) 'Trust the people! populism and the two faces of democracy' *Political Studies* 47 p2–16.

Carey, M. (1995) 'Comment: concerns in the analysis of focus group data' *Qualitative Health Research* 5 (4), pp. 487–95.

Chapman, D. and Cowdell, T. (1998) *New Public Sector Marketing* (London: Financial Times Pitman Publishing).

Christensen, T. and Laegreid, P. (2002) *New Public Management: The Transformation of Ideas and Practice* (Aldershot: Ashgate).

Clarke, H.D, Sanders, D., Stewart, M.C. and P.F. Whiteley (2002) 'Downs, Stokes and Modified Rational Choice: Modelling Turnout in 2001' in L. Bennie, C. Rallings, J. Tonge and P. Webb (eds.) *British Elections and Parties Review*, volume 12 (London: Frank Cass), pp. 28–47.

Clarke, H., Stewart, M., and P. Whiteley (1998) 'Political Change and Party Choice: Voting in the 1997 General Election' in D. Denver, J. Fisher, P. Cowley, and C. Pattie (eds.) *British Elections and Parties Review, Volume 8: The 1997 General Election* (London: Frank Cass), pp. 9–34.

Corrigan, P. (1997) *The Sociology of Consumption* (London: Sage).

Cousins, L. (1990) 'Marketing planning in the public and non profit sectors' *European Journal of Marketing* 24 (7), pp. 15–30.

Crewe, I. (1986) 'On the death and resurrection of class voting: some comments on *How Britain Votes*' *Political Studies* 35, pp. 620–38.

Crouch, C. (1997) 'The terms of neo-liberal consensus' *Political Quarterly*, pp. 352–360.

———. (2000) *Coping with Post-democracy* (London: Fabian Society).

———. (2004) *Post Democracy* (Cambridge: Polity).

Crozier, M., Huntington, S.P., and S. Watanuki (1975) *The Crisis of Democracy: Report to the Trilateral Commission on the Governability of Liberal Democracies* (New York: New York University Press).

Curtice, J. and Semetko, H. (1994) 'Does It Matter What the Papers Say?' in A. Heath et al *Labour's Last Chance? The 1992 Election and Beyond* (London: Dartmouth), pp. 43–63.

Dahl, R. (1961) *Who Governs? Democracy and Power in an American City* (New Haven and London: Yale University Press).

Dahl, R. (1982) *Dilemmas of Pluralist Democracy* (New Haven, CT: Yale University Press).

Dalton, R. (1996) *Citizen Politics: Public Opinion and Political Parties in Advanced Industrial Democracies* (Chatham, NJ: Chatham House Publishers).

———. (2004) *Democratic Challenges, Democratic Choices: The Erosion of Political Support in Advanced Industrial Democracies* (Oxford: Oxford University Press).

Dant, T. (1991) *Knowledge, Ideology and Discourse: A Sociological Perspective* (London: Routledge).

Davis, A. (2002) *Public Relations Democracy: Public Relations, Politics and the Mass Media in Britain* (London: Sage).

Day, G. (1999) *The Market Driven Organisation: Understanding Attracting, and Keeping Valuable Customers* (New York: Free Press).

Deacon, D. and Golding, P. (1994) *Taxation and Representation: The Media, Political Communication and the Poll Tax* (London: John Libbey).

Denver, D. (2003) *Elections and Voters in Britain* (Basingstoke: Palgrave).

Deshpande, R., Farley, J.U. and F. E. Webster Jr. (1993) 'Corporate culture, customer orientation, and innovativeness in Japanese firms: a quadrad analysis' *Journal of Marketing* 57, pp. 23–27.

Dickinson, R., Herbst, A., and J. O'Shaughnessy (1986) 'Marketing concept and customer orientation' *European Journal of Marketing* 20 (10), pp. 18–23.

Dowding, K. (1991) *Rational Choice and Political Power* (Aldershot: Edward Elgar).

Dowling, G. (2004) *The Art and Science of Marketing. Marketing for Marketing Managers* (Oxford: Oxford University Press).

Downs, A. (1957) *An Economic Theory of Democracy* (New York: Harper and Row).

———. (1991) 'Social Values and Democracy' in K Renwick Monroe (ed.) *The Economic Approach to Politics: A Critical Reassessment of the Theory of Rational Action* (New York: HarperCollins), pp. 143–70.

Drucker, P. (1954) *The Practice of Management* (New York: Harper and Row).

———. (1974) *Management: Tasks, Responsibilities and Practices* (London: Heineman).

Duckler, M. (2003) 'How extendible is your brand? A four-step road map can help find the answer' *Marketing Management* 12 (6), pp. 28–34.

Dunleavy, P. (1987) 'Class dealignment in Britain revisited' *West European Politics* 10, pp. 400–419.

———. (1997) 'Introduction: 'New Times' in British Politics' in P. Dunleavy, A. Gamble, I. Holliday, and G. Peele (eds.) *Developments in British Politics 5* (London: Macmillan), pp. 1–19.

Dunleavy, P. and Husbands, C. (1985) *British Democracy at the Crossroads* (London: George Allen and Unwin).

Dunleavy, P. and O'Leary, B. (1987) *Theories of the State* (London: Macmillan).

Dunleavy, P. and Ward, H. (1981) 'Exogenous voter preferences and parties with state power' *British Journal of Political Science* 11, pp. 351–80.

———. (1991) 'Party Competition—the Preference Shaping Model' in P. Dunleavy *Democracy, Bureaucracy and Public Choice* (Hemel Hempstead, UK: Harvester Wheatsheaf), pp. 112–46.

Edwards, T. (2000) *Contradictions of Consumption: Concepts, Practices and Politics in Consumer Society* (Buckingham: Open University Press).

Egan, J. (1999) 'Political Marketing: Lessons from the Mainstream' *Journal of Marketing Management* 15, pp. 495–503.

Ellis, P.D. (2006) 'Market orientation and performance: a meta-analysis and cross-national comparisons' *Journal of Management Studies* 43 (5), pp. 1089–107.

Elster, J. (1986) 'Introduction' in J. Elster (ed.) *Rational Choice* (Oxford: Basil Blackwell) pp. 1–34.

Evans, J.A. (2004) *Voters and Voting: An Introduction* (London: Sage).

Evans, J.R. and Berman, B. (1994) *Marketing* 6th edition (London: Macmillan).

Exworthy, M. and Halford, S. (eds.) (1999) *Professionals and the New Managerialism in the Public Sector* (Buckingham: Open University Press).

Fairclough, N. (2000) *New Labour, New Language?* (London: Routledge).

Farrell, D. and Wortman, M. (1987) 'Parties strategies in the electoral Market: political marketing in West Germany, Britain and Ireland' *European Journal of Political Research* 15, pp. 297–318.

Farrell, D., McAllister, I. and D. Studlar (1998) 'Sex, Money and Politics: Sleaze and the Conservative Party in the 1997 Election' in D. Denver, J. Fisher, P. Cowley, and C. Pattie (eds.) *British Elections and Parties Review, volume 8: The 1997 General Election* (London: Frank Cass), pp. 80–94.

Farrell, M.A. (2000) 'Developing a market-oriented learning organization' *Australian Journal of Management* 25 (2), 201–22.

Feeny, D., Berkes, F., McCay, B. and J.M. Acheson (1990) 'The tragedy of the commons: twenty two years later' *Human Ecology* 18 (1), pp. 1–19.

Ferejohn, J. and Fiorina, M. (1974) 'The Paradox of Not Voting: A Decision Theoretic Analysis' *American Political Science Review* 68, pp. 525–36.

Fern, E.F. (2001) *Advanced Focus Group Research* (London: Sage).

Finlayson, A. (2003) *Making Sense of New Labour* (London: Lawrence Wishart).

Finlayson, A. and Martin, J. (2006) 'Poststructuralism' in C. Hay, M. Lister, and D. Marsh (eds.) *The State. Theories and Issues* (Basingstoke: Palgrave), pp. 155–71.

Fiorina, M. P. (1976) 'The voting decision: instrumental and expressive aspects' *The Journal of Politics* 38 (2), pp. 390–413.

————. (1989) *Retrospective Voting in American National Elections* (New Haven, CT: Yale University Press).

Fiorina, M.P. and Shepsle, K.A. (1982) 'Equilibrium, Disequilibrium and the General Possibility of a Science of Politics' in P.C. Ordeshook and K. A. Shepsle (ed.) *Political Equilibrium* (The Hague, Netherlands: Kluwer-Nijhoff), pp. 49–64.

Fisher, S.L. (1980) 'The Decline of Parties Thesis and the Role of Minor Parties' in P. H. Merkl (ed.) *West European Party Systems. Trends and Prospects*, pp. 609–13.

Fitchett, J. (2004) 'The fantasies, orders and roles of sadistic consumption: game shows and the service encounter' *Consumption, Markets and Culture* 7 (4), pp. 285–306.

Fox, K.F.A and Kotler, P. (1980) 'The marketing of social causes: the first 10 years' *Journal of Marketing* 44, pp. 24–33.

Franklin, B. (1994) *Packaging Politics* (London: Edward Arnold).

————. (2001) 'The Hand of History: New Labour, News Management and Governance' in S, Ludlam and M. Smith (eds.) *New Labour in Government* (Basingstoke: Palgrave), pp. 130–44.

Franklin, M. (1992) 'Britain' in M. Franklin, T.T. Mackie and H. Valen (eds.) *Electoral Change. Responses to Evolving Social and Attitudinal Structures in Western Countries* (Cambridge: Cambridge University Press), pp. 101–22.

————. (2002) 'The Dynamics of Electoral Participation' in L. LeDuc, R.G. Niemi and P. Norris (eds.) *Comparing Democracies, volume 2: New Challenges to the Study of Elections and Voting* (London: Sage) pp. 148-68.

————. (2004) *Voter Turnout and the Dynamics of Electoral Competition in Established Democracies since 1945* (Cambridge: Cambridge University Press).

Franklin, M.N. (1985) *The Decline of Class Voting* (Oxford: Oxford University Press).

————. (1996) 'Electoral Participation' in L. LeDuc, R.G. Niemi and P. Norris (eds.) *Comparing Democracies: Elections and Voters in Global Perspective* (Thousand Oaks, CA: Sage) pp. 216–35.

Frazier, G.L., Spekman, R.E., O'Neal, C.R. (1991) 'Just-in-time exchange relationships in industrial markets' in B. Enis, K. Cox and M. Mokwa (eds.) *Marketing Classics* 8th edition (New Jersey: Prentice Hall).

Frey, J. and Fontana, A. (1991) 'The group interview in social research' *Social Science* 28, pp. 175–87.

Fukuyama, F. (1992) *The End of History and the Last Man* (London: Hamish Hamilton).

Gaber, I. (1995) 'Driving the news or spinning out of control: politicians, the media and the battle for the news agenda' Inaugural lecture *London Goldsmiths* 30 November.

Gaber, I. (1998) 'A world of dogs and lamp-posts' *New Statesman* 19th June, p14.

————. (2004) 'Alastair Campbell, exit stage left. A new chapter in political communications or just another spin?' Paper presented to the PSA Conference, University of Lincoln, Lincoln, UK April 2004.

Gabriel, Y. and Lang, T, (1997) *The Unmanageable Consumer* (London: Sage).

Galbraith, J.K. (1999) *The Affluent Society* (London: Penguin).

Gamble, A. (1974) *The Conservative Nation* (London: Routledge and Regan Paul).

————. (1998) 'After the Watershed, the Conservative Eclipse' in A. Coddington and M. Perryman (eds) The Moderniser's Dilemma (London: Lawrence and Wishart Limited) pp. 15–31.

Garnett, M. (1996) *Principles and Politics in Contemporary Britain* (London: Longman).

Godelier, M. (1972) *Rationality and Irrationality in Economics* (London: NLB).

Goldman, A.E. (1962) 'The group depth interview' *Journal of Marketing Research* 26, pp. 61–68.

Goldman, A.E. and McDonald, S.S. (1987) *The Group Depth Interview: Principles and Practice* (Englewood Cliffs, NJ: Prentice Hall).

Goodin, R. and Dryzek, J. (1980) 'Rational participation: the politics of relative power' *British Journal of Political Science* 10, pp. 273–92.

Goodwin, J. and Horowitz, R. (2002) 'Introduction: the methodological strengths and dilemmas of qualitative sociology' *Qualitative Sociology* 25 (1), pp. 33–47.

Gould, P. (1998) *The Unfinished Revolution* (London: Little, Brown and Company).

———. (2002) 'Labour Party Strategy' in J. Bartle, S. Atkinson and R. Mortimore (eds.) *Political Communications. The General Election Campaign of 2001*(London: Frank Cass), pp. 57–68.

Gray, J. (1984) *Hayek on Liberty* (Oxford: Blackwell).

Green, D. and Shapiro, I. (1994) *Pathologies of Rational Choice Theory. A Critique of Applications in Political Science* (New Haven and London: Yale University Press).

Greenley, G. (1995a) 'Market orientation and company performance: empirical evidence from UK companies' *British Journal of Management* 6, pp. 1–13.

———. (1995b) 'Invited comment on the market orientation content of "a critical review of research in marketing"' *British Journal of Management* 6 (special issue), pp. 87–88.

Gwin, J. (1990) 'Constituent analysis: a paradigm for marketing effectiveness in the not-for-profit organisation' *European Journal of Marketing* 24 (7), pp. 43–48.

Habermas, J. (1989) *The Structural Transformation of the Public Sphere: An Inquiry into a Category of Bourgeois Society* (translated by Thomas Burger) (Cambridge: Polity).

———. (1997) *Legitimation Crisis* (Cambridge: Polity).

Hacking, I. (1999) *The Social Construction of What?* (Cambridge, MA: Harvard University Press).

Hackley, C.E. (1999) 'Tacit knowledge and the epistemology of expertise in strategic marketing management' *European Journal of Marketing* 33 (7/8), pp. 720–36.

Hall, P.A. (1993) 'Policy paradigms, social learning and the state: the case of economic policymaking in Britain' *Comparative Politics* 25 (3), pp. 275–96.

Hall, P.A. (1999) 'Social capital in Britain' *British Journal of Political Science* 29, pp. 417–61.

Hall, S. (1983) 'The Great Moving Right Show' in S. Hall and M. Jacques (eds.) *The Politics of Thatcherism* (London: Lawrence Wishart), pp. 19–39.

Hall and RCR Taylor (1996) 'Political science and the three new institutionalisms' *Political Studies* 44, pp. 936–57.

Hardin, G. (1968) 'The tragedy of the commons' *Science* 162, pp. 1243–48.

Hardin, R. (1982) *Collective Action* (Baltimore: Johns Hopkins University Press).

Harman, H. (2006) 'A new deal for democracy' *Speech to the Hansard Society* 16 January 2006. www.dca.gov.uk/speeches/2006/sp060116.htm.

Harris, L.C. and Ogbonna, E. (2001) 'Strategic human resource management, market orientation, and organizational performance' *Journal of Business Research* 51 (2), pp. 157–66.

Harris, P. and Wring, D. (2001) 'Editorial. the marketing campaign. the 2001 British general election' *Journal of Marketing Management* 17, pp. 909–12.

Harrop, M. (1986) 'The Press and Post-war Elections' in I. Crewe and M. Harrop (eds.) *Political Communications: The General Election Campaign of 1983* (Cambridge: Cambridge University Press), pp. 137–49.

———. (1990) 'Political Marketing' *Parliamentary Affairs* 43 (3), pp. 277–91.

Hay, C. (1994) 'Labour's Thatcherite revisionism: playing the "politics of catch-up"' *Political Studies* 42 (4), pp. 700–707.

———. (1997) 'Blaijorism: towards a one-vision polity?' *Political Quarterly*, pp. 372–78.

———. (1999) *The Political Economy of New Labour* (Manchester: Manchester University Press).

———. (2002) *Controversies in Political Analysis* (London: Palgrave).

———. (2004a) '"Taking ideas seriously" explanatory political analysis' *British Journal of Politics and International Relations* 6 (2), pp. 142–49.

———. (2004b) 'Theory, stylised heuristic or self-fulfilling prophecy? the status of rational choice theory in public administration' *Public Administration* 82, pp. 2–33.

———. (2007) *Why We Hate Politics* (Cambridge: Polity).

von Hayek, F. (1991) *The Road to Serfdom* (London: Routledge).

Hayes, B.C. and McAllister, I. (1996) 'Marketing politics to voters: late deciders in the 1992 British election' *European Journal of Marketing* 30 (10/11), pp. 134–46.

Heath, A., Jowell, R., and J. Curtice (1985) *How Britain Votes* (Oxford: Pergamon Press).

Heath, A., Jowell, R., Curtice, J., Evans, G., Field, J., and S. Witherspoon (1991) *Understanding Political Change* (Oxford: Pergammon Press).

Heath, A., Jowell, R., and Curtice, J., with B. Taylor (eds.) (1994) *Labour's Last Chance? The 1992 Election and Beyond* (Aldershot: Dartmouth).

Heath, A.F., Jowell, R.M. and J. Curtice (2001) *The Rise of New Labour. Party Policies and Voter Choices* (Oxford: Oxford University Press).

Heath, A. and Park, A. (1997) 'Thatcher's Children?' in R. Jowell et al (eds.) *British Social Attitudes: The Fourteenth Report, The End of Conservative Values?* (Aldershot: Gower), pp. 1–22.

Heath, A. and Taylor, B. (1999) 'New Sources of Abstention' in G. Evans and P. Norris (eds.) *Critical Elections: British Parties and Voters in Long-term Perspective* (London: Sage), pp. 164–80.

Heffernan, R. (2002) '"The possible as the art of politics": understanding consensus politics' *Political Studies* 50, pp. 742–60.

Held, D. (1997) *Models of Democracy* 2nd edition (Oxford: Polity Press).

Henn, M., Weinstein, M. and D. Wring (2002) 'A generation apart? youth and political participation in Britain' *British Journal of Politics and International Relations* 4 (2), pp. 167–92.

Henneberg, S.C.M. (2002) 'Understanding Political Marketing' in N.J. O'Shaughnessy, (ed.) *The Idea of Political Marketing* (Westport, CT: Praeger), pp. 93–170.

Henneberg, S. (2004) 'The views of an *advocatus dei*: political marketing and its critics' *Journal of Public Affairs* 4 (3), pp. 225–43.

Henneberg, S.C.M. (2006) 'Leading or following? a theoretical analysis of political marketing postures' *Journal of Political Marketing* 5 (3), pp. 29–46.

Henneberg, S.C. and O'Shaughnessy, N.J. (2007) 'Prolegomena to theory and concept development in political marketing' *Journal of Political Marketing* special issue 6 (2/3), pp. 1–4.

Hetherington, M. (1999) 'The effect of political trust on the presidential vote 1968–96' *American Political Science Review* 93, pp. 311–26.

Higgins, M. (forthcoming) *The Media and Its Public* (Maidenhead: Open University Press).

Himmelweit, H.T., Humphreys, P., and M. Jaeger (1985) *How Voters Decide* (Milton Keynes, UK: Open University Press).

Hindmoor, A. (2006) 'Public Choice' in C. Hay, M. Lister, and D. Marsh (eds.) *The State. Theories and Issues* (Basingstoke: Palgrave), pp. 79–97.

Hinich, M.J., Ledyard, J., and P. Ordeshook (1972) 'Nonvoting and the existence of equilibrium under majority rule' *Journal of Economic Theory* 4, pp. 144–53.

Hinich, M.J. and Munger, M.C. (1997) *Analytical Politics* (Cambridge: Cambridge University Press).

Hooley, G., Lynch, J.E., and J. Shepherd (1990) 'The marketing concept: putting theory into practice' *European Journal of Political Marketing* 24 (9), pp. 7–24.

Hooley, G., Cox, T., Fahy. J., Shipley, D., Beracs, J., Fonfara, K., and B. Snoj (2000) 'Market orientation in the transition economies of Central Europe: tests of the Narver and Slater market orientation scales' *Journal of Business Research* 50, pp. 27–85.

Hotelling, H. (1929) 'Stability in competition' *The Economic Journal* 39 (1), pp. 41–57.

Houston, F. (1986) 'The marketing concept: what it is and what it is not' *Journal of Marketing* 50 (April), pp. 81–87.

Howarth, D., Norval, A.J., and Y. Stavrakakis (eds.) (2000) *Discourse Theory and Political Analysis: Identities, Hegemonies and Social Change* (Manchester: Manchester University Press).

Hunt, S.D. (1976) 'The nature and scope of marketing' *Journal of Marketing* 40 pp. 17–28.

Hydén, L.C. and Bülow, P.H. (2003) 'Who's talking: drawing conclusions from focus groups—some methodological considerations' *International Journal of Social Research Methodology* 6 (4), pp. 305–21.

Isin, E. (2002) *Being Political* (Minneapolis: University of Minnesota Press).

Jackman, R.W. (1993) Response: response to Aldrich's "rational choice and turnout". rationality and political participation' *American Journal of Political Science* 37 (1), pp. 279–90.

Jameson, F. (1990) ' Postmodernism and Consumer Society' in H. Foster (ed.) *Post Modern Culture* (London: Pluto), pp. 111–25.

Jaworski, B.J. and Kohli, A.K. (1993) 'Market orientation: antecedents and consequences' *Journal of Marketing* 57, pp. 53–70.

Jaworski, B.J., and Kohli, A.K. (1996) 'Market orientation: review, refinement and roadmap' *Journal of Market-Focused Management* 1, pp. 119–35.

Johnasen, H.P.M. (2005) 'Political marketing: more than persuasive techniques, an organizational perspective' *Journal of Political Marketing* 4 (4), pp. 85–105.

John, P. (1999) 'Ideas and interests; agendas and implementation: an evolutionary explanation of policy change in British local government finance' *British Journal of Politics and International Relations* 1 (1), pp. 39–62.

Jones, D.G.B. and Monieson, D.D. (1990) 'Early development of the philosophy of marketing thought' *Journal of Marketing* 54 (January), pp. 102–13.

Jones, G. (2005) 'Labour worries in marginals may just be a ploy' *The Telegraph* 4th May.

Jones, N. (1997) *Campaign 1997* (London: Indigo).

Kaase, M. and Newton, K. (1995) *Beliefs in Government* (Oxford: Oxford University Press).

Katz, R. and Mair, P. (1995) 'Changing models of party organisation and party democracy: the emergence of the cartel party' *Party Politics* 1 (1), pp. 5–28.

Kavanagh, D. (1980) 'Political culture of Great Britain: the decline of civic culture' in G.A. Almond and S. Verba (eds.) *The Civic Culture Revisited* (London: Sage), pp. 129–76.

——. (1992) 'The United Kingdom' in D. Butler and A. Ranney (eds.) *Electioneering. A Comparative Study of Continuity and Change* (Oxford: Clarendon Press), pp. 70–87.

——. (1995) *Election Campaigning. The New Marketing of Politics* (Oxford: Blackwell).

——. (1997) 'The Labour Campaign' in P. Norris and N. Gavin (eds.) *Britain Votes 1997* (Oxford: Oxford University Press), pp. 25–33.

Keat, R. (1994) 'Scepticism, Authority and the Market' in R. Keat, N. Whiteley, and N. Abercrombie (eds.) *The Authority of the Consumer* (London: Routledge).

Keith, R. (1960) 'The marketing revolution' *Journal of Marketing* (January) 24 (1), pp. 35–38.

Kelley, S. (1956) *Professional Public Relations and Political Power* (Baltimore: Johns Hopkins).

Kelley, S., Ayres, R., and W. Bowen (1967) 'Registration and voting: putting first things first' *American Political Science Review* 86, pp. 929–38.

Kennedy, M.M. (1994) 'Out of focus groups' *Across the Board (Conference Board Inc)* 31 (5), pp. 10–12.

Kerr, P. (2001) *Postwar British Politics: From Conflict to Consensus* (London: Routledge).

King, A. (1975) 'Overload: problems of governing in the 1970s' *Political Studies* 23 pp. 284–96.

King, D. (1987) *The New Right. Politics, Markets and Citizenship* (London: Macmillan).

——. (1997) 'The Polarisation of American Parties and Mistrust in Government' in J.S. Nye, P.D. Zelikow, and D.C. King (eds.) *Why People Don't Trust Government* (Cambridge, MA: Harvard University Press), pp. 155–78.

King, G., Keohane, R.O., and Verba, S (1994) *Designing Social Inquiry: Scientific Inference in Qualitative Research* (Princeton, NJ: Princeton University Press).

Kirchheimer, O. (1966) 'The Transformation of Western European Party Systems' in J. Palombara and M. Weiner (eds.) *Political Parties and Political Development* (Princeton, NJ: Princeton University Press), pp. 177–200.

Kitchen, P.J. (2003) *The Rhetoric and Reality of Marketing: An International Managerial Approach* (Basingstoke: Palgrave).

Kitzinger, J. (1994) 'The methodology of focus groups: the importance of interaction between research participants' *Sociology of Health and Illness* 16 (1), pp. 103–21.

Kitzinger, J. and Barbour, R.S. (1999) 'Introduction: The Challenge and Promise of Focus Groups' in R.S. Barbour and J. Kitzinger (eds.) *Developing Focus Group Research: Politics, Theory and Practice* (London: Sage), pp. 156–72.

Klapper, J. (1960) *The Effects of Mass Communication* (Glencoe, IL: Free Press).

Klingeman, H.D. and Fuchs, D. (1995) *Citizens and the State* (Oxford: Oxford University Press).

Knack, S. (1992) 'Civic norms, social sanctions, and voter turnout' *Rationality and Society* 4, pp. 133–56.

Kohli, A.K. and Jaworski, B.J. (1990) 'Market orientation: the construct, research propositions and managerial implications' *Journal of Marketing* 54, April pp. 1–18.

Kotler, P. (1972) 'A generic concept of marketing' *Journal of Marketing* 36, pp. 46–54.

Kotler, P. (1975) 'Overview of political candidate marketing' *Advances in Consumer Research* 2, pp. 761–69.

———. (1979) 'Strategies for introducing marketing into nonprofit organisations' *Journal of Marketing* 43 pp. 37–44.

———. (1982) 'Voter Marketing: Attracting Votes' in P. Kotler (ed.) *Marketing for Non Profit Organisations* (Englewood Cliffs, NJ: Prentice Hall).

———. (1984) *Marketing Management: Analysis, Planning, and Control* (Englewood Cliffs, NJ: Prentice Hall).

Kotler, P. and Andreasen, A. (1991) *Strategic Marketing for Non-Profit Organizations* 4th Edition (Englewood Cliffs, NJ: Prentice Hall).

———. (1996) *Strategic Marketing for Non-Profit Organisations* 5th edition (Englewood Cliffs, NJ: Prentice Hall).

Kotler, P. and Armstrong, G. (1996) *Principles of Marketing* (Englewood Cliffs, NJ: Prentice Hall).

Kotler, P. and Kotler, N. (1999) 'Political Marketing. Generating Effective Candidates, Campaigns and Causes' in B. Newman (ed.) *Handbook of Political Marketing* (London: Sage) pp. 3–18.

Kotler, P. and Levy, S. (1969) 'Broadening the concept of marketing' *Journal of Marketing* 33 pp. 10–15.

Kotler, P., Wong, V., Saunders, J., and G. Armstrong (2005) *Principles of Marketing* (Harlow, UK: Prentice Hall).

Kotler, P. and Zaltman, C. (1971) 'Social marketing: an approach to planned social change' *Journal of Marketing* 35, pp. 8–12.

Krueger, R.A. (1994) *Focus Groups: A Practical Guide for Applied Research* (London: Sage).

Krueger, R.A and Casey, M.A. (2000) *Focus Groups. A Practical Guide for Applied Research* 3rd edition (London: Sage).

Laclau, E. and Mouffe, C. (1985) *Hegemony and Socialist Strategy: Towards a Radical Democratic Politics* (London: Verso).

———. (1987) 'Post-Marxism without apologies' *New Left Review* (November/December), pp. 79–106.

Lancaster, G. and Massingham, L. (1993) *Essentials of Marketing* (London: McGraw Hill).

Langford, B.E., Schoenfeld, G., and G. Izzo (2002) 'Nominal grouping sessions vs focus groups' *Qualitative Market Research* 5 (1), pp. 58–71.

Lasswell, H.D. (1936) *Politics: Who Gets What, When, How* (New York: McGraw Hill).

Laufer, R. and Paradeise, C. (1990) *Marketing Democracy. Public Opinion and Media Formation in Democratic Societies* (New Brunswick, NJ: Transaction Publishers).

Laver, M. (1997) *Private Desires, Political Action: An Invitation to the Politics of Rational Choice* (London: Sage).

———. (1998) 'Party policy in Britain 1997: results from an expert survey' *Political Studies* 46, pp. 336–47.

Lawson, K. and Merkl, P. (eds.) (1988) *When Parties Fail: Emerging Alternative Organizations* (Princeton, NJ: Princeton University Press).

Lawther, S., Hastings, G.B and R. Lowry (1997) 'De-Marketing: putting Kotler and Levy's ideas into practice' *Journal of Marketing Management* 13, pp. 315–25.

Ledyard, J.O. (1981) 'The Paradox of Voting and Candidate Competition: A General Equilibrium Analysis' in G. Horwich and J. Quirk (eds.) *Essays in Contemporary Fields of Economics* (West Lafayette, IN: Purdue University Press), pp. 54–80.

Ledyard, J.O. (1984) 'The pure theory of large two candidate elections' *Public Choice* 44, pp. 7–41.

Lees-Marshment, J. (2001a) *Political Marketing and British Political Parties. The Party's Just Begun* (Manchester, UK: Manchester University Press).

———. (2001b) 'The marriage of politics and marketing' *Political Studies* 49 (4) pp. 692–713.

———. (2006) 'Political Marketing Theory and Practice: A Reply to Ormrod's Critique of the Lees-Marshment Market-Oriented Party Model' *Politics* 26 (2), pp. 119–25.

Leftwich, A. (ed.) (2004) *What Is Politics?* 2nd edition. (Cambridge: Polity).

Leininger, M. (1994) 'Evaluation Criteria and Critique of Qualitative Research Studies' in J.M. Morse (ed.) *Critical Issues in Qualitative Research Methods* (Thousand Oaks, CA: Sage), pp. 95–115.

Levitt, T. (1960) 'Marketing myopia' *Harvard Business Review* (July–August), pp. 3–23.

Levy, S. (1959) 'Symbols for sale' *Harvard Business Review* (July–August), pp. 117–24.

Lewis, J., Inthorn, S., and K. Wahl-Jorgensen (2005) *Citizens or Consumers? What the Media Tell Us about Political Participation* (Maidenhead: Open University Press).

Leys, C. (2001) *Market Driven Politics. Neoliberal Democracy and the Public Interest* (London: Verso).

Lijphart, A. (1999) *Patterns of Democracy: Government Forms and Performance in Thirty- Six Countries* (New Haven, CT: Yale University Press).

Lilleker, D. and Lees-Marshment, J. (2005) *Political Marketing. A Comparative Perspective* (Manchester, UK: Manchester University Press).

Lindblom, C.E. (1977) *Politics and Markets* (New York: Basic Books).

Lipset, S.M. and Rokkan, S. (1966) 'Cleavage Structure, Party Systems and Voter Alignments: An Introduction' in S.M. Lipset and S. Rokkan (eds.) *Party Systems and Voter Alignment* (New York: Free Press), pp. 1–64.

Lister, M. (2007) 'Institutions, inequality and social norms: explaining variations in participation' *British Journal of Politics and International Relations* 9 (1), pp. 20–35.

Lock, A. and Harris, P. (1996) 'Political marketing—vive la difference' *European Journal of Marketing* 30 (10/11), pp. 28–29.

Louw, E. (2005) *The Media and Political Process* (London: Sage).

Lovelock, C.H. and Weinberg, C.B. (1988) *Public and Non-Profit Marketing* (Danvers, MA: Boyd and Fraser).

Lukes, S. (1974) *Power: A Radical View* (London: Macmillan).

Lunt, P. and Livingstone, S. (1996) 'Rethinking the focus group in media and communication research' *Journal of Communication* 46 (2), pp. 79–120.

Lury, A. (1994) 'Advertising—Moving beyond the Stereotypes' in R. Keat, N. Abercrombie and N. Whiteley (eds.) *The Authority of the Consumer* (London: Routledge).

Maarek, P. J. (1995) *Political Marketing and Communication* (London: John Libbey and Company).

Mackie, T. and Franklin, M. (1992) 'Electoral Change and Social Change' in M. Franklin, T.T. Mackie and H. Valen (eds.) *Electoral Change. Responses to Evolving Social and Attitudinal Structures in Western Countries* (Cambridge: Cambridge University Press), pp. 33–60.

Mancini, P. and Swanson, D.L. (1996) 'Politics, Media and Modern Democracy: Introduction' in D.L. Swanson and P. Mancini (eds.) *Politics, Media and Modern Democracy: An International Study of Innovations in Electoral Campaigning and Their Consequences* (Westport, CT: Praeger), pp. 1–28.

Mandelson, P. (1997) 'Coordinating government policy' Speech delivered to the conference on Modernising the Policy Process, Regent's Park Hotel, 16th September cited in Franklin, B. (2001) 'The Hand of History: New Labour, News Management and Governance' in S. Ludlam and M.J. Smith (eds.) *New Labour in Government* (Basingstoke: Palgrave), pp. 130–44.

Mannheim, K. (1936) *Ideology and Utopia* (London: Routledge and Kegan Paul).

Marion, G. (2006) 'Marketing ideology and criticism: legitimacy and legitimation' *Marketing Theory* 6 (2), pp. 245–62.

Marquand, D. (2004) *Decline of the Public* (Cambridge: Polity).

Marsden, D. and Littler, D. (1996) 'Evaluating alternative research paradigms: a market-oriented framework' *Journal of Marketing Management* 12 (7), pp. 645–55.

Marsh, D. (1994) 'Explaining Thatcherism: beyond unidimensional explanation' Paper presented at the PSA Swansea, UK, April 1994.

Marsh, D. and Furlong, P. (2002) 'A Skin, Not a Sweater: Ontology and Epistemology in Political Science' in D. Marsh and G. Stoker (ed.) *Theory and Methods in Political Science* 2nd edition (Basingstoke: Palgrave Macmillan), pp. 17–44.

Marsh, D. and Savigny, H. (2005) 'Political science as a broad church: the search for a pluralist discipline' *Politics* 24 (3), pp. 155–68.

Marshall, T.H. (1950) *Citizenship and Social Class* (Cambridge: Cambridge University Press).

Marx, K. (1994) 'The Economic and Political Manuscripts' in L. Simon (ed.) *Karl Marx. Selected Writings* (Indianapolis/Cambridge: Hackett Publishing Company).

Mauser, G. (1983) *Political Marketing* (New York: Praeger).

McCombs, M.E. and Shaw, D.L. (1972) 'The agenda setting function of the press' *Public Opinion Quarterly* 36 (2), pp. 176–87.

McCracken, G. (1986) 'Culture and consumption: a theoretical account of the structure and movement of the cultural meaning of consumer goods' *Journal of Consumer Research* 13, pp. 71–84.

McDonald, M.D., Mendes, S.M., and I. Budge (2004) 'What are elections for? conferring the median mandate' *British Journal of Political Science* 34, pp. 1–26.

McDonald, W.J. (1993) 'Focus group research dynamics and reporting: an examination of research objectives and moderator influences' *Journal of the Academy of Marketing Science* 21 (2), pp. 161–64.

McGinnis, J. (1968) *The Selling of the President, 1968* (New York: Trident Press).

McGrath, J.E., Martin, J., and Kulka, R.A. (eds.) (1982) *Judgement Calls in Research* (Beverley Hills, CA: Sage).

McKenna, R. (1991) 'Marketing is everything' *Harvard Business Review* (January–February), pp. 65–79.

McKitterick, J.B. (1957) 'What Is the Marketing Management Concept?' in F.M. Bass (ed.) *The Frontiers of Marketing Thought and Science* (Chicago: American Marketing Association), pp. 71–82.

McManus, J.H. (1994) *Market Driven Journalism* (London: Sage).

Merton, R.K. (1987) 'The focussed interview and focus groups: continuities and discontinuities' *Public Opinion Quarterly* 51 (4) pp. 550–66.

Merton, R.K., Fiske, M., and P.L. Kendall (1956) *The Focused Interview* (Glencoe: UK Free Press).

Merton, R.K and Kendall, P.L. (1946) 'The focussed interview' *American Journal of Sociology* 51, pp. 541–57.

Miles, M.B. and Huberman, A.M. (1984) *Qualitative Data Analysis: A Sourcebook of New Methods* (Beverly Hills, CA: Sage).

Mill, J.S. (1961) *A System of Logic* (London: Longmans).

Miller, A. and Listhaug, O. (1999) 'Political Performance and Institutional Trust' in P. Norris (ed.) *Critical Citizens: Global Support for Democratic Governance* (Oxford: Oxford University Press).

Miller, W.I.L., Clarke, H.D., Harrop, M., Leduc, L., and P.F. Whiteley (1990) *How Voters Change* (Oxford: Clarendon Press).

Minogue, M., Polidano, C., and D. Hulme (eds.) (1998) *Beyond the New Public Management: Changing Ideas and Practices in Governance* (Cheltenham: Edward Elgar).

Moon, N. (1999) *Opinion Polls. History Theory and Practice* (Manchester, UK: Manchester University Press).

Moorman, C. and Rust, R.T. (1999) 'The role of marketing' *Journal of Marketing* 63, pp. 180–97.

Morgan, D.L. (1988) *Focus Groups and Qualitative Research* (Newbury Park, CA: Sage).

———. (1993) *Successful Focus Groups* (Newbury Park, CA: Sage).

———. (1995) 'Why things (sometimes) go wrong in focus groups' *Qualitative Health Research* 5 (4), pp. 516–23.

Morgan, D.L. and Spanish, M.T. (1984) 'Focus groups: a new tool for qualitative research' *Qualitative Sociology* 7, pp. 253–70.

MORI opinion polls 1999, accessed via *www.mori.co.uk*, 16th July 2004.

Morris, D. (1999) *Behind the Oval Office. Getting Re-elected against All Odds* (Los Angeles: Renaissance Books).

Morrisson, D. (1998) *The Search for a Method: Focus Groups and the Development of Mass Communication Research* (Luton, UK: University of Luton Press).

Morrison, D.E. (2003) 'Good and Bad Practice in Focus Group Research' in V. Nightingale and K. Ross (eds.) *Critical Readings: Media and Audiences* (Maidenhead: Open University Press), pp. 111–30.

Moynihan, D. and Titley, B. (1995) *Advanced Business* (Maidenhead, UK: Open University Press).

Mueller, D.C. (1979) *Public Choice* (Cambridge: Cambridge University Press).

Nagler, J. (1991) 'The effect of registration laws and education on U.S. voter turnout' *American Political Science Review* 85, pp. 1393–406.

Narver, J.C. and Slater, S.F. (1990) 'The effect of a market orientation on business profitability' *Journal of Marketing* 54, pp. 20–35.

Needham, C. (2005) 'Brand leaders: Clinton, Blair and the limitations of the permanent campaign' *Political Studies* 53 (2), pp. 343–61.

Negrine, R. and Lilleker, D.G. (2002) 'The professionalization of political communication' *European Journal of Communication* 17 (3), pp. 305–23.

Newman, B. (1994) *The Marketing of the President. Political marketing as Campaign Strategy* (London: Sage).

———. (1999) 'Introduction' in B. Newman (ed.) *Handbook of Political Marketing* (London: Sage), pp. 3–18.

———. (2001) 'Commentary: image-manufacturing in the USA: recent US presidential elections and beyond' *European Journal of Marketing* 35 (9/10), pp. 966–70.

Newton, K. (2006) 'Political support: social capital, civil society and political and economic performance' *Political Studies* 54 (4), pp. 846–64.

Newton, K. and Brynin, M. (2001) 'The national press and party voting in the UK' *Political Studies* 49, pp. 265–85.

Niffenegger, P. (1989) 'Strategies for success from the political marketers' *Journal of Consumer Marketing* 6, pp. 45–61.

Nimmo, D. (1970) *The Political Persuaders* (Englewood Cliffs, NJ: Prentice Hall).

———. (1999) 'The Permanent Campaign: Marketing as a Governing Tool' in B. Newman (ed.) *Handbook of Political Marketing* (Thousand Oaks, CA: Sage), pp. 73–88.

Niskanen, W.A. (1971) *Bureaucracy and Representative Government* (Chicago: Aldine).

———. (1973) *Bureaucracy: Servant or Master?* (London: Institute of Economic Affairs).

Norris, P. (1999) 'Institutions and Political Support' in P. Norris (ed.) *Critical Citizens: Global Support for Democratic Governance* (Oxford: Oxford University Press), pp. 1–30.

———. (2000) *A Virtuous Circle. Political Communication in Postindustrial Societies* (Cambridge: Cambridge University Press).

———. (2001) 'Apathetic Landslide: The 2001 British General Election' in P. Norris (ed.) *Britain Votes 2001* (Oxford: Oxford University Press), pp. 1–25.

Norris, P., Curtice, J., Sanders, D., Scammell, M., and H. Semetko (1999) *On Message: Communicating the Campaign* (London: Sage).

Norris, P. and Evans, G, (1999) 'Introduction: Understanding Electoral Change' and 'Conclusion: Was 1997 a Critical Election?' in G. Evan and P. Norris (eds.) *Critical Elections. British Parties and Voters in Long-Term Perspective* (London: Sage), pp xix–xl, 259–71.

Novotny, P. (2000) 'From Polis to Agora. The marketing of political consultants' *Press/ Politics* 5 (3), pp. 12–26.

O'Cass, A. (1996) 'Political marketing and the marketing concept' *European Journal of Marketing* 30 (10/11), pp. 45–61.

———. (2001) 'Political marketing. An investigation of thee political marketing concept and political market orientation in Australian politics' *European Journal of Marketing* 35 (9/10), pp. 1103–25.

O'Driscoll, A. and Murray, J.A. (1998) 'The changing nature of theory and practice in marketing: on the value of synchrony' *Journal of Marketing Management* 14, pp. 391–416.

O'Leary, R. and Iredale, I. (1976) 'The marketing concept: quo vadis?' *European Journal of Marketing* 10 (3), pp. 146–57.

O'Shaughnessy, N. (1987) 'America's political market' *European Journal of Marketing* 21 (4), pp. 60–66.

————. (1990) *The Phenomenon of Political Marketing* (London: Macmillan).

————. (1999) 'Political Marketing and Political Propaganda' in B. Newman (ed.) *Handbook of Political Marketing* (London: Sage), pp. 725–40.

————. (2001) 'The marketing of political marketing' *European Journal of Marketing* 35 9/10, pp. 1047–57.

O'Shaughnessy, N.J. and Henneberg, S.C. (2007) 'The selling of the President 2004: a marketing perspective' *Journal of Public Affairs* 7, pp. 249–68.

O'Toole, T., Lister, M., Marsh, D., Jones, S., and A. McDonagh (2003) 'Tuning out or left out? Participation and non-participation among young people' *Contemporary Politics* 9 (1), pp. 45–61.

Olson, M. (1965) *The Logic of Collective Action* (Cambridge, MA: Harvard University Press).

————. (1989) 'How Ideas Affect Societies: Is Britain the Wave of the Future?' in *Ideas, Interests and Consequences* (London: Institute of Economic Affairs), pp. 23–50.

Olssen, M. and Peters, M.A. (2005) 'Neoliberalism, higher education and the knowledge economy: from free market to knowledge capitalism' *Journal of Education Policy* 20 (3), pp. 313–45.

Ormrod, R. (2006) 'A critique of the Lees-Marshment market-oriented party model' *Politics* 26 (2), pp. 110–18.

Palfrey, T.R. and Rosenthal, H. (1983) 'A strategic calculus of voting' *Public Choice* 41, pp. 7–53.

Pakulski, J. (1997) 'Cultural citizenship' *Citizenship Studies* 1 (1), pp. 73–86.

Palmer, J. (2002) 'Smoke and Mirrors: is that the way it is? themes in political marketing' *Media, Culture and Society* 24, pp. 345–63.

Parry, G., Moyser, G., and Day, N. (1992) *Political Participation and Democracy in Britain* (Cambridge: Cambridge University Press).

Parsons, S. (2005) *Rational Choice and Politics. A Critical Introduction* (London: Continuum).

Pattie, C. (2001) 'New Labour and the Electorate' in S. Ludlam and M.J. Smith (eds.) *New Labour in Government* (Basingstoke: Macmillan), pp. 32–54.

Pattie, C. and Johnston, R. (2001a) 'A low turnout landslide: abstention at the British general election of 1997' *Political Studies* 49 (2), pp. 286–305.

Pattie, C. and Johnston, R. (2001b) 'Losing the voters' trust: evaluations of the political system and voting at the 1997 British general election' *British Journal of Politics and International Relations* 3 (2), pp. 191–222.

Pattie, C., Seyd, P., and P. Whiteley (2003) 'Civic attitudes and engagement in modern Britain' *Parliamentary Affairs* 56, pp. 616–33.

Pelham, A.M. and Wilson, D.T. (1996) 'A longitudinal study of the impact of market structure, firm structure, strategy, and market orientation culture on dimensions of small firm performance' *Journal of the Academy of Marketing Science* 24 (1), 27–43.

Pilcher, J. and Wagg, S. (eds.) (1996) *Thatcher's Children? Politics, Childhood and Society in the 1980s and 1990s* (London: Falmer Press).

Pimlott, B. (1997) 'New Labour, new era' *Political Quarterly*, pp. 325–34.

Plott, C.R. (1991) 'A Comparative Analysis of Direct democracy, Two Candidate Elections and Three Candidate Elections in an Experimental Environment' in T. R. Palfrey (ed.) *Laboratory Research in Political Economy* (Ann Arbor: University of Michigan Press), pp. 11–31.

Poguntke, T. (1996) 'Anti-party sentiment—conceptual thoughts and empirical evidence: explorations into a minefield' *European Journal of Political Research* 29, pp. 319–44.

Popkin, S. (1994) *The Reasoning Voter: Communication and Persuasion in Presidential Campaigns* 2nd edition (Chicago: University of Chicago Press).

Prior, M. (2005) 'News vs. entertainment: how increasing media choice widens gaps in political knowledge and turnout' *American Journal of Political Science* 49 (3), pp. 577–92.

Protherough, R. and Pick, J. (2003) *Managing Britannia* (Exeter: Imprint Academic).

Putnam, R.D. (1995) 'Tuning in, tuning out: the strange disappearance of social capital in America' *Political Science and Politics* 28, pp. 664–83.

Putnam, R. (2000) *Bowling Alone: The Collapse and Revival of American Community* (New York: Simon and Schuster).

Pyper, R. (2001) *New Public Management in Britain* (London: Macmillan).

Qualter, T. (1985) *Opinion Control in the Democracies* (Hampshire: Macmillan).

Quester, P.G., McGuigan, R.L., Perrault, W.D. and E.J. McCarthy (2004) *Marketing* (Macquarie Park, NSW: McGraw Hill).

Reid, D.M. (1988) 'Marketing the political product' *European Journal of Marketing* 22 (9), pp. 34–47.

Riker, W. and Ordeshook, P. (1973) *Introduction to Positive Political Theory* (Englewood Cliffs, NJ: Prentice Hall).

Robinson, M.J. (1976) 'Public affairs television and the growth of political malaise: the case of "the selling of the Pentagon"' *American Political Science Review* 70, pp. 409–32.

Rook, D. (2003) 'Out-of-focus-groups' *Marketing Research* 15 (2), pp. 10–15.

Rose, R. and Peters, B.G. (1977) *Can Government Go Bankrupt?* (New York: Basic Books).

Rosenblum, M. (1993) *Who Stole the News?* (New York: Wiley).

Rothschild, M. (1979) 'Marketing communications in nonBusiness situations—or why it's so hard to sell brotherhood like soap' *Journal of Marketing* (Spring 43), pp. 11–20.

Sackman, A. (1992) 'The marketing organisation model: making sense of modern campaigning in Britain' Paper presented at UK PSA Annual Conference in Belfast, April. Cited in Wring, 1997.

———. (1996) 'The learning curve towards New Labour: Neil Kinnock's corporate party 1983–92' *European Journal of Marketing* 30 (10/11), pp. 147–58.

Sarlvik, B. and Crewe, I. (1983) *Decade of Dealignment* (Cambridge: Cambridge University Press).

Sartori, G. (1976) *Parties and Party Systems: A Framework for Analysis* (Cambridge: Cambridge University Press).

Scammell, M. (1994) 'The phenomenon of political marketing: the Thatcher contribution' *Contemporary Record* 8 (1), pp. 23–43.

Scammell, M. (1995) *Designer Politics. How Elections Are Won* (London: Macmillan).

———. (1996) 'The odd couple: marketing and Maggie' *European Journal of Marketing* 30 (10/11), pp. 122–34.

———. (1999) 'Political marketing: lessons for political science' *Political Studies* 47 (4), pp. 718–39.

Schattschneider, E.E. (1960) *The Semi-Sovereign People: A Realist's View of Democracy in America* (New York: Holt, Rhinehart and Winston.

Schumpeter, J.A. (1947) *Capitalism, Socialism and Democracy* 2nd edition (London: Unwin).

Scott, A.M. (1970) *Competition in American Politics. An Economic Model* (New York: Holt, Rinehart and Winston).

Scrivens, E. and Witzel, M.L. (1990) 'Editorial' *European Journal of Marketing* 24 (7), pp. 5–14.

Scullion, R. (forthcoming) 'The Impact of the Market on the Character of Citizenship, and the Consequences of This for Political Engagement' in D.G. Lilleker, M. Passera, and R. Scullion (eds.) *Voters or Consumers: Imagining the Postmodern Electorate* (Cambridge: Cambridge University Press).

Searing, D.D., Conover, P.J., and I. Crewe (2003) 'Citizenship in the age of liberalism' *Parliamentary Affairs* 56, pp. 634–51.

Seyd, P. (2001) 'The Labour Campaign' in P. Norris (ed.) *Britain Votes 2001* (Oxford: Oxford University Press), pp. 43–59.

Shakespeare, S. (2005) 'They seem to be campaigning for the sake of it' *The Observer* 17th April.

Shama, A. (1976) 'The marketing of political candidates' *Journal of the Academy of Marketing Sciences* 4, pp. 764–77.

Shapiro, B. (1973) 'Marketing for nonprofit organisations' *Harvard Business Review* 51 (September–October), pp. 123–32.

Sheth, J., Gardner, D., and D. Garrett (1988) *Marketing Theory. Evolution and Evaluation* (New York: John Wiley and Sons).

Simon, H.A. (1982) *Models of Bounded Rationality* volumes 1–2 (Cambridge, MA: MIT Press).

Simons, J. (2000) 'Ideology, imagology and critical thought: the impoverishment of politics' *Journal of Political Ideologies* 5 (1), pp. 81–103.

Slater, S.F and Narver, J.C. (1994) 'Does competitive environment moderate the market orientation–performance relationship' *Journal of Marketing* 58, pp. 46–55.

Slater, S.F. and Narver, J.C. (2000) 'The positive effect of a market orientation on business profitability: a balanced replication' *Journal of Business Research* 48 (1), pp. 69–73.

Smith, A. (1776, 1828) *An Enquiry into the Nature and Causes of the Wealth of Nations* (Edinburgh: Adam and Charles Black).

Smith, G. (2001) 'The 2001 general election: factors influencing the brand image of political parties and their leaders' *Journal of Marketing Management* 17, pp. 989–1006.

———. (2006) 'Competitive analysis, structure and strategy in politics: a critical approach' *Journal of Public Affairs* 6 pp. 4–14.

Smith, G. and Hirst, A. (2001) 'Strategic political segmentation. A new approach for a new era of political marketing' *European Journal of Marketing* 35 (9/10), pp. 1058–73.

Smith, G. and Saunders, J. (1990) 'The application of marketing to British politics' *Journal of Marketing Management* 5 (3), pp. 295–306.

Smith, M. (1995) 'Pluralism' in D. Marsh and G. Stoker (eds.) *Theory and Methods in Political Science* (London: Macmillan) pp. 209–27.

———. (2006) 'Pluralism' in C. Hay, M. Lister and D. Marsh (eds.) *The State. Theories and Issues* (Basingstoke: Palgrave), pp. 21–38.

Smith, M.A. (1995) 'Ethics in focus groups: a few concerns' *Qualitative Health Research* 5 (4), pp. 478–87.

Smith, W.R. (1956) 'Product differentiation and market segmentation as alternative marketing strategies' *Journal of Marketing* 21, pp. 3–8.

Solomon, M. (1983) 'The role of products as social stimuli: a symbolic interactionist perspective' *Journal of Consumer Research* 10, pp. 319–29.

Sparrow, N. and Turner, J. (2001) 'The permanent campaign: The integration of market research techniques in developing strategies in a more uncertain political climate' *European Journal of Marketing* 35 (9/10), pp. 984–1024.

Stanton, W.J., Miller, K., and R.J. Layton (1991) *Fundamentals of Marketing* (New York: McGraw Hill).

Stanyer, J. (2003) 'Politics and the media: A crisis of trust?' *Parliamentary Affairs* 57 (2), pp. 420–34.

Steiner, P.O. (1952) 'Program patterns and preferences, and the workability of competition in radio broadcasting' *The Quarterly Journal of Economics* 66 (2), pp. 194–223.

Stevenson, N., (2003) *Cultural Citizenship. Cosmopolitan Questions* (Maidenhead: Open University Press).

Stewart, D.W. and Shamdasani, P.N. (1990) *Focus Groups: Theory and Practice* (Newbury Park, CA: Sage).

Stoker, G. (2006) *Why Politics Matters. Making Democracy Work* (Basingstoke: Palgrave).

Street, J. (2001) *Mass Media, Politics and Democracy* (Basingstoke: Palgrave).

———. (2004) 'Celebrity politicians: popular culture and political representation' *British Journal of Politics and International Relations* 6 (4), pp.435–52.

Strömbäck, J. (2007) 'Antecedents of political market orientation in Britain and Sweden: analysis and future research propositions' *Journal of Public Affairs* 7, pp. 79–89.

Strother, R. (2003) 'Tell your customers that you've listened, learned and responded' *Media Asia* 28th November, p16.

Taggart, P. (1996) *The New Populism and New Politics: New Protest Parties in Sweden in a Comparative Perspective* (London: Macmillan).

Taylor, G. (1997) *Labour's Renewal? The Policy Review and Beyond* (London: Macmillan).

Taylor, M. (2006) *Rationality and the Ideology of Disconnection* (Cambridge: Cambridge University Press).

Taylor-Gooby, P. and Lawson, R. (1993) *Markets and Managers: New Issues in the Delivery of Welfare* (Buckingham: Open University Press).

Temple, M. (2000) *How Britain Works: From Ideology to Output Politics* (London: Macmillan).

———. (2006) 'Dumbing down is good for you' *British Politics* 1 (2), pp. 257–73.

Tollison, R. and Willett, T.D. (1973) 'Some simple economics of voting and not voting' *Public Choice* 16, pp. 59–71.

Touraine, A. (2000) *Can We Live Together?* (Cambridge: Polity).

Trustrum, L. (1989) 'Marketing concept: concept and function' *European Journal of Marketing* 23 (3), pp. 48–56.

Tsebelis, G. (1990) *Nested Games: Rational Choice in Comparative Politics* (Berkeley, CA: University of California Press).

Tullock, G. (1967) *Toward a Mathematic of Politics* (Ann Arbor: University of Michigan Press).

———. (1976) *The Vote Motive* (London: Institute for Economic Affairs).

Uhlaner, C.J. (1989) 'Rational turnout: the neglected role of groups' *American Journal of Political Science* 33, pp. 390–422.

Uncles, M. (2000) 'Market orientation' *Australian Journal of Management* 25 (2), ppi–ix.

Underwood, D. (1995) *When MBAs Rule the Newsroom* (New York: Columbia University Press).

Underwood, R.L. (2003) 'The communicative power of product packaging: creating brand identity via lived and mediated experience' *Journal of Marketing Theory and Practice* 10 (7), pp. 62–76.

Verba, S. and Nie, N. (1972) *Participation in America: Political Democracy and Social Equality* (New York: Harper and Row).

Von der Hart, H.W.C. (1990) 'Government organisations and their customers in the Netherlands: strategy, tactics and operations' *European Journal of Marketing* 28 (3), pp. 63–71.

Walsh, K. (1994) 'Marketing and public sector management' *European Journal of Marketing* 28 (3), pp. 63–71.

———. (1995) *Public Services and Market Mechanisms: Competition, Contracting and the New Public Management* (Basingstoke: Macmillan).

Walvis, T. (2003) 'Avoiding advertising research disaster: advertising and the uncertainty principle' *Brand Management* 10 (6), pp. 403–9.

Ward, H. (1995) 'Rational Choice Theory' in D. Marsh and G. Stoker (eds.) *Theory and Methods in Political Science* (London: Macmillan), pp. 76–93.

Wattenberg, M.P. (1990) *The Decline of American Political Parties, 1952–1988* (Cambridge, MA: Harvard University Press).

Weatherford, M.S. (1992) 'Measuring political legitimacy' *American Political Science Review* 86 (1), pp. 149–66.

Webb, P. (1995) 'Are British political parties in decline?' *Party Politics* 95 (3), pp. 299–322.

Webster, C. (1992) 'What kind of marketing culture exists in your service firm? An audit' *Journal of Services Marketing* 6, pp. 54–67.

Webster, F. (1988) 'Rediscovering the marketing concept' *Business Horizons* 31 (May–June), pp. 29–39.

Webster, F. (1992) 'The changing role of marketing in the corporation' *Journal of Marketing* 56 (October), pp. 1–17.

Weibull, J.W. (1995) *Evolutionary Game Theory* (Cambridge, MA: MIT Press).

Weldon, T.D. (1953) *The Vocabulary of Politics* (Harmondsworth: Penguin).

Wellhofer, E.S. (1990) 'Contradictions in market models of politics: the case of party strategies and voter linkages' *European Journal of Political Research* 18, pp. 9–28.

Wellner, A. (2003) 'The new science of focus groups' *American Demographics* 25 (2), pp. 29–34.

Wendt, A. (1987) 'The agent-structure problem in international relations theory' *International Organization* 41 (3), pp. 335–70.

Wensley, R. (1993) '"The voice of the consumer?": speculations on the limits to the marketing analogy' *European Journal of Marketing* 24 (7), pp. 49–60.

———. (1995) 'A critical review of research in marketing' *British Journal of Management* 6 (special issue), pp.63–82.

Whiteley, P. (1995) 'Rational choice and political participation—evaluating the debate' *Political Research Quarterly* 48 (1), pp. 211–34.

Whiteley, P. (2003) 'The state of participation in Britain' *Parliamentary Affairs* 56, pp. 610–15.

Wickham-Jones, M. (1995) 'Recasting social democracy: a comment on Hay and Smith' *Political Studies* 43 (4), pp. 698–702.

Wilkinson, S. (1998) 'Focus group methodology: a review' *International Journal of Social Research Methodology* 1, pp. 181–203.

Williams, R. (1989) 'The Idea of a Common Culture' in R. Gable (ed) *Resources of Hope* (London: Verso), pp. 32–38.

Wintour, P. (2004) 'Media blamed for loss of trust in government' *The Guardian* 6th May.

——. (2005) 'Campaign planners buy into supermarket tactics' *www.spinwatch.org.*

Wintour, P. and White, M. (2005) 'Private poll reveals Labour fears' *The Guardian* 27th April.

Wolfinger, R. and Rosenstone, S. (1980) *Who Votes?* (New Haven, CT: Yale University Press).

Woolgar, S. (2004) 'Marketing ideas' *Economy and Society* 33 (4), pp. 448–62.

Worcester, R.M. (2005) 'The day after the election' *The Observer* 5th August.

Wright, T. (1998) 'Inside the Whale: The Media from Parliament' in J. Seaton (ed.) *Politics and the Media: Harlots and Prerogatives at the Turn of the Millennium* (Oxford: Blackwell), pp. 19–27.

Wring, D. (1996) 'Political marketing and party development in Britain. A "secret" history' *European Journal of Marketing* 30 (10/11), pp. 100–111.

——. (1997) 'Reconciling marketing with political science: theories of political marketing' *Journal of Marketing Management* 13, pp. 651–63.

——. (1999) 'The Marketing Colonization of Political Campaigning' in B. Newman (ed.) *Handbook of Political Marketing* (London: Sage), pp. 41–54.

——. (2001) 'Labouring the point: operation victory and the battle for a second term' *Journal of Marketing Management* 17, pp. 913–27.

——. (2002) 'Images of labour: the progression and politics of party campaigning in Britain' *Journal of Political Marketing* 1 (1), pp. 23–37.

——. (2003) 'Focus group follies? qualitative research and British Labour party strategy' Paper presented at the World Congress of the International Political Science Association, Durban, South Africa, July.

——. (2005) *The Politics of Marketing the Labour Party* (Basingstoke: Palgrave Macmillan).

Yanai, N. (1999) 'Why do political parties survive?' *Party Politics* 5 (1), pp. 5–17.

Yorke, D.A. and Meehan, S.A. (1986) 'ACORN in the political marketplace' *European Journal of Marketing* 20 (8), pp. 63–76.

Zikmund, W. and D'Amico, M. (1989) *Marketing* (New York: Wiley).

Websites

www.ama.org

www.electoralcommission.org.uk/files/dms/MORIAPEreportFinal_20376-14906__E__N__S__W__.pdf

www.statistics.gov.uk

www.ipsos-mori.com/publications/rd/new-rules-of-engagement.shtml

www.ipsos-mori.com/publications/rmw/whomdowetrust.shtml

Index